Mastering SAP® ERP HCM
Organizational Management

 **PRESS**

SAP PRESS is a joint initiative of SAP and Galileo Press. The know-how offered by SAP specialists combined with the expertise of the Galileo Press publishing house offers the reader expert books in the field. SAP PRESS features first-hand information and expert advice, and provides useful skills for professional decision-making.

SAP PRESS offers a variety of books on technical and business related topics for the SAP user. For further information, please visit our website: *www.sap-press.com*.

Martin Esch, Junold Anja
Authorizations in SAP ERP HCM
2008, 344 pages
978-159220-165-6

Hans-Jürgen Figaj, Richard HaÐmann, and Anja Junold
HR Reporting with SAP
2007, 431 pages
978-1-59229-172-4

Jeremy Masters and Christos Kotsakis
SAP ERP HCM Performance Management
2007, 302 pages
978-1-59229-124-3

Jeremy Masters and Christos Kotsakis
Implementing Employee and Manager Self Service
October 2008, approx. 300 pages
978-1-59229-188-5

Sylvia Chaudoir

Mastering SAP® ERP HCM
Organizational Management

Galileo Press

Bonn • Boston

ISBN 978-1-59229-208-0

© 2009 by Galileo Press Inc., Boston (MA)

1st Edition 2009

Galileo Press is named after the Italian physicist, mathematician and philosopher Galileo Galilei (1564–1642). He is known as one of the founders of modern science and an advocate of our contemporary, heliocentric worldview. His words *Eppur si muove* (And yet it moves) have become legendary. The Galileo Press logo depicts Jupiter orbited by the four Galilean moons, which were discovered by Galileo in 1610.

Editor   Jenifer Niles

Copy Editor   Ruth Saavedra

Cover Design   Tyler Creative

Layout Design   Vera Brauner

Production   Iris Warkus

Typesetting   Publishers' Design and Production Services, Inc.

Printed and bound in Canada

Contents at a Glance

Contents

4 Infotypes in Organizational Management **69**

5 Working with Relationships **81**

11 Integration of OM with other SAP Components 299

Appendices 321

Preface

I've been a consultant and trainer in human resources information systems for quite some time. Over the years in which I have been working with SAP systems, Organizational Management has been a part of just about every implementation project in which I've been involved. It's hard to find another component that can have such a forceful impact on the success of other components, and I'm very passionate about working with my customers to ensure that how they design and manage their organizational structure will meet their needs now as well as in the future.

This book came about based on the advice I give my customers. I probably work with only a handful of customers each year through implementation projects, short term consulting, and training. And as much as I communicate my messages to these customers, it became apparent to me that there was a need to share this information with a much broader audience. So the idea for this book was born. This book is a composite of nearly 15 years of designing (and sometimes redesigning), implementing, testing, and supporting HCM solutions. My experience as a trainer, consultant, and strategist has helped very diverse customers become successful with their HCM software. The examples are real, and the tips and advice are exactly the same as those provided to the customers I work with today.

I've written this book for anyone and everyone. No prior knowledge of SAP software, and in particular SAP ERP HCM is required, so the book is for both new and experienced users of SAP. The topics provided are meant to give you both a solid understanding of Organizational Management basics and how the component is designed to work, as well as how to take your implementation to the next level. Whether you are new to SAP's HCM solution or have been a user for many years, I hope that you will find reading this book a good investment of your time.

I'll turn my words now to thank the many people that have supported me in the realization of this work. I truly appreciate the words of encouragement and excitement that my friends and colleagues have shared with me during this time. Thanks in particular to my friend and colleague Steve Turner, who graciously provided me access to his reference system. And of course I want to give many thanks to my family. Thanks to my husband Leo, who patiently supported me through the writing process and only asked a couple dozen times if I was finished yet. Thanks to my children Nick and Marina, who were incredibly tolerant when I would disappear for hours on end and were always happy to see me again when I surfaced for air and hugs. And last but not least thanks to my publisher, Galileo Press, and to Jenifer Niles in particular, who was incredibly supportive of me and helped guide me through the publishing of this book.

Sylvia Chaudoir
San Mateo, CA
May 2008

Whether your company is large or small, public or private, with employees in the United States only or global, if you're planning on implementing SAP ERP HCM, then Organizational Management is for you. The design and implementation of this central SAP ERP HCM component can help make or break any SAP ERP HCM installation.

1 Introduction

1.1 Organizational Management is for Everyone

With the vast array of functionality provided by SAP® in its suite of applications, it's sometimes difficult to know where to begin. With SAP ERP Human Capital Management (HCM), also referred to as SAP Human Resources (HR), this is no less complicated. There are literally dozens of functions that you can implement and use, and nearly 75 country-specific versions to meet specific regulatory and reporting needs.

With all of this functionality, however, certain functions are central in design and focus. The Organizational Management (OM) component is one such example. OM is a core component to the SAP ERP HCM functions, and has integration ties to almost every SAP ERP HCM component that exists. As such, it is one of the areas where you should focus your attention early on in any implementation of SAP ERP HCM.

To most effectively implement and use the functions of SAP ERP HCM, it is important to have an understanding of the different aspects of the system. Keeping in mind these different viewpoints will help you develop a plan for implementing the system functions so that you can include only the information you will actually use to get the most back out of it. These different views include:

▶ The *process* view that you'll use to create, manage, and maintain the information. SAP provides a vast array of business processes to handle all aspects of personnel management. In many cases there are multiple choices for the process to use to support any given function. You can also tailor the processes to meet your company's particular business practices and policy needs. This choice provides freedom in implementation but also introduces some complexity. Deciding which process to use, how to use the process, how to configure or customize it to meet your specific requirements, and who will use the process are among the necessary tasks in implementation. In some cases the process will be very straightforward, and the function in the SAP system will closely match what you may be doing today. In other cases, either the SAP function or your business process may have to change to be effective. We'll explore all of these process dimensions throughout this book.

▶ The *data* view is a bit more granular than the process view, and primarily serves to help you understand the various information structures in SAP ERP HCM and how the data drives the various functions. Knowing the process by which the data is created is helpful, but knowing how that data is then stored and later accessed will help you get the most out of it. We'll look at the various data components and how the data is created and stored, as well as how it is accessed and reported.

▶ The *technical* view focuses on the technical aspects of implementing OM, primarily the customizing activities that are necessary in an implementation to best design the processes and data that you'll use. Where configuration settings must be made, the options available will be explained and best practices outlined.

1.1.1 Using the SAP Implementation Guide

As just mentioned, throughout this book we'll discuss the technical concepts in addition to the data and process concepts. The technical components primarily consist of the configuration and setup tasks that are necessary to use the OM functions described. For most functions, the configuration steps are uniformly accessed via the SAP Implementation Guide (IMG).

The various IMG tasks are described in detail in each of the relevant chapters, including detailed instructions on how to configure each of the tables contained therein. In the IMG, the path **Personnel Management • Organizational Management** will take you to the section where all of the IMG tasks detailed in this book can be found (Figure 1.1). From the IMG section for OM, multiple configuration topics are presented, each of which will be discussed in one or more relevant chapters throughout this book. Where a particular customizing topic or activity is called out, the IMG path to the activity and any corresponding transaction code will also be provided.

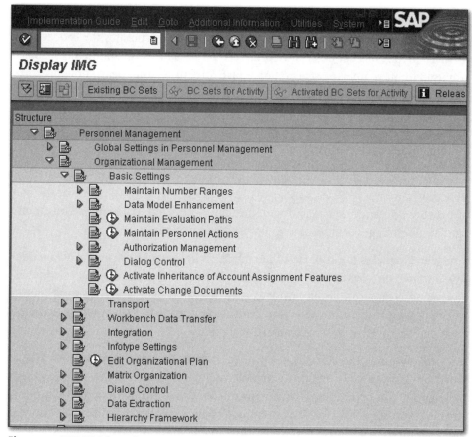

Figure 1.1 SAP IMG Steps for Organizational Management

1.2 Structure of This Book

The chapters of this book go into detail about each of their respective topics. Each chapter discusses both the process and data viewpoints described in Section 1.1 where applicable, and delves into the technical aspects of implementation, configuration, and customization.

Chapter 2 provides an overview of the SAP Business Suite of applications, in particular, focusing on SAP ERP and within that the functions of SAP ERP HCM. It provides a baseline of knowledge of how the SAP ERP HCM component is structured and functions, and lays the foundation for understanding what OM does within and for that function.

Chapter 3 explains the basic concepts behind OM. It discusses what object-oriented design principles are and how SAP ERP HCM incorporates the concept into OM. The types of data objects used in OM are explained, including how objects are used to make up the organizational plan structure. You'll learn how organizational units, jobs, positions, and persons work together to represent your company structure with the SAP system. This chapter also reviews additional objects such as users and tasks provided by SAP for various functions within SAP ERP HCM and in non-HR functions in SAP.

Chapter 4 looks at the infotype concept that is used throughout the SAP ERP HCM function and how it's used to store data. We'll explain in detail some of the concepts that rule and regulate infotype behavior. Effective dates, time constraints, and number ranges will be among the topics reviewed.

Chapter 5 explains the concept of relationships in the object-oriented data model. We'll show you how objects are related to one another and how that relationship is used to create a multidimensional organizational plan. We'll also outline the various tasks needed to create your own relationships to provide further dimension and perspective to the organizational plan.

As a follow-up to the discussion on relationships, **Chapter 6** goes on to discuss how to report on your organizational data using evaluation paths. You'll find out how evaluation paths use relationships to connect seemingly unrelated information. We'll discuss what SAP delivers out of the box, how evaluation paths can be customized or even created using the implementation tools, and how they are then used in reporting.

With the basic concepts covered, **Chapter 7** takes a detailed look at some specific infotypes that store the organizational plan data you'll be creating in OM. Some infotypes are core and common across different objects, and so are discussed in depth so a broad understanding can be achieved. We'll also look at some specific infotypes that are used in the United States to meet some very specific functional requirements.

The various methods for creating and maintaining the organizational data elements are described in **Chapter 8**. For as many data elements as there are, there are just as many means to access the data. This chapter explains what the available transactions are, and discusses how to get to each and what it does and how it works. We'll also discuss what works best, the limitations of the interface, and pros and cons of each interface. The chapter also features a functional comparison table of each interface option with recommendations for different use cases.

Chapter 9 is a follow-up to Chapter 8, explaining the Object Manager user interface concept, as well as how to customize the user interface to meet the needs of your various enterprise users. This is a detailed technical explanation of the Object Manager screen layout, what is delivered in the standard, what you can change, and how to change it. We'll discuss why you should change the objects list and how to remove standard and add new objects. You'll learn how to add new infotypes and how to remove infotypes you won't use or don't want. The ABAP function modules that are used in the OM search function, how to add new search criteria to objects, how to remove standard search criteria, and Q&A on whether to create custom searches is also provided. Lastly, we'll discuss what data are available to display and how to change the display of the data.

Chapter 10 is a review of some of the technical tools and processes that will help you set up your system to begin creating the OM structure and use to its fullest extent. You'll learn about utilities that are available to validate the consistency of your organizational plan setup, ensuring that the necessary configuration and master data is in place. We'll also discuss mechanisms for sharing data between SAP systems. Finally, this chapter provides valuable information on the authorization options you can use to secure access to the OM structure.

Chapter 11 is a discussion about integration of OM to the other functions within SAP ERP HCM: Personnel Administration, Personnel Development, Training & Event Management, Compensation Management, Recruitment, and Employee and Manager Self-Service. A review of how OM is integrated with other SAP components is also provided. What object types, infotypes, and relationships are created and used in the process, how the integration itself occurs, what to watch out for when integrating a new component into the data model, and best practices for initial design when considering whether to implement the component are provided.

1.2.1 SAP Release Version

The material in this book is based on the latest SAP release at the time of publishing, which is SAP ERP 6.0. It's important to note, however, that the OM component in SAP ERP HCM has existed for some time now, and the general concepts concerning how the component functions as well as how it is configured have remained the same for several releases.

All users of the OM component are encouraged to read through each chapter to gain an understanding of the topics. It's likely that you can apply the information to your own release as well as to SAP ERP 6.0. Much of the benefit in the OM functions is gained by experimenting with the configuration and data model concepts that are available in all SAP release versions.

1.2.2 A Brief Word on Terminology

Throughout this book there's a lot of SAP jargon. We've used several terms so far, and we're still only in Chapter 1. The name SAP itself is an acronym, so SAP is clearly no stranger to the concept. SAP ERP HCM functions are no different. Traditionally, the SAP ERP HCM components have a two- or three-letter acronym that is commonly referred to in documentation and by users of the system. For example, in the Employee Management space, some of the components are:

▶ OM – Organizational Management

▶ PA – Personnel Administration

▶ MSS – Manager Self-Service

A complete list of the SAP ERP HCM–related component acronyms is provided in Appendix G. For the purposes of this book, we'll often refer to the two- or three-letter acronyms above and in the appendix when referring to HCM components.

So, let's move on to Chapter 2 and get started with our exploration of Organizational Management in SAP ERP HCM.

Of all the applications in the SAP ERP software, Human Capital Management (HCM) can be the most complex. Rich in functionality and complicated by country regulatory and process requirements, SAP ERP HCM offers a wide-ranging structure and design options. In this chapter, we'll give you a brief overview of SAP ERP and the specific offerings in SAP ERP HCM.

2 SAP HCM Overview

The SAP Business Suite is a comprehensive collection of business applications, which includes core enterprise applications, industry-specific solutions, and composite applications. These applications are based on the SAP NetWeaver® platform, which is both an integration and application platform.

2.1 SAP Business Suite: Enterprise Applications Overview

One of the primary marketing messages for the SAP Business Suite is that it's a comprehensive family of adaptive business applications, rapidly adjusting while continuing to perform well to meet the needs of the customer. SAP provides best-of-breed functionality in a variety of different business areas, each built for complete integration with the others and including industry-specific functionality and virtually unlimited scalability.

Because business requirements change regularly, application software changes frequently as well. To help customers adapt easily to these changes, SAP provides product version updates regularly to keep up with regulatory changes and to enhance production functionality to help customers manage their business processes more effectively. However, keeping track of these new versions and names can be somewhat confusing, so throughout this book, we'll refer to the naming conventions SAP adopted for its products from 2007 onward. For example, the new application name SAP ERP 6.0 was previously known as SAP ERP 2005, which was named for the year in which it was released. Similarly, SAP NetWeaver 7.0 replaces the name SAP NetWeaver 2004s.

So let's take a look at SAP ERP 6.0 (Figure 2.1).

Figure 2.1 SAP ERP Overview

2.1.1 The SAP ERP Foundation

The SAP ERP applications provide functionality for enterprise resource planning, including the core business functions that most customers think about when they first implement SAP. Generally, these functions are targeted toward large enterprises, and can apply to companies regardless of their global presence or industry.

SAP provides a complex range of solutions through these various products. The solutions are meant to provide both back-office and front-line user software applications. With them you can run virtually any and every aspect of a business. SAP ERP is a tightly integrated global software solution that gives customers a better way to manage corporate processes and assets.

	End-User Service Delivery			
Analytics	Strategic Enterprise Management	Financial Analytics	Operations Analytics	Workforce Analytics
Financials	Financial Supply Chain Management	Financial Accounting	Mgmt. Accounting	Corporate Governance
Human Capital Management	Talent Management	Workforce Process Mgmt.		Workforce Deployment
Procurement and Logistics Execution	Procurement	Supplier Colaboration	Inventory and Warehouse Mgmt.	Out- and Inbound Logistics	Transportation
Product Developmt. and Manufacturing	Production Planning	Manufacturing Execution	Enterprise Asset Management	Product Development	Lifecycle Data Management
Sales and Service	Sales Order Management	Aftermarket Sales and Service	Professional Service Delivery	Foreign Trade	Incentive & Commission Mgmt.
Corporate Services	Real Estate Management	Project Portfolio Management	Travel Management	Environment, Health & Safety	Quality Management
SAP NewtWeaver	People Integration	Information Integration	Process Integration	Application Platform

Figure 2.2 SAP ERP Solution Map

While the solution map in Figure 2.2 outlines various functions included in the SAP ERP solution, there are really four main application functions that make up the product:

▸ **SAP ERP Financials** includes financial accounting, financial and management reporting, corporate governance and compliance, capital management, and corporate performance management. SAP ERP Financials applications have been at the core of most U.S. and global implementations of SAP systems, and will likely remain so for some time.

▸ **SAP ERP Human Capital Management** includes employee management processes for human resource management, personnel administration, and payroll functions. The various functions take a person from applicant to hired employee, through the employment life cycle, and all the way to retirement or termination.

▸ **SAP ERP Operations** incorporates processes for companies to provide products and services to customers. Procurement and logistics execution, product development and manufacturing, sales, and service delivery are among the functions supported.

▸ **SAP ERP Corporate Services** includes many corporate functions that typically fall outside the above three groups. Real estate management, asset management, product and portfolio management, environment, health and safety management, and quality management are some examples of these functions. Whether centralized or decentralized, these corporate administrative services can be managed within SAP ERP.

In addition, **SAP NetWeaver** is the integration and application platform upon which all SAP Business Suite applications are based. It's composed of multiple technical components and tools for running the SAP applications.

These core components make up most of the functionality provided by SAP ERP and are marketed and sold through a variety of different mechanisms.

2.1.2 SAP Specialized Business Solutions

In addition to SAP ERP, SAP also provides products for enhanced functions in the following areas.

- ▶ **SAP Product Lifecycle Management (PLM)**
  Functionality to manage, track, and control product-related information over the product lifecycle. SAP PLM provides enhanced product development and manufacturing processes designed to get products to market faster.

- ▶ **SAP Customer Relationship Management (CRM)**
  Functionality for marketing, sales, and service functions. SAP CRM gives companies tools to help obtain and retain customers, build relationships and gain insight into customers, and implement customer-focused strategies to help improve customer loyalty.

- ▶ **SAP Supply Chain Management (SCM)**
  Functionality to enable adaptive supply chain networks. SAP SCM changes traditional supply chains from linear or sequential processes to more demand-driven and proactive network processes.

- ▶ **SAP Supplier Relationship Management (SRM)**
  Functionality to optimize procurement operations, improving sourcing and purchasing processes.

In each of these specialized products, SAP has taken specific process requirements and developed application functions beyond the base SAP ERP solution to meet the needs of each process. In all cases, very tight integration is built into the new functions with the core application areas in SAP ERP. This allows customers to leverage any existing implementation of SAP ERP solutions and extend the functionality where it is most needed. Because these products are newer, many are implemented well after the initial SAP ERP implementation.

Example

Many customers implementing SAP in the 1990s implemented Sales and Distribution components. With an initial release in 1999, customers are enhancing their sales functions with further implementations of SAP CRM. Similarly, many customers that have implemented SAP ERP Financials components are now enhancing their SAP solution by implementing Enterprise Buyer Procurement or Strategic Enterprise Management. In either situation, the later release of a component is well integrated into the base component, helping customers get the most benefit out of both.

In any case, it works well regardless of when the components are installed. It's really just a matter of implementation timing.

So let's take a look at the SAP ERP HCM components to get an idea of how they can each help improve your business processes.

2.2 SAP HCM Components in Depth

Throughout this book, we'll be focusing on the SAP ERP HCM component. SAP ERP HCM is used for managing all aspects of the employee lifecycle. From attracting and hiring employees, training and ongoing personnel and event transactional management, to payment and termination, the SAP ERP HCM solution is a unified suite for all people-related processes.

The SAP ERP HCM strategy is similar to SAP ERP in that it provides a comprehensive and global solution that can be utilized by companies of virtually any size, geography, or industry. Similar to the SAP ERP components, SAP ERP HCM is made up of multiple major functions. The various SAP ERP HCM components can be implemented together, or they can be implemented independently or sequentially one after another. To increase HR process efficiencies, SAP ERP HCM automates what SAP refers to as three key processes:

- **Workforce Process Management**
  These are the "core" HR transaction functions most people not only think of first but also implement first in SAP ERP HCM. Employee or personnel administration, organizational management, benefits administration, time management, and payroll are among the processes included.

- **Talent Management**
  These enhanced people-management functions range from recruitment and applicant management, training and event management, to personnel development and compensation administration.

- **Workforce Analytics**
  These are reporting and analysis options associated with HR, and come in the form of hundreds of predefined reports and key performance indicators (KPIs).

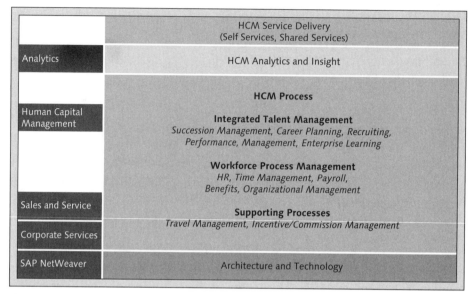

Figure 2.3 SAP ERP HCM Solution Map

Figure 2.3 shows an overlay of SAP ERP HCM functions on the SAP ERP Solution Map in Figure 2.2. This overlay identifies where the various functions or SAP ERP HCM components fulfill and integrate with other areas of SAP ERP, providing more rich functionality in those areas.

Let's take a look at each of these components and examine their basic functions a little further.

2.2.1 Workforce Process Management is "Core"

Workforce Process Management is the core component of any SAP ERP HCM implementation. These transactional functions provide support for all basic employee and personnel information management. The SAP ERP HCM solution uses a central database approach to establish the identity of a person, typically an employee, and to relate all information that HR and the company may need to perform transactions and record data for that person.

People are assigned a sequential person number that is typically system generated but can also be entered manually. It is around this central person ID concept that the information is entered and stored and later accessed for reporting and analysis (Figure 2.4).

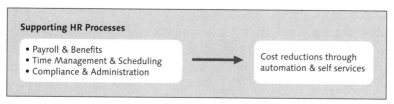

Figure 2.4 Workforce Process Management Enables Cost Reductions

Employee Administration

Employee Administration, also referred to as Personnel Administration (PA), includes the personnel management processes that take an employee from "hire to retire." Employee personal and job-related information is tracked through the various events that occur in the employee's lifecycle, and is stored in a number of different records, called infotypes in SAP ERP HCM, which collectively make up the employee's personnel file in the SAP system. The infotype concept is discussed more thoroughly in Chapter 4. These personnel records are referenced, linked, and enhanced throughout the various components within SAP ERP HCM to perform the functions in those areas.

Organizational Management

Organizational Management is the component that we will focus on in this book, but at a high level it's basically a mechanism to depict your organization in SAP systems. The organization from an HR perspective is created and managed, allowing organizational group differentiation to be represented in the other HR processes. All organizational units form the basis of the structure, whether it's a company, division, function, department, or work unit. The level of detail or granularity is completely up to you to define, so the system is very flexible. Jobs and positions are defined to represent the various types of roles that exist within those organizations.

Benefits Administration

Employee benefit plan enrollments and participation are managed via *Benefits Administration*. Benefits plans are first configured to include all details of the plans offered. This includes plan types and options, such as a medical PPO versus HMO plans, with individual or family coverage. Financial components of the plans can incorporate employee and employer costs and varying coverage levels, and can take into account flexible credits that the company may offer. Benefits can be grouped for different populations within the company into different benefit programs that the employee can select to enroll. Employees enroll in the various benefits through annual open enrollment periods or through event-related transactions, such as marriage or the birth of a child. The company can then report on participation, interact with benefits providers or carriers through interfaces, or pay and bill for benefits through integration with SAP ERP Financials third-party remittance functions. The component also includes functions for managing retiree benefits and COBRA administration for after employees are terminated or otherwise lose benefits coverage.

Time Management

Time off as well as time worked is tracked and accounted for in *Time Management*. Functions exist to create and assign various work schedules to employees, defining both their working hours and nonworking hours, such as holidays, breaks, and meals. Time can then be recorded by the employee directly or for the employee by another person. Time recording is done a number of ways, depending on the operations of your company. You can record time actively, meaning that all working time as well as time off is entered into the system. In the United States this type of time reporting can be completed by nonexempt personnel, who have to report time worked in order to be paid correctly.

You can also record time on an exception basis, meaning you are assumed to be working your scheduled hours unless you say otherwise. In this scenario, you typically only report absences, such as sick time or vacation. Additionally, the SAP system can accept time from other systems, such as time clock or card systems. A number of SAP partner organizations provide time entry solutions that integrate data into SAP ERP HCM. Once the data is entered, it's then processed to validate the entries against rules that have been configured in the system. The various time rules ensure that employees aren't entering time when they shouldn't and that if an employee works certain hours, they are credited appropriately. Time Management includes capabilities to charge time to projects, orders, or other cost elements, providing a means to do labor-related accounting.

Payroll Processing

Finally, employees are paid through country-specific *Payroll Processing* routines. In the payroll component, additional personnel records are created that provide information on the various payments, deductions, and taxes that apply to the employee. These records, along with information from the other personnel modules (Employee Administration, Benefits, Time Management), are read and processed according to complex payroll functions and rules. There are more than 50 country-specific payroll programs provided that allow companies to pay employees and ensure legal compliance and reporting for the countries in which they do business. Fully integrated to SAP ERP Financials, the payroll results are transferred to banking, general ledger, accounts payable, and cost accounting functions to provide end-to-end employee finance processing.

2.2.2 Talent Management is about Managing Talent

Talent Management encompasses enhanced functions of SAP ERP HCM (Figure 2.5). Many customers don't implement these components with an initial SAP ERP HCM implementation unless they are replacing an entire HRMS platform that also included these functions. This is probably because these components require additional configuration and process setup beyond the general employee processing.

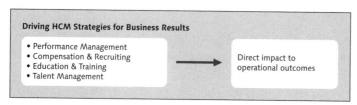

Figure 2.5 Talent Management Puts Talent to Best Use

E-Recruitment

E-Recruitment and applicant management begin person-related processing before the person is ever an employee. E-Recruitment is where requisitions for open jobs or positions are created and posted for applicants to apply. Depending on how the opening is defined, the applicant can be evaluated systematically against the requirements of the requisition and ranked or selected for applicant processing. Applicant Management takes the recruiting functions through all stages of candidate screening and selection. Once people are selected for hire, the candidate information can be passed via integration programs to PA.

Enterprise Learning Management

Enterprise Learning Management is a multifunction component that encompasses everything training related, from designing and creating training content to classroom delivery and results measurement. Authoring tools are used to create training courses and tests and to conduct online virtual learning events. SAP provides its own tools and partners with other companies offering this software. The learning solution provides a learning environment for all of your organization's training needs.

Performance Management

Performance Management allows companies to align team and individual goals with corporate goals and strategies. Employee reviews and appraisals can be standardized and uniformly processed throughout the organization, allowing you to tie compensation to employee performance results. The functions provided are targeted to support a performance-oriented compensation process.

Compensation Administration

Compensation Administration allows you to administer multiple pay strategies: stock and other long-term or incentive payments, variable merit and bonus pay plans, and performance- or competency-based fixed pay. You can use Compensation Management to create both centralized and decentralized budgets, and plan and administer compensation adjustments within those budgets at the manager level. Pay grades and salary structures are defined to identify the internal value of jobs and positions in your organization. Internal salary data analysis and external salary survey participation tools enable companies to conduct comparative salary package evaluation to ensure marketplace competitiveness.

Personnel Development

Personnel Development incorporates both career and succession planning. Career planning allows you to plan and implement specific personnel and training measures to promote the professional development of your employees. Qualifications for general or specific roles in the organization can be specified. Personnel development sets out to ensure that all of the employees in all of the functional areas in your company are qualified to the standards required at present, and will remain so in the future, all while taking into account the employees' qualifications, preferences, and aspirations. Succession planning uses this same information to create, implement, and evaluate succession planning scenarios.

2.2.3 Workforce Analytics Reporting

Workforce Analytics delivers workforce analytical and reporting tools, as well as strategic planning and alignment functions. Components include standard reports, ad hoc reporting, and evaluations based on KPIs. These tools empower companies to develop workforce strategies, analyze results, and perform ongoing monitoring via a wide range of reports and analyses to ensure optimal performance (Figure 2.6).

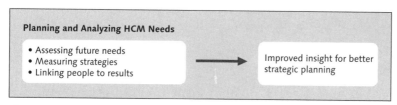

Figure 2.6 Workforce Analytics Provides Insight

SAP provides some important figures such as time to hire, employee turnover and retention rates, progress against corporate goals, training program effectiveness, and compensation program measures. One of the key benefits of the Workforce Analytics components is that data is up to the minute, providing direct visibility into the workforce and its operations. Integration with the other SAP ERP components is another key advantage for SAP ERP HCM analytics. SAP HCM processes are better planned and designed up front through financial and operational data integration. Additionally, allowing integration of actual financial and business results into the HR analysis provides complete transparency into opportunities and measurement of the strategy performance. Rather than hoping you have the right information at the right time to make critical business decisions, SAP ERP HCM analytics ensures that you do have it and can answer whatever challenges and questions come your way.

2.2.4 The SAP ERP HCM Big Picture

At the end of the day, the important thing to remember about the SAP ERP HCM solution is that it is a complete solution (Figure 2.7). A carefully designed and properly executed SAP ERP HCM solution can offer far more than transactional cost reductions.

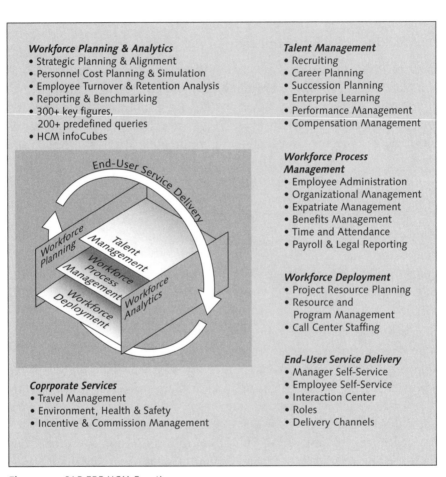

Workforce Planning & Analytics
- Strategic Planning & Alignment
- Personnel Cost Planning & Simulation
- Employee Turnover & Retention Analysis
- Reporting & Benchmarking
- 300+ key figures, 200+ predefined queries
- HCM infoCubes

Talent Management
- Recruiting
- Career Planning
- Succession Planning
- Enterprise Learning
- Performance Management
- Compensation Management

Workforce Process Management
- Employee Administration
- Organizational Management
- Expatriate Management
- Benefits Management
- Time and Attendance
- Payroll & Legal Reporting

Workforce Deployment
- Project Resource Planning
- Resource and Program Management
- Call Center Staffing

Coprporate Services
- Travel Management
- Environment, Health & Safety
- Incentive & Commission Management

End-User Service Delivery
- Manager Self-Service
- Employee Self-Service
- Interaction Center
- Roles
- Delivery Channels

Figure 2.7 SAP ERP HCM Functions

SAP ERP HCM allows you to transform your traditional HR functions into a comprehensive human capital program. This can achieve employee productivity enhancements, and it can impact business results by ensuring that all employees contribute their full potential and further the objectives of the business. Whether you implement all or parts, the functions provided can help HR deliver value to the company through the SAP ERP HCM processes in a program that integrates people, process, and technology.

2.3 Conclusion

We've discussed the SAP ERP HCM components at a fairly high level, but clearly, a significant amount of functionality is provided by these components. In the next chapter we'll begin to take a closer look at OM, its design principles, and the data elements that make up the organizational plan.

The basic data structures in Organizational Management are based on object design. Once you master the fundamental design principles covered in this chapter, you can design with confidence that your plan will be successful.

3 Organizational Management Basics

Core to the SAP ERP HCM Employee Management functionality is Organizational Management (OM). The functions in OM allow you to create and manage the organizational structure of the company. The organizational plan, as it's called in SAP systems, is used to carry out various business processes within the applications. The organizational plan represents the various groups and departments of the organization, the roles and positions in those areas, and the people and tasks. The organizational plan differs from other organizational elements in SAP systems, such as the company code or cost center structures in finance, or the personnel areas and subareas in Personnel Administration (PA). These other structures have specific settings that control how processes flow in the SAP transactions. The organizational plan is data that is purely representative of how you view your organizational structure.

3.1 The Backbone of SAP ERP HCM

OM is considered the basis for the SAP ERP HCM functions in the SAP system, and enables you to implement and use the SAP ERP HCM functions for PA, Recruitment, Personnel Development, Performance Management, Compensation Management, Training and Event Management, Personnel Cost Planning, and Manager Self-Service. OM also forms the basis for the SAP Business Workflow, creating the foundation for assigning and routing tasks to an employee. As such, it is imperative that the organizational structure be given a good deal of forethought and consideration in its design. Having the right number of levels as well as the right level of detail in the structure of the organizational plan will set the foundation for how many processes will function throughout SAP ERP HCM. Too little detail can result in the need for manual processes and human intervention when processing personnel transactions or in reporting. But too much detail can be both a process and a maintenance nightmare.

3.2 Object-Oriented Data Management in SAP Systems

It's best to start at the concept level when explaining how OM is structured. SAP chooses object-oriented data modeling to depict organizational structures and to distribute work in the application, so understanding these concepts will help you plan the design of your organization most effectively. Of course, object-oriented programming and object technology in general are by no means new in the world of software, and they are certainly not specific to SAP. But let's take a look at object-oriented programming.

By definition, object-oriented programming (OOP) is a programming paradigm that uses "objects" and their interactions to design applications and computer programs[1]. OOP has roots dating back to the 1960s, and has been in active use in programming languages since the early 1990s. Development languages such as C++ and Java, among others, use object technology concepts in their design. In OOP, each object is treated as a separate and reusable entity, with a distinct role or responsibility. When joined, these objects work together to provide a complete functional program.

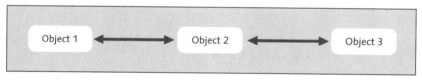

Figure 3.1 Related Objects

The OOP approach is used in the organizational model and in other areas of SAP systems; however, ABAP (the language supported by SAP) can be developed using object orientation (OO) or not. In the past few years, SAP has been using OO technology to develop GUI controls and some BASIS tasks, but many people who develop in ABAP still don't use OO; they only use the objects developed by SAP in their code. And even the objects developed by SAP are usually mixed with non-OO code.

---

1 *www.wikipedia.org*– "Object-oriented programming"

However, object data concepts are used in a number of functional areas within SAP systems. They are most widely used in HCM, but objects are also used in Authorizations, Finance, Sales and Distribution, Production Planning, and Workflow, which is used in virtually every SAP function. Although we'll examine some of the detailed integration points in the final chapter, the point to remember is that objects provide both repeatability and flexibility, and objects are here to stay.

3.3 Object Technology in OM

Taking the OOP concept to SAP ERP HCM, OM uses an object-oriented data model to represent the organizational structures. Each component of the organization is created as an individual object with its own role and responsibilities, as well as detailed information defining the object. When these objects are related to one another, they form the entire company's organizational structure. Nuances of the structure are defined by the data details of each object, as well as how the objects are related to one another.

This object-oriented data modeling approach to creating the organization in SAP systems provides an extreme level of flexibility. Because you can create objects on your own, you can freely design the breadth and depth of the organization to suit your own needs. If your needs are simple, you can create a relatively basic organizational structure with only those elements and details that are absolutely necessary to support the business processes you need. On the other hand, if your needs are complex, you can create a very detailed organizational structure with lots of object information to support complex requirements.

Example
Many customers who don't implement SAP ERP HCM still implement OM to support SAP Business Workflow. The organizational structure in OM provides the basis for routing workflow approval tasks. Because information on all employees is not present in SAP ERP HCM, a basic OM structure is built consisting of only those users that have approval tasks. This simple structure is all the enterprise needs to process workflows correctly.

In OM, object technology is at the center of the application design. Certain types of objects are used to create the organizational plan. The organizational plan is a representation of the functional structure of your enterprise, and is made up of various objects that are then related to one another. At the core, organizational units, jobs, and positions are the objects needed to create a basic organizational structure. When these objects are created and then related to one another, the underlying structure of the company is complete. Combine this basic structure with people, and you have a fully functional organizational plan.

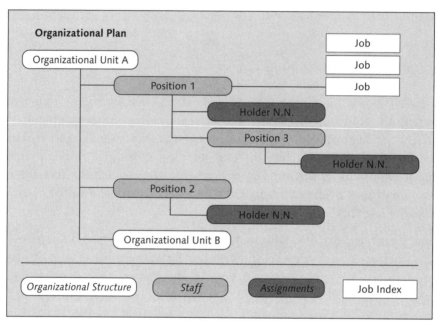

Figure 3.2 Object-Oriented Organizational Plan

Figure 3.2 shows a basic organizational plan example. The organizational structure depicts the functional organization, represented by a higher-level organizational unit with a subordinate-level organizational unit. Also represented in the organizational plan are reporting structures between the staff in an enterprise. Staff can be equals, such as position 1 and 2, or a staff member can report to another, such as position 3 reports to position 1. Each position is in turn assigned to a person, who is the holder of that particular role. Last, the position can be linked to a job index.

Example

Thinking of your own company, the two organizational units in Figure 3.2 can represent a department and a subdepartment function. Organizational unit A may be Human Resources, and organizational unit B may be Benefits. Positions 1 and 2 may be benefits managers, both linked to the job manager. This same concept applies across the enterprise.

3.4   HR Data Objects in OM

The organizational plan in an SAP system is created by defining various object types and by assigning attributes to them and relating them to one another. Over 100 standard objects are delivered with the SAP system, but only certain objects are generally used to create the organizational plan within SAP ERP HCM. Some of these objects are depicted in Figure 3.3.

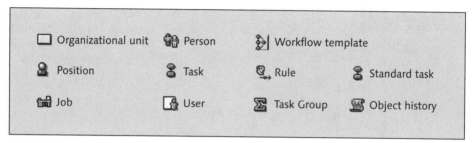

Organizational unit	Person	Workflow template	
Position	Task	Rule	Standard task
Job	User	Task Group	Object history

Figure 3.3   Most Common SAP Organizational Objects

SAP objects are generally defined with three characteristics:

▶ A one- or two-character object identifier

▶ A text description of the object

▶ A graphic representing the object

For example, the object type O is for organizational unit, and is generally depicted with a box. Each object type has unique information for these three characteristics. SAP has reserved the A-ZZ name range for its delivered object types. Customers can create their own object types in the 1-99 number range. This is discussed in more detail in Section 3.6.5.

The IMG provides a number of views to help you understand how objects work in the system. In the primary IMG view, accessible via the IMG path **Personnel Management • Organizational Management • Basic Settings • Data Model Enhancement • Maintain Object Types**, the object type is defined with its one-to-two character code and text. This is depicted in Figure 3.4. Alternatively, you can access this via Transaction Code OOOT. Optional elements are the organizational object type and ICON assignment.

> **Note**
>
> Over 1300 types of organizational objects are delivered by SAP and control the components the object can have. Keep in mind that not all organizational objects are used in HR and so they may not be relevant for your particular implementation.

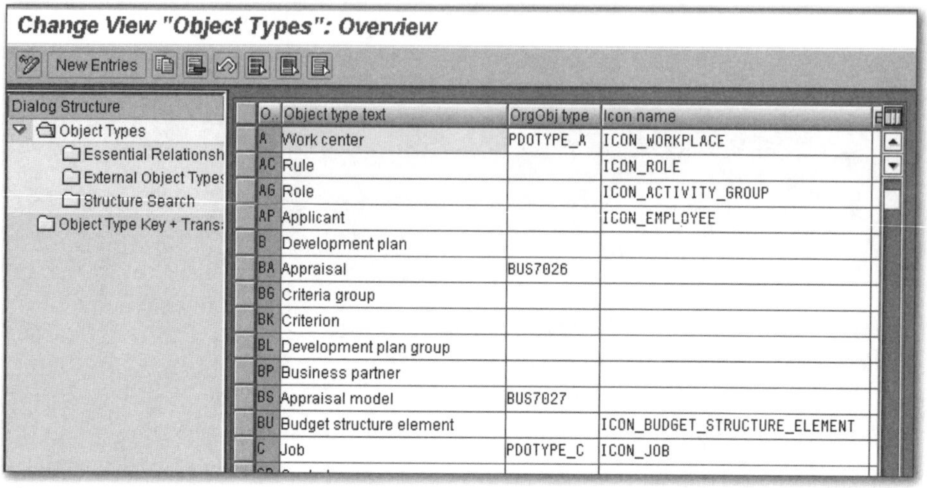
Change View "Object Types": Overview
New Entries
Dialog Structure
Object Types
Essential Relationsh
External Object Types
Structure Search
Object Type Key + Trans
O..
Object type text
OrgObj type
Icon name
A
Work center
PDOTYPE_A
ICON_WORKPLACE
AC
Rule
ICON_ROLE
AG
Role
ICON_ACTIVITY_GROUP
AP
Applicant
ICON_EMPLOYEE
B
Development plan
BA
Appraisal
BUS7026
BG
Criteria group
BK
Criterion
BL
Development plan group
BP
Business partner
BS
Appraisal model
BUS7027
BU
Budget structure element
ICON_BUDGET_STRUCTURE_ELEMENT
C
Job
PDOTYPE_C
ICON_JOB

Figure 3.4 IMG: OM Object Types

An organizational object type is a correspondingly named object type in the Business Object Repository, used in SAP Business Workflow. It is defined by basic data including key fields, attributes, methods with parameters and exceptions (i.e., activities that can be performed for an object), events, and implementation in the program code.

Icons are available from SAP, and are assigned to the object type so that in the OM processes a visual distinction can be made between similarly named object types. For example, if a job and a position are both named Manager, you can tell them apart by the icons displayed next to them.

You can utilize the additional IMG views by selecting an object type and then double-clicking on the further views for additional customizing activities. The additional IMG activities in Figure 3.4 will be reviewed in later sections. For now, let's move on to the basic organizational plan structure elements.

3.5 Basic Organizational Plan Structure Elements

In a basic organizational plan structure, organizational units, jobs, and positions are used to define the company organizational structure. In addition, the cost center object provides an integration point to SAP Financial Controlling, and the person object integrates PA. All of these objects set the stage for SAP Business Workflow functions, which utilize task objects. By defining these basic organizational elements, the essential structure of the company and personnel hierarchy is defined in the SAP system and can be used to perform transactions and to manage the workforce.

3.5.1 Organizational Unit ☐

At the center of an organizational plan are organizational units (object key O), arranged in a hierarchy that mirrors the structure of your enterprise. An *organizational unit* is a functional unit that can represent anything that you define as important in representing your company. Examples of organizational units can include parent company, subsidiary, division, function, departments, and work groups. Organizational units can mirror other organizational-type units that are created in other SAP components, such as company code or business area in SAP ERP Financials, but they should be designed to differ from these structures and, in particular, to represent the human resources perspective of the organizations.

> **Tip**
>
> Many customers wonder whether they should simply mirror the cost center structure that is set up in SAP ERP Controlling. While at first glance this may seem a simple structure that easily translates to how personnel are organized, in many companies the cost center structure is too broad. Keep in mind that organizational units should represent work-related functions, not simply financial control units. Organizational units can have a many-to-one relationship with cost centers, so you are not limited by the breadth or depth of the cost center hierarchy when building the organizational hierarchy. A good rule of thumb is to have separate organizational units at each manager position.

An organizational structure depicts the hierarchy in which the various organizational units at your enterprise are arranged. SAP provides sample data delivered with the SAP system, shown in Figure 3.5. You create your own organizational structure by creating and maintaining organizational units, and then creating relationships between the units. In implementation, your company organizational charts can provide a solid basis from which to design the organizational structure, including reporting relationships.

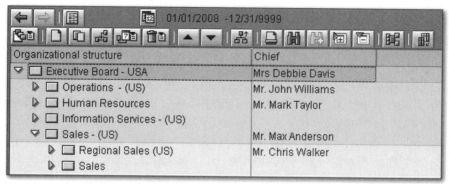

Figure 3.5 Sample SAP Organizational Structure

The organizational unit is technically the only required component of an organizational plan from the SAP system's point of view. After creating the various organizational units and relating them to one another, the basis of the organizational plan is complete. Any other elements, including jobs and positions, are considered optional. Practically, however, most customers don't consider an organizational plan complete with just organizational units. There are few processes that rely solely on organizational units, so it's not wise to stop there.

In addition to the typical one-dimensional organizational plan, you can depict a multidimensional *matrix* organization. A matrix organization can represent relationships between both functions and disciplines. In this scenario, multiple hierarchies of the organizational units exist in the SAP system, providing different viewpoints of the organizational plan. This functionality is particularly useful for organizations that do project-based reporting. Projects can be defined as organizational units and reported on separately from the usual hierarchical structure.

> **Tip**
>
> When creating matrix reporting hierarchies for project management organizations or other purposes, it's best to use a relationship other than A/B 002 (Reports to/Is line supervisor of). Most processes and standard reports in SAP systems assume that the A/B 002 relationship links an employee and the manager responsible for his pay, performance, and development. To keep these manager processes separate, many customers use relationship A/B 088 (Dotted line reports to/Dotted line supervises) to represent matrix organizations. The dotted line reporting relationship more accurately describes the reporting structure in a project-oriented hierarchy.

Infotypes for Organizational Units

The following infotypes are generally used to define the organizational units in OM, but you can choose additional infotypes as needed. The infotypes' uses and purposes are explained in detail in Chapter 7.

- Object (Infotype 1000)
- Relationship (Infotype 1001)
- Description (Infotype 1002)
- Department/Staff (Infotype 1003)
- Account Assignment Features (Infotype 1008)
- Work Schedule (Infotype 1011)
- Cost Planning (Infotype 1015)
- Standard Profiles (Infotype 1016)
- PD Profiles (Infotype 1017)
- Cost Distribution (Infotype 1018)
- Required Positions (Infotype 1019)
- Site Dependent Info (Infotype 1027)
- Address (Infotype 1028)
- Mail Address (Infotype 1032)

Critical Relationships for Organizational Units

Organizational units generally are defined with the following relationships:

- To other organizational units via A/B 002 (Reports To / Is Line Manager of) [See Figure 3.6 for an example of this.]
- To positions via A/B 003 (belongs to/includes)
- To a master cost center (object key K) via relationship A 011 (cost center assignment) or distributed across multiple cost centers via relationship A 014 (cost center distribution)

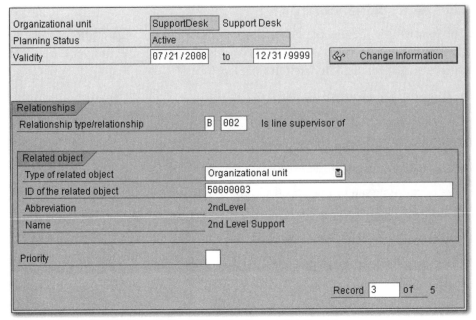

Figure 3.6 Building the Organizational Hierarchy through Relationships

3.5.2 Job

Jobs (object key C) are categorizations of functions in an enterprise. A *job* is described in general terms, and can be performed by multiple individuals within the company. For example, Administrative Assistant or Manager is a job. A job is defined by both a short and long text description, as shown in Figure 3.7. Jobs are further defined by the assignment of characteristics that document the requirements and the work performed in that job.

When you create and maintain jobs, they are listed in a *job index*. Jobs are the basis from which multiple positions can be created with similar tasks or attributes. When you create a new position, you relate it to a job that already exists in the job index.

> **Example**
>
> Your job index may contain several management jobs: Associate Manager, Manager, Senior Manager, Associate Director, and Director. When you create a new position, IT Application Support Manager, the position can be linked to the job Manager in the job index.

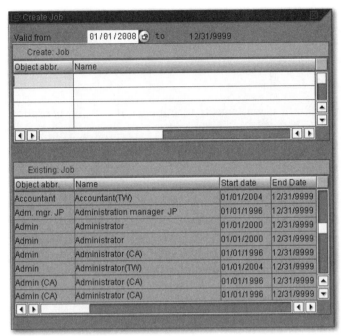

Figure 3.7 Creating Jobs in the SAP System

When positions are created, they will generally inherit the characteristics of the job. This allows you to create a job more broadly and define attributes that can apply to anyone performing the tasks and duties of the job. For example, a manager may be responsible for managing, coaching, and developing personnel; for conducting performance reviews; and for hiring employees. Additional requirements can be based on the specific function area in which that particular manager works, for which additional requirements can be defined at the position level. Similarly, the job can be assigned a general salary grade and level, but the compensation can vary depending on the geographic region in which the position exists.

Infotypes for Jobs

The following infotypes are generally used to define jobs in OM, but you can choose additional infotypes as needed. The infotypes' uses and purposes are explained in detail in Chapter 7.

- ▶ Object (Infotype 1000)
- ▶ Relationship (Infotype 1001)

▶ Description (Infotype 1002)

▶ Cost Planning (Infotype 1015)

▶ Standard Profiles (Infotype 1016)

▶ PD Profiles (Infotype 1017)

Additional infotypes are utilized if you choose to implement the Compensation Administration component in HR.

▶ Planned Compensation (Infotype 1005)

▶ Job Evaluation Results (Infotype 1050)

▶ Salary Survey Results (Infotype 1051)

Critical Relationships for Jobs

Jobs generally are defined with the following relationships:

▶ To positions via A/B 007 (describes / is described by)

▶ To tasks via A/B 007 (describes / is described by)

▶ To another job via A/B 041 (is the same as)

3.5.3   Position 🧑

Positions (object key S) provide the key to integration with PA, because they are the organizational object that is directly assigned to people in the SAP system. A *position* differs from a job in that it is distinct and specific. A position represents a job that can be occupied by a person (employee) in the staff assignments of an organizational unit. Jobs are used as a basis for creating positions with similar tasks and responsibilities. In addition to inheriting the job characteristics, positions can inherit information from the organizational unit to which it is assigned. Additionally, you can define further information that is specific only to that one position. Maintaining precise tasks, responsibilities, and attributes of the position directly allows you to further define its characteristics.

Positions have a dual role in the organizational plan. First, you represent the personnel capacity (i.e., headcount) of an organizational unit using positions. Separate positions need to be created for all employees within the enterprise. By representing the current status of an organizational unit and foreseeable requirements, you create the basis for distributing work to people throughout your organization.

Only after you've created a position, can you assign people or users and in so doing complete what are called staff assignments in OM. A staff assignment structure is displayed in Figure 3.8.

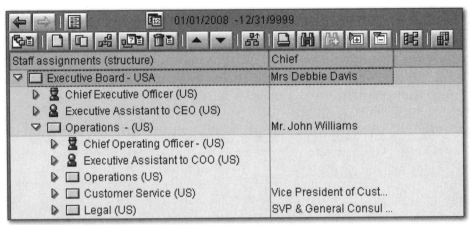

Figure 3.8 Sample SAP Organizational Plan with Positions (IDES)

You can take the staff assignment to a more detailed level by defining *chief positions* in the organization. These are positions to which all other positions in the organizational unit report. The chief position is a key attribute in the organizational plan that controls certain functions in Manager Self-Service, and is represented by the icon.

Second, to represent the hierarchical reporting relationship of the enterprise, relationships are created among positions and between positions and holders. Holders can be either employees or users in the SAP system. A reporting structure depicts the position hierarchy in your enterprise. You create a reporting structure by relating positions to one another. Similarly, you can create a matrix organizational structure by relating positions to more than one organizational unit.

Example

If your enterprise has a highly structured project management organization, you may benefit from using matrix relationships to depict project assignments. Positions are assigned to their "home" organizational unit, representing the employee and manager relationship. Positions are secondarily assigned to a project and can also report to a project manager. In this way, you can do dual-reporting on the organizational and project hierarchies.

Positions are generally assigned to organizational units and holders on a one-to-one basis. That is, a position belongs to one organizational unit, and is filled by one person at one given time. Positions do allow flexibility in this regard, however. In the assignment of relationships to positions, there is the ability to assign a percentage allocation. This allows a position to be split or shared among multiple organizations or persons.

As shown in Figure 3.9, the details for the position include the assignment of a holder, in this case at 100%. Allocation at less than 100% for multiple individuals would result is multiple people being listed.

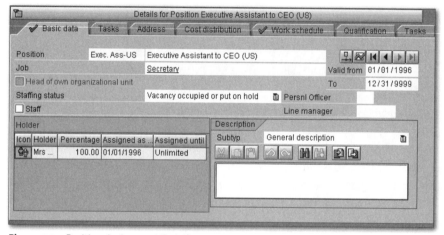

Figure 3.9   Position Assignment Details

As a general rule, allocation of a position should never exceed 100%, but in some instances it may be allowed. If a person is knowingly taking on a new position and will be training his replacement, you can choose to over-allocate the position at 200% during the transition period when the training occurs. Then, once the incumbent leaves the position for a new one, the allocation will drop back to 100%.

Vacancy Management

It's important to note the significance of the Vacancy Infotype (1007) when discussing position management. A *vacancy* identifies positions that are currently vacant and can be selected for future occupancy. Whether you utilize the Vacancy infotype depends on how your company views unoccupied positions. If you consider any unoccupied position to be vacant and available to be filled, you don't necessarily need to create a Vacancy infotype for each unfilled position. Rather, a system-wide flag can be set that will recognize any unoccupied position as a vacancy. If, however, you don't consider an unoccupied position to be a vacancy, you must utilize the Vacancy infotype so that the system recognizes a true opening.

As seen in Figure 3.10, the Staffing Status field shows that the Vacancy for the position has been filled. The staffing status of a vacancy is determined by the extent to which a vacancy is occupied as a percentage value.

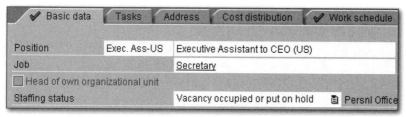

Figure 3.10   Staffing Status of Position Showing Vacancy Occupied

Vacancies can have one of three status values: vacant (0% occupied), occupied (100%), or reserved (partially occupied or completely reserved). Vacancies can be created from either OM or from the SAP Recruitment component. Any vacancies created in OM are marked with a P in the Maintained in OM field of the Vacancy view (V_T750X).

Infotypes for Positions

The following infotypes are generally used to define positions in OM, but you can choose additional infotypes as needed. The infotypes' uses and purposes are explained in detail in Chapter 7.

- Object (Infotype 1000)
- Relationship (Infotype 1001)
- Description (Infotype 1002)
- Department/Staff (Infotype 1003)
- Vacancy (Infotype 1007)
- Account Assignment Features (Infotype 1008)

- Authorities and Resources (Infotype 1010)
- Work Schedule (Infotype 1011)
- Obsolete (Infotype 1014)
- Cost Planning (Infotype 1015)
- Standard Profiles (Infotype 1016)
- PD Profiles (Infotype 1017)
- Cost Distribution (Infotype 1018)
- Address (Infotype 1028)
- Mail Address (Infotype 1032)
- SAP Organizational Object (Infotype 1208)

Additional infotypes are used in Compensation Administration.

- Planned Compensation (Infotype 1005)
- Job Evaluation Results (Infotype 1050)
- Salary Survey Results (Infotype 1051)

Critical Relationships for Positions

Positions must always be defined with the following relationships:

- To an organizational unit via A/B 003 (belongs to/includes)
- To a job via A/B 007 (describes / is described by)

Positions can also be defined with these relationships:

- An organizational unit via relationship A 012 (reports to)
- Another position via relationship A/B 002 (reports to / is line manager of)
- A holder (one or more persons or users) via relationship A/B 008 (holder)
- Tasks via relationship A/B 007 (describes / is described by)
- A work center via relationship A/B 003 (belongs to / includes)
- A master cost center via relationship A 011 (cost center assignment) or with multiple cost centers via relationship A 014 (cost center distribution)

3.5.4 Person

The *Person* (object key P) is the employee in PA that is the holder of the position in the organizational plan. By assigning the employee to a position, you implement integration between OM and PA. Integration is carried out from both OM and PA perspectives in the SAP system. Multiple records are maintained when a person is assigned to a position. As previously mentioned, a position can have a vacancy assigned to it.

Figure 3.11 Vacancy Delimit Action Request

Once selected and assigned to a person, the vacancy can be delimited, as shown in Figure 3.11. In PA, only the position is selected as the integration point to OM. The position can be maintained from one of two infotypes. In PA, Infotype 0000 Actions, shown in Figure 3.12, the position is entered in the Organizational Assignment section of the screen. When saved, this data is transferred to Infotype 0001 Organizational Assignment, creating a record of the same effective starting and ending period.

Create Actions

Organizational assignment		
Position	10000666	Human Resources Manager
Personnel area	1010	Headquarters
Employee group	1	Company Employee
Employee subgroup	U2	Salary

Figure 3.12 PA Infotype 0000 Actions Integration to Position

In the Organizational Assignment infotype (Figure 3.13), the percentage allocation can be adjusted for the position assignment if necessary.

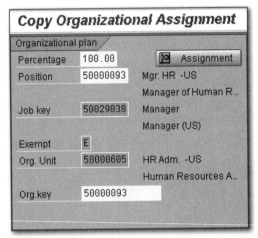

Figure 3.13 PA Infotype 0001 Organizational Assignment Integration Point

If not entered in Infotype 0000 Actions, the position can also be entered at this point, or it can be changed. In either case, the infotype records 0000 and 0001 remain in sync at all times. This data sync occurs when the records are saved in the system. It's important to note in Infotype 0001 Organizational Assignment that in addition to the position, the job and organizational unit are also displayed, but these cannot be edited. These fields are populated dynamically, inherited from the objects that are related to the position. If no job or organizational unit were related to the position, the fields would be blank. If a change in job or organization is required, it must be carried out through a change in the position.

In OM, the assignment of a position to a person is stored as a relationship in OM Infotype 1001. The relationship A/B 008 Holder represents this assignment, and is the point of integration between the two objects: position and person.

3.5.5 Cost Center

The cost center (object key K) is an unusual object in OM. Objects can be one of two types: internal object types whose master data records are in database tables belonging to SAP ERP HCM or external object types whose master data records belong to other application areas. A *cost center* is an external object from the SAP Financials Controlling component that is used to represent the origin of costs. When you assign a cost center to an organizational plan object, you determine where costs that are incurred by the object are to be charged.

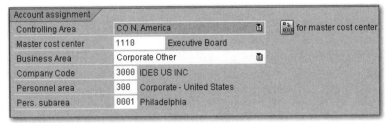

Figure 3.14 Master Cost Center Assignment

Assignment of cost centers in the organizational plan is heavily reliant on the inheritance concept. Programs and processes that rely on a cost center start with the immediately related organizational objects and look for a related cost center. A directly related cost center is called a *master cost center*, shown in Figure 3.14. If one is not found, the programs work their way up the organizational reporting hierarchy until they find a valid cost center assignment.

All cost center assignments are made via one relationship: A 011 cost center assignment. This relationship can be made at the organizational unit, position, or work center, although organizational unit is most common. As a best practice, organizational units at the highest level are assigned the cost center, because all organizational units below or reporting to that organizational unit will inherit that same cost center. This practice simplifies maintenance. Any exceptions can be made at a lower-level organizational unit. Similarly, cost center exceptions can also be assigned to individual positions.

Multiple cost center assignments can be made to OM objects through Infotype 1018 Cost Center Distribution. In this infotype, multiple cost centers can be listed and assigned a percentage allocation for the charges. If the object has a master cost center assigned, it will be displayed here so that the total allocation cannot exceed 100%. If you use multiple cost center distribution, keep in mind that the inheritance principle applies to this as well: All subordinate organizational objects will use this allocation if they do not have a master cost center assignment or their own cost distribution records.

3.6   Objects Beyond the Basics

As previously mentioned, SAP delivers over a hundred objects. Although we won't discuss all of them, some objects are important to know and understand in designing your organizational plan, because they will affect how other functions within SAP ERP HCM and other SAP application areas can be used.

3.6.1   User 🔳

A user (object key US) is an SAP technical user ID corresponding to an individual who can perform various processes and functions. The *user* object is typically not a component of the basic organizational plan; however, it does have some specific uses in OM relating to workflow and authorizations.

In SAP Business Workflow, a user can be assigned workflow tasks and activities. In this scenario, a user can be a person or it can be a system user responsible for background or batch processing. This is common in many processes throughout SAP ERP HCM, where long-running processes can be scheduled after normal business hours, and where notifications of process warnings or errors must be managed. Relating the scheduled workflow task to a nonperson user ID allows the system to run independently of people starting or stopping the process. More information regarding SAP Business Workflow integration is described in Section 11.2.

Note

Keep in mind that while user (US) and external person (H) objects allow you to route workflow tasks within SAP ERP, these objects don't work for Manager Self-Service (MSS) components in the SAP NetWeaver Portal. The system requires a valid personnel number (PERNR) in the PA component for MSS functions to work.

In authorization management, a user is a central object. Users are assigned authorization roles and profiles that control access and permissions to perform certain functions. Where people other than person objects are required, the user object can be used to represent that person in the organizational plan.

Example

Your enterprise may not choose to create personnel records for contingent labor in the SAP ERP HCM application; however, you would like to represent these people in the organizational plan. You can choose to create users for contingent personnel and relate those users to positions, thereby creating a more complete organizational structure.

3.6.2 Task 🗿

A task is a duty or responsibility that is performed by employees in your enterprise. *Tasks* are used in the SAP Business Workflow component to manage the flow of data, information, and requests for action through the system. The main purpose of workflow is to get the right tasks to the right processor in the organization.

Workflow uses four types of tasks:

Object Type	Object Description
T	Tasks (customer-defined tasks)
TS	Standard tasks
WF	Workflow tasks (customer-defined)
WS	Workflow templates

SAP provides a number of standard tasks and workflow templates in the delivered system. These standard tasks provide out-of-the-box workflow functionality in most application areas where SAP ERP HCM processes require approvals. Examples of this include absence approvals, requisition approvals, employment and salary verification, and payment requests. Workflow tasks and templates that you create in your own implementation are defined with a separate object type, either T or WF.

OM provides the framework for routing tasks to individuals in the organization. Tasks are assigned to objects in the organizational plan: organizational units, jobs, and positions. Workflow searches the relationships of these objects to the holders, persons, or users, to determine who can then complete the tasks.

Example

The task Approve Purchase Requisition can be assigned to certain management personnel in the organization. You can choose to relate this task to the Job Manager, in which case any position linked to that job can inherit the task, or you can choose to only relate the task to those positions marked as head of the organizational unit (chief positions). All people related to these jobs or positions are assigned the approval task. The task Create Purchase Order can then be assigned to the organizational unit Purchasing, which enables any person in the department to process the approved purchase requisition and create a purchase order.

Workflow tasks can also be assigned directly to users and people; however, this isn't necessary if the organizational plan is set up correctly. It's far more advantageous to use organizations, jobs, and positions to assign workflow tasks, because the relationships from tasks to those objects don't need to be changed as people move in, out, and around the organization. If you assign tasks to specific people or user objects, the task relationship will likely need to be maintained, updated, and reassigned to someone else when the person moves to another role in the company.

3.6.3 Work Center 🪑

A work center (object type A) is a physical location where work is carried out in your organization. A *work center* can be defined broadly, such as California, or it can be defined specifically, such as office 0504-123A. Once created, work centers are generally assigned to organizational units and/or positions, identifying the part of the company that is responsible for the work center and what role and ultimately what person perform the work.

Work centers are primarily used in non-SAP ERP HCM application modules. Production planning, in particular, is a heavy user of the work center concept. Logistics work centers can be tied to the work center object in OM to tie back to the position and person associated with that work center. Work centers are used for scheduling, costing, capacity planning, and simplifying operations maintenance.

3.6.4 Other Objects

In addition to the objects just described, many other delivered object types are provided, some of which are shown in Figure 3.15. Most objects are not described in any SAP configuration or process documentation. Rather, the object types are tied to specific functionality in the various SAP ERP HCM components.

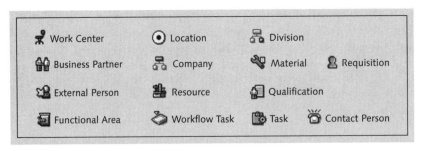

Figure 3.15 Additional OM Object Types

Table 3.1 lists some of the widely used object types per component.

HCM Component	Commonly Used Object Types	
ALL	CP	Central person
	P	Person
	O	Organizational unit
	S	Position
	US	User
Recruitment	RA	Advertisement
	NA	External candidate
	NB	Requisition
	NC	Job posting
	ND	Application
	NE	Candidacy
	NF	Talent group
Compensation Management	C	Job
	JF	Job family
Training and Event Management	AP	Applicant
	H	External person
	KU	Customer
	KI	Interested party
	PT	Contact person
	U	Company
	BP	Business partner
	L	Business event group
	D	Business event type
	E	Business event
	F	Location
	R	Resource type
	G	Resource
	M	Material

Table 3.1 Object Types Used by Component

HCM Component	Commonly Used Object Types	
Personnel Development	LB	Career
Succession Planning	BL	Development plan group
Appraisals	B	Development plan
	BS	Appraisal model
	BA	Appraisal
	BG	Criteria group
	BK	Criterion
	Q	Qualification
	QB	Qualification bundle
	QK	Qualification group
	QP	Requirements profile
Business Workflow	A	Work center
	TG	Task group
	T	Task
	TS	Standard task
	WF	Workflow task
	WS	Workflow template
	AC	Rule

Table 3.1 Object Types Used by Component (cont.)

3.6.5 Creating Your Own Objects

In some cases, despite creative use of the OM objects delivered by SAP, the standard objects provided are not sufficient to meet your business needs. In this case, you can create your own objects. The IMG activities provide the steps necessary to enhance the existing data model with custom objects. There are five relatively simple steps:

1. Access the IMG via Transaction SPRO

2. In the section **Personnel Management • Organizational Management**, expand the **Data Model Enhancement** section and choose Maintain Object Types, as shown in Figure 3.16.

Figure 3.16 IMG: Maintain Object Types

3. Select the New Entries button to get a blank entry screen.

4. Enter the two-character ID (1-99) for your new object and a text description, and select an icon to represent your object (Figure 3.17).

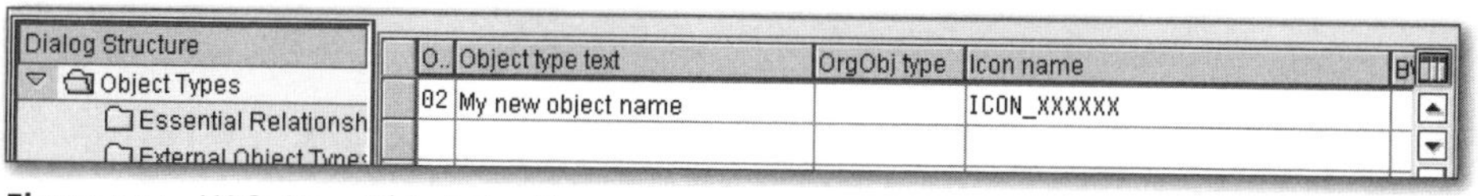

Dialog Structure	O..	Object type text	OrgObj type	Icon name	B	
▽ 🗀 Object Types	02	My new object name		ICON_XXXXXX		
🗀 Essential Relationsh						
🗀 External Object Type						

Figure 3.17 IMG: New Object Creation

5. Save your entry.

3.7 Plan Versions

A key concept in the organizational plan design is the plan version. A *plan version* is a designated area where you create and work with different sets of information in OM. You can create several organizational plans utilizing different plan versions. Each plan version can have information, objects, or infotypes, from any or all of the components from SAP ERP HCM. This provides you with the following options in OM:

▶ In one plan version, you represent your current valid organizational plan, which you use for your current business processes (for example, in the reporting hierarchy, workflow, personnel planning). In this plan version, you conduct the day-to-day business of the organization.

▶ In additional plan versions, you can depict organizational plans as planning scenarios (for example, in playing out a reorganization of certain functions or departments). In these plan versions, you are essentially modeling what might be possible in a particular plan scenario.

You can further compare the current organizational plan with the planning scenarios and transfer data from the simulated structures into the current organizational plan. This comparison ability allows you to identify and analyze the impact of the different organizational plan on any or all of its components. Experimentation is one of the best means to determine if a new organizational plan design will work for your enterprise.

Plan versions are defined by a two-character status indicator and description. You differentiate between plan versions by assigning each a unique code, and then creating organizational data within or assigning data to that code. The data in one plan version is not related in any way to data in another plan version, so you are free to create, manipulate, or delete the data within a plan version without fear of impacting other plan versions.

Plan versions are user-defined, two-character alphanumeric codes. These are maintained in the plan version table in the SAP IMG. By default, SAP delivers plan version 01 as the current and active plan version and plan version 02 as an alternate. You are free to create as many additional plan versions as you deem necessary.

It's important to note that there can be only one active plan version at any given time. The active plan version is the version that is considered the productive data used in the system. From this plan version, the daily business processes throughout SAP ERP HCM and other applications will use the data and objects. You have to mark a plan version as the active plan version through the IMG customizing activities. Once set, the Active flag in the Plan Versions customizing table is set, as shown in Figure 3.18. This table is accessible via the IMG or through Transaction Code OOPV.

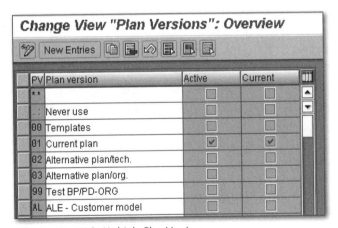

Figure 3.18 IMG: Multiple Plan Versions

The active plan version is set in the system switch table for OM, known technically as Table T77S0. As shown in Figure 3.19, you enter the plan version for the active plan in the open field Value abbr. for the table key PLOGI PLOGI. Once saved, this becomes the active plan version.

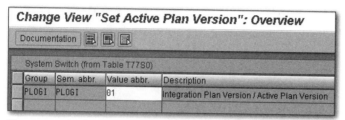

Figure 3.19 IMG: Setting the Active Plan Version

Plan version 01 is by default the active plan version in the SAP client in which you are working. Usually, this plan version remains the active plan throughout a company's use of SAP HR.

Tip
It has been my experience that customers use alternate plan versions for modeling and testing new scenarios. When the plan is finalized, it will be implemented in the active plan version rather than the active plan version switched to another value.

3.8 Organizational Plan Status

To streamline the organizational planning processes, SAP provides a *status* setting for objects and data records within the organizational plan. You can use the status to control creation and editing of the plan information. There are five possible status values:

- Active
- Planned
- Submitted
- Approved
- Rejected

The status identifies the current state of the object or data record in the organizational plan. Objects with varying status values can exist within the same plan version. The five status values have different meanings in the SAP system. The status values and their meanings are shown in Table 3.2.

Status (Value)	Status Definition
Active (1)	This indicates that an object is currently operable. You have unrestricted activities in active status. You can create, change, display, delimit, delete, and list active objects.
Planned (2)	This indicates that an object is proposed or projected, but not currently operable. You can create, change, display, delimit, delete, and list planned objects.
Submitted (3)	This indicates that an object has been submitted for review and subsequent approval or rejection. This is only an intermediary state for an object. You cannot create or make changes to objects in submitted status.
Approved (4)	This indicates that an object, previously sumitted for review, is accepted or authorized. Approving sets or changes the status immediately to active, after which you can edit the object (create, change, display, delimit, delete, and list) freely.
Rejected (5)	This indicates that an object is rejected or turned down. You can only display objects with rejected status; however, you can change the status to planned so that you can work with the object again.

Table 3.2 Status Values and Definitions

Status values can either be preset or set by the user, depending on which transaction is used to maintain OM data. The maintenance modes are described in full in Chapter 8. Table 3.3 outlines what you can do with statuses.

Maintenance Mode	Possible Status Settings
Simple maintenance	The default status *active* is applied to all records you create or maintain. You cannot change or reassign another status in this mode.
Detail maintenance	You can apply different status values to objects and records one at a time. The status is set during the creation or editing process itself. If a particular user uses the same status value most of the time, you can set the default for that user to that specific status value.
Structural graphics	Similar to simple maintenance, a default status is applied that you cannot change. You can, however, change the default to another status value. Although this will set the status value for newly created records and information, it can't be changed in structural graphics mode.

Table 3.3 Status Options

Figure 3.20 is an example of detail maintenance for an organizational unit object. As you can see, different tabs represent the various status settings the object can have. A check in the infotype name indicates if the infotype is maintained in that status value for the object being maintained.

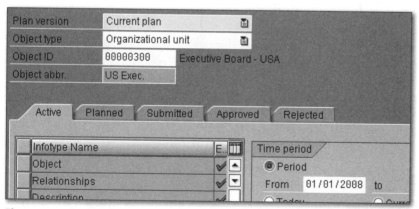

Figure 3.20 Status Tabs in OM Detail Maintenance

Many customers use status values to decentralize the data maintenance of OM objects and records. For example, a department HR manager may be able to *submit* a new organizational unit, which may then be *reviewed* by his higher-level organization head. The record may then be routed to HR operations to approve and make the record *active* in the system. This use of statuses and related workflow routing can serve to involve all users and consumers of the organizational plan data in its design and maintenance.

Example

You may choose a multistep process to create a new position. Managers in organizational units can plan new positions and submit to their group director for approval. When the director approves the position request, an HR operations analyst can evaluate the position request to determine whether all information needed to incorporate the new position into the organizational plan is complete. If correct, the new position is activated and available to fill.

In addition to changing the object status through detail maintenance, which is typically the destination transaction for workflow routing, you can change the status programmatically. Report RHAKTI00, Change Object Status, can be used to change the status for selected objects or infotype records. More information on this report can be found in Chapter 9.

3.9   Object Number Ranges

When creating objects in the OM component, data is given an eight-character identification number. Figure 3.21 provides an example of this for object 10000002 USA Company. This object ID number can be assigned by the user, or it can be system-generated. Generally, it's standard practice for the system to auto-generate the ID numbers for objects so that specific meaning is not built into the ID itself. If you build logic into the ID number, there is a greater chance that the logic you have used will fail in the future. For example, you may run out of a particular number prefix, or your company may reorganize and render the numbering convention obsolete.

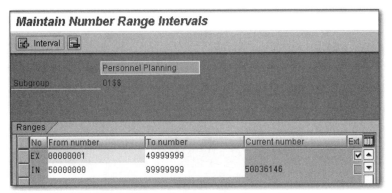

Figure 3.21 IMG: Number Range for Active Plan Version 01

The number range object for personnel planning encompasses all of the organizational objects created in OM. The technical number range object ID is RP_ PLAN (Personnel Planning), and is used to set the number range values. Number range configuration may be accessed via the IMG or through Transaction OONR. A generic number range is delivered for all plan versions and objects, as well as for the active plan version 01. An example of this is represented in Figure 3.21.

The number range for personnel planning objects uses a four-character subobject xxyy:

▶ xx: The first two characters correspond to the plan version.

▶ yy: The second two characters correspond to the object ID.

SAP uses the dollar sign ($) in this number range object to represent a wildcard character. Using this convention, Figure 3.21 provides the number range for all objects ($$) in plan version 01. The number range contains both an internal and external number range. External numbers are those the users can create themselves. The internal number range is used for automatic or system-generated object ID numbers. The number range itself provides the lower and upper limit of numbers available in the range. Also displayed is the current number in use.

Tip

In your implementation project, you may need to modify the number range values often as you create and delete test data. If the objects you create start at the beginning of the number range, you'll want to reset the current number to the initial values in the range.

You can create number ranges for any plan version and object type combination using the subgroup convention. Figure 3.22 provides examples of number range combinations using various plan versions and object types.

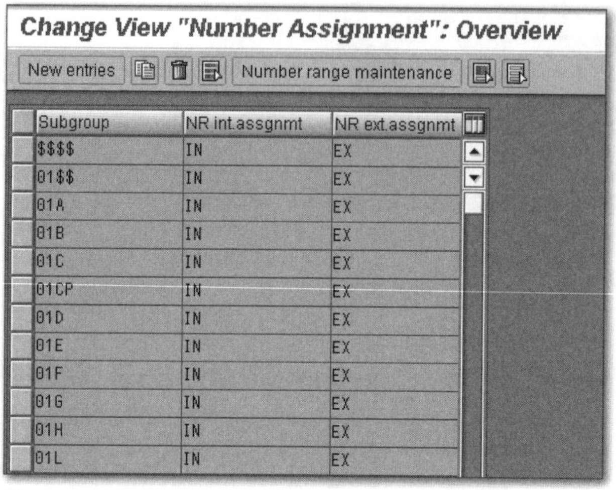

Change View "Number Assignment": Overview

Subgroup	NR int.assgnmt	NR ext.assgnmt
$$$$	IN	EX
01$$	IN	EX
01A	IN	EX
01B	IN	EX
01C	IN	EX
01CP	IN	EX
01D	IN	EX
01E	IN	EX
01F	IN	EX
01G	IN	EX
01H	IN	EX
01L	IN	EX

Figure 3.22 IMG: OM Number Range Subgroups

Finally, it's important to note that the number range subobject $$$$ provides the number range for all other plan versions and objects not otherwise specified by their own subobject. Any plan versions or objects for which you have not created a specific number range subobject will share this number range.

It's critical to keep the $$$$ and $$01 number range subgroups in mind when setting up plan- or object-specific ranges, such as 01A in Figure 3.22. Some customers have attempted to enforce the use of internal number range assignment for the objects in their organizational plan by deleting the external range values in their specific object subgroups. Simply deleting the external number range, however, doesn't work. They have forgotten that the $$$$ and $$01 ranges will also set an external number range, thereby rendering the deletion ineffective.

> **Tip**
>
> To truly force internal number range assignment for an object type, it's a best practice to set the external number range to one specific number value and create a placeholder object with a validity period outside your organizational plan to prevent someone from accidentally using it. Figure 3.23 shows how this number range configuration should be set.

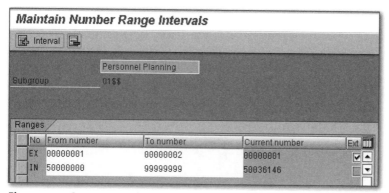

Figure 3.23 Setting a Number Range for Forced Internal Assignment

3.10 Conclusion

In this chapter we've explained the basic concept of object-oriented design and how it's used to create the organizational plan in OM. Organizational units, jobs, positions, and persons are some of the many organizational objects that work together to represent the enterprise structure of your company in the SAP system. Now you have an understanding of how data is structured around these objects. In the next chapter we'll discuss a central data storage principle that is used throughout SAP ERP HCM: the infotype.

Although data in OM is based on objects, it's stored and organized in a particular fashion specific to the SAP ERP HCM application and used throughout the component. In this chapter we'll explain the OM infotype concept, which is used to arrange the data about the organizational objects.

4 Infotypes in Organizational Management

Infotypes have been mentioned in earlier chapters, but in this Chapter we'll look at them more closely.

4.1 The Infotype Concept

An infotype is a collection of fields or attributes related to a particular type of content. The term *infotype* is specific to SAP ERP HCM, and is not used in any other part of the SAP applications. In database terms, infotypes represent a data structure or set of related data records. Each time data is stored in an infotype, a corresponding database record is created.

From the user's perspective, an infotype is a data entry screen with fields for employee or business information. For example, street, city, state, and zip code are fields related to an address, which can be the employee's home address or a business location. Usually, infotypes present users with one data entry screen; however, they can sometimes consist of multiple data screens that have to be completed together. Users can use infotypes create, modify, copy, delimit, or delete data. Infotypes also present users with two options for the data: a single entry screen and a list screen. On a single entry screen, one infotype record is created or changed or may be deleted. With a list screen, all the data records for a person or object are displayed in a list.

Each infotype enables you to define a particular set of details or characteristics for an object. Every time an infotype is created for an object, you create an infotype record. Once these records are made, you can display, change, copy, delimit, or delete them. Infotype records can be made limitlessly for an object. You can even create several of the same infotype records for an object. For example, an object can have several relationship infotype records that define how that object is linked to other objects in the organizational plan.

Figure 4.1 provides a sample single entry screen in OM for Infotype 1000, called the Object infotype, for an organizational unit. In this infotype, the object is described by an abbreviation and a long text name, as well as a language. The language key is important for global enterprises, because it allows organizations to be defined once and given names in multiple languages for ease of hierarchical reporting in a specific country.

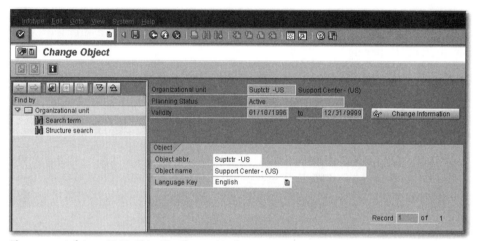

Figure 4.1 Infotype 1000 Object in Change Mode

One additional item to note is the Change Information icon, which is present in all infotypes. This function displays the creation or edit audit trail for the infotype, listing the user ID and date and time stamp when the infotype record was last changed. This can be important in researching data integrity issues or identifying the last person to edit the information.

4.2 Infotypes for OM

From the technical perspective, it's important to understand three things about infotypes. First is the sheer number of infotypes that are available for use. Nearly

150 infotypes are used throughout OM. The SAP Implementation Guide (IMG) provides a number of configuration options for infotypes. You probably won't change any of these settings in your implementation, but it's useful to understand what the options allow.

The IMG activities are accessible in one of two ways: via Transaction Code OOIT or via the IMG path **Personnel Management · Organizational Management · Basic Settings · Data Model Enhancement · Infotype Maintenance · Maintain Infotypes**. The main Infotypes view provides the full listing of infotypes provided by SAP, as shown in Figure 4.2. If you create your own custom infotypes, they'll be listed here as well. An infotype is technically defined in the SAP data dictionary by a four-character (nnnn) table structure.

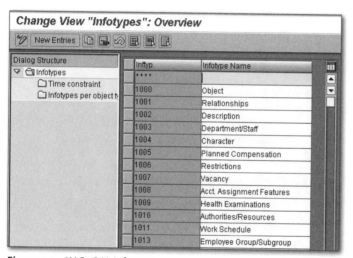

Figure 4.2 IMG: OM Infotypes

Numbered name ranges exist for infotype structures depending on the component. Each infotype is defined by a four-digit number that uniquely identifies it.

▶ 0000 – 0999: Employee Information

▶ 1000 – 1999: Organization Management

▶ 2000 – 2999: Time Management

▶ 4000 – 4999: Recruitment

▶ 9000 – 9999: Reserved for customer infotypes

> **Note**
>
> Although the number ranges identify the infotype function generally, some infotypes are used in multiple components. For example, Infotype 0002 Personal Data is used in Personnel Administration and Recruitment, and Infotype 1007 Vacancy is used in Organizational Management and Recruitment.

The second element to understand is which infotypes are used by which objects. Within OM some infotypes are only relevant for certain object types, whereas other infotypes can be edited for all object types. The Vacancy infotype is, for example, only relevant for positions. You can learn this information one of two ways. The first is to navigate through the various functions in OM and try to determine which infotypes get used. It could take days, if not weeks, to try to figure this out yourself, so we don't recommend this method. Rather, rely on the second method, which is simply to look in the IMG. To navigate within the IMG view, select the infotype in the initial view, and the objects that use this infotype are displayed in Infotypes per object type.

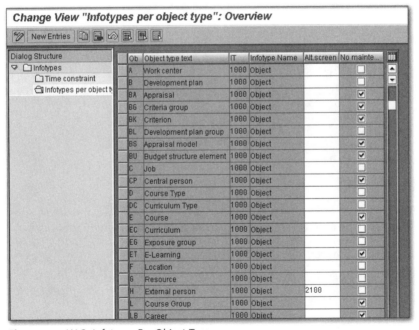

Figure 4.3 IMG: Infotypes Per Object Type

There's no easy way to get a listing from the IMG of all the infotypes that are used by a particular object. Figure 4.3 shows the list of object types that use one specific infotype, in this case the Object Infotype 1000. Using this method, you need to select each of the 150+ infotypes separately and then find out which objects use it in the second view. It is a bit tedious but gets the job done nonetheless.

> **Tip**
>
> If you have broad access in a sandbox or development system, you can use the Data Browser Transaction Code SE16 or General Table Display Transaction SE16N to view the infotype table directly. Table T777I stores information regarding infotypes per object type. By viewing the Table T777I contents directly via Transaction Code SE16 or SE16N, you can more easily get a listing of the infotypes that are used by each object type.

In this view of the infotypes is an indication of whether any alternate data entry screen is used to maintain the data. In general, most infotypes use screen 2000 for single entry maintenance. In some cases, a special screen is provided with enhanced features or functions for data entry of that particular object type. That special screen is listed here.

Also in this customizing view is the checkbox for No Maintenance of an object. This checkbox identifies whether an infotype can be maintained directly through the expert mode in OM, meaning that you can call an infotype directly to create it. If an object is checked in this fashion, the infotype is instead maintained using a specific transaction, usually in conjunction with that component's processes.

> **Example**
>
> Object type BA Appraisal is maintained via the Performance Management functions. Through those specific transactions, the Object infotype is created in the background. It's not possible to create the object directly in expert mode.

4.3   Infotype Subtypes

Infotype records can be further broken down into what are called *subtypes*, or categories of a particular infotype. For example, the Schedule infotype can have subtypes for Main or Alternative schedule models. Whether or not an infotype has a subtype depends on how the infotype is structured. Not all infotypes use subtypes.

> **Tip**
>
> You can determine which infotypes use a subtype by looking at the infotype table structure. OM infotypes are technically named HRPnnnn, where nnnn is the four-character infotype number (Figure 4.4). Using either the Data Dictionary Transaction SE11 or the Data Browser/Display Transactions SE16 or SE16N, you can view the table fields to see if Subtype (SUBTY) is an available field.

Change View "Subtypes": Overview

Inftyp.	Infotype Name	Subtyp	Subtype text
1002	Description	5002	Condition
1002	Description	5020	Description on Web
1002	Description	6000	Testing Procedure
1002	Description	6001	Input Data
1002	Description	6002	Result
1009	Health Examinations	0001	Health exclusions
1009	Health Examinations	0002	Health examinations
1010	Authorities/Resources	0001	Authority/pwr of attorney
1010	Authorities/Resources	0002	Technical resources
1010	Authorities/Resources	0050	Supervisory instance
1011	Work Schedule	0001	Salaried employees
1011	Work Schedule	0002	Hourly Paid Employees
1011	Work Schedule	ALL	All work schedule groups
1015	Cost Planning		Normal case
1015	Cost Planning	0001	National average
1015	Cost Planning	0002	Regional Survey
1015	Cost Planning	0003	Industry Survey
1015	Cost Planning	0004	Company Appraisals
1019	Quota planning	*	
1019	Quota planning	0001	First planning (2003)
1019	Quota planning	0002	Second planning (2003)
1019	Quota planning	0003	First planning (2004)

Figure 4.4 IMG: Infotype Subtypes

The Subtypes customizing view can be accessed via the IMG path **Personnel Management • Organizational Management • Basic Settings • Data Model Enhancement • Infotype Maintenance • Maintain Subtypes** or directly via Transaction OOSU. Subtypes are defined by a four-character alphanumeric code, and are usually part of the infotype key. The infotype key determines when a new database record needs to be created. Each time a new key is generated, a new database record is generated. Subtype codes can have meaning built into them to aid in selection or reporting, or they can be defined by nondescript codes such as 0001, 0002, and so on.

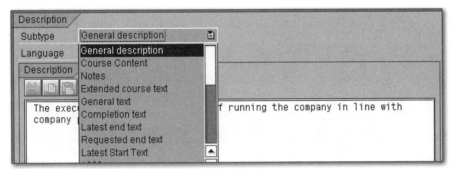

Figure 4.5 Infotype Subtype Selection

Some infotypes rely heavily on subtypes. Infotype 1001 Relationships records are built entirely with subtypes. Each type of relationship functions as a separate subtype for the infotype, allowing for multiple records to be created with varying relationships.

4.4   Infotype Effective Dates

An important concept throughout SAP ERP HCM infotypes is that of effective dating, or the validity period. When you create new data, old data is not necessarily lost. Infotype records have a starting and an ending effective date, defining the period for which the information is valid. Throughout the life of the data, new records can be created with new starting effective dates. The system acts to delimit or shorten the validity period of the previous record so that the new record becomes valid.

4.4.1   Example: Changing an Object Name

Throughout the next few pages, we'll look at an in-depth example of changing an object name. If you look back at Figure 4.1, you'll see that the validity period for the example shown is from 01/10/1996 through 12/31/9999. The organizational unit Support Center – (US) was created on, or is valid starting on, 01/10/1996, and will continue to be valid through the end time, 12/31/9999. Let's say you want to change the name of this organizational unit in the beginning of the year.

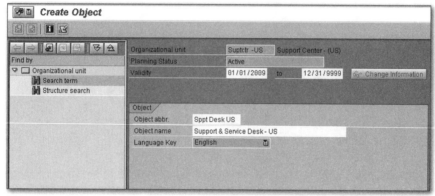

Figure 4.6 Copy an Organizational Unit to Change the Name

In Figure 4.6, the Create function is selected for the Object infotype, and a new effective date of 1/1/2009 has been entered to change both the short and long text names of the organizational unit.

> **Tip**
>
> When creating a new record, it's usually recommended to copy the previous record rather than starting from a blank screen. So, you can retain the information you want to keep and just change what you want more easily. In this case, because we're changing everything, we're using Create instead of Copy.

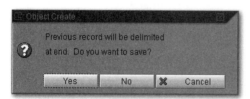

Figure 4.7 Object Delimit Confirmation Prompt

When you save the data, you'll be presented with a pop-up window, shown in Figure 4.7. Creating the new record prompts the system to delimit the previous record. Delimiting a record in SAP means that the previous record that used to end on 12/31/9999 will now be shortened to a new end date. The new end date is typically the day before the new record being created.

In displaying all records for this infotype, we can see that the original record has been given a new end date, and the new record with the new effective date is also present (see Figure 4.8). The original description of the infotype is preserved for historical purposes, and the new record with the altered short and long names has been added. The validity start and end dates are also part of the infotype key. Each time new dates are created, a new infotype record is created.

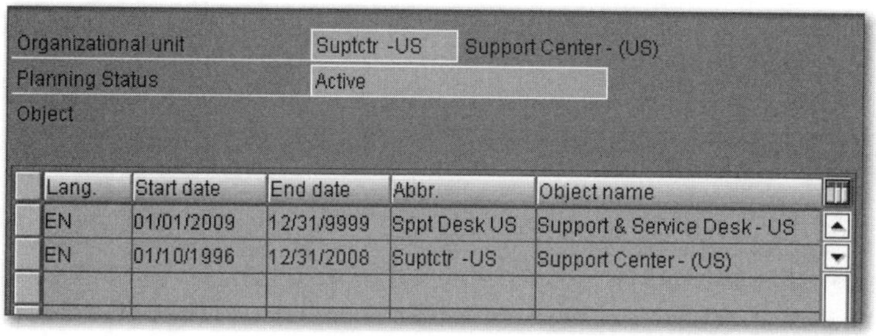
Organizational unit
Suptctr -US
Support Center - (US)
Planning Status
Active
Object
Lang.
Start date
End date
Abbr.
Object name
EN
01/01/2009
12/31/9999
Sppt Desk US
Support & Service Desk - US
EN
01/10/1996
12/31/2008
Suptctr -US
Support Center - (US)

Figure 4.8 List View of New and Delimited Infotype

So, HR data is automatically time delimited, allowing for evaluation of past, current, and future events. This behavior is dynamic throughout the SAP ERP HCM system. How and even whether an infotype record is delimited depends on the infotype being created and on how the time controls are defined for that infotype. This concludes our in-depth example of changing an object name.

4.5 Time Constraints

As mentioned in Section 4.1.2, there are three IMG elements that are important to understanding infotypes. The third element is the time constraint. A time constraint prevents information in the system from conflicting. Figure 4.7 shows how the time constraint of an object and infotype combination is configured in the IMG. You can access the time constraint customizing view from either the Maintain Infotypes or Maintain Subtypes IMG activity. The time constraint setting defines and controls whether an infotype *must* always exist, can have time gaps between records, or can exist multiple times. This setting is either made at the infotype level generically, or can be defined by subtype for all infotypes.

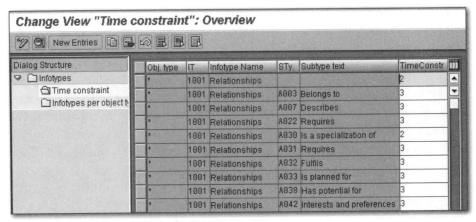

Figure 4.9 IMG: Object and Infotype Time Constraints

Note
A position can only be defined by one job at a time. Having a position linked to more than one job would not make sense. So, when a new relationship record is created between a position and a job, the previous record is delimited. On the other hand, a position can have multiple relationships to qualification requirements objects. It certainly makes sense that a position has multiple requirements tied to it. Examples include communication skills, proficiency in software programs, decision making, and customer focus. Therefore, in this case, the addition of a new qualification record for a position may not delimit the older one. The multiple qualifications can coexist.

There are four possible settings for the time constraint value, and each affects how many of the infotypes can exist, how conflicting validity periods are handled by the system, and how the infotype can be edited (Table 4.1).

Value	Time Constraint Setting
0	A maximum of one infotype record of the same type and for the same object can exist in the same period of time.
	No changes can be made to the record.
1	A maximum of one infotype record of the same type and for the same object can exist in the same period of time.
	No gaps can exist between the records. Some changes to be made to the attributes of the record.

Table 4.1 Time Constraint Options for Infotypes

Value	Time Constraint Setting
2	A maximum of one infotype record of the same type and for the same object can exist in the same period of time. Gaps can exist between valid records.
3	Multiple infotype records of the same type and for the same object can exist in the same period of time. Gaps can exist between valid records.

Table 4.1 Time Constraint Options for Infotypes (cont.)

When discussing infotype time constraints and gaps, a visual example is useful. Figure 4.10 is a simple illustration of how Infotype 1000 has time constraint 1: A record must always exist without gaps, but you can edit it.

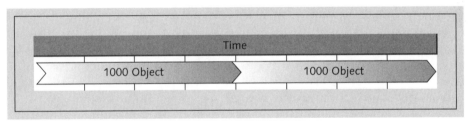

Figure 4.10 An Object Must Always Exist

Note
Infotype 1000 Object defines the existence of an object, so it must always be present for the object to exist. If the object was created with a typo in the short or long description, you coulc edit it to correct the name. Alternatively, changing the name altogether at a point in time would require that the first record be delimited and a new record created with the new name. In this case, the new record has a new validity period, but there are no gaps over time.

Relationships have time constraint 2 or 3, depending on the type of relationship. Some relationships should always exist, whereas others can have a gap between the validity periods of two records, as shown in Figure 4.11.

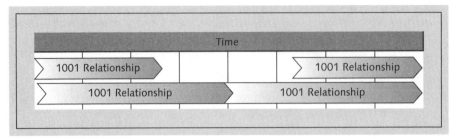

Figure 4.11 Relationships Can Always Exist or Can Have Gaps

Note

For positions, Infotype 1001 Relationships should always exist with subtype A002 Reports To linked to an organizational unit. This relationship defines where the position fits into the organizational hierarchy. An active position should never exist as a single entity unrelated to an organizational unit, so the system expects that at any given period of time this relationship will exist. This is time constraint 2.

Alternatively, for jobs, Infotype 1001 Relationships may or may not exist with subtype A007 Describes linked to a position. You can have a job Network Specialist IV that is defined in your job index, but you cannot currently have a position that is defined by that job. The relationship only exists when there is a valid position that can be linked to the job by this relationship, so there may be gaps over time. This is time constraint 3.

Regardless of your particular requirements, the time constraints work together to control the system reactions for the various object types. Understanding how time constraints work will help you determine why certain infotypes are created in a particular manner. Time constraints are used throughout SAP ERP HCM wherever infotypes are used, so understanding this concept in the OM context will help you apply it to other SAP ERP HCM components as well.

4.6 Conclusion

In this chapter, we've explained how OM data is stored in the SAP system. Data that is related is organized in infotypes, a term that applies to both data entry screens and data structures. Every time a record is created for an OM object, an infotype record is created. The infotype is a key concept in SAP ERP HCM, because it's used throughout the function. Now that you have an understanding of how infotypes work, let's explore another key facet of the OM function design: relationships.

Relationships take your OM objects and bring them to life. By relating objects to one another, you add dimension to the organizational plan and enable it to truly reflect your enterprise. In this chapter we'll explain relationships, which are used to link organizational objects together.

5   Working with Relationships

Relationships enable you to depict multidimensional dependencies between various objects. A relationship defines the link between one object and another, which takes the organizational plan from a static list of individual objects to a relational and hierarchical depiction of the organization. Relationships indicate, for example, that a job and position are linked together, and that an organizational unit and position are linked together.

5.1   Relationships in OM

Relationships between the various objects you create in OM form the organizational plan that represents your enterprise. Without relationships, all you have are individual and isolated pieces of information.

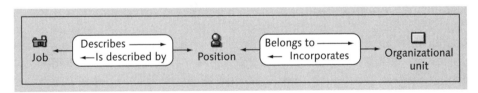

Figure 5.1   Multidirectional Relationships in OM

In the example in Figure 5.1, note that two sets of dual relationships are defined for the three object types listed: job, position, and organizational unit. The first set contains two relationships between a job and a position. The second set contains two relationships between a position and an organizational unit.

5.1.1 Relationships are Passive or Active

Relationships have some basic characteristics that are important to understand. Relationships are first defined generically by a three-character numeric code (nnn), as shown in Figure 5.2. You can access the customizing table via the IMG path **Personnel Management • Organizational Management • Basic Settings • Data Model Enhancement • Relationship Maintenance • Maintain Relationships**. You can also access this customizing view directly via Transaction Code OOVK. Over 150 standard relationship types are defined in SAP, any of which can be used with nearly any object type.

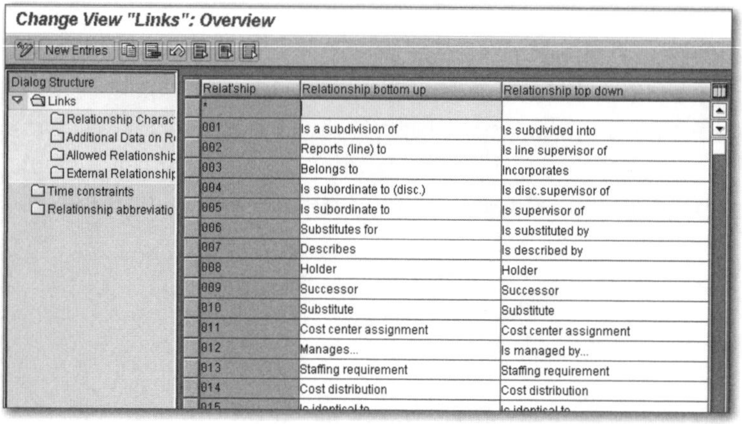

Relat'ship	Relationship bottom up	Relationship top down
001	Is a subdivision of	Is subdivided into
002	Reports (line) to	Is line supervisor of
003	Belongs to	Incorporates
004	Is subordinate to (disc.)	Is disc.supervisor of
005	Is subordinate to	Is supervisor of
006	Substitutes for	Is substituted by
007	Describes	Is described by
008	Holder	Holder
009	Successor	Successor
010	Substitute	Substitute
011	Cost center assignment	Cost center assignment
012	Manages...	Is managed by...
013	Staffing requirement	Staffing requirement
014	Cost distribution	Cost distribution
015	Is identical to	Is identical to

Dialog Structure
- Links
  - Relationship Charac
  - Additional Data on R
  - Allowed Relationship
  - External Relationship
  - Time constraints
  - Relationship abbreviatio

Figure 5.2 IMG: Relationships Defined

> **Note**
>
> The relationship code is given both a bottom-up and a top-down description.

Relationships are almost always bidirectional or reciprocal, although in certain circumstances they are unidirectional. By giving the relationship this dual description, the system knows which text to display when the relationship code (nnn) is paired with the bottom-up or top-down indicator.

Relationships are defined as either active or passive in the SAP system. Looking back to Figure 5.1, the job has the active relationship to the position; the job describes the position. The position has the passive relationship to the job; the position is described by the job. In this case, the position has the active relationship to the organizational unit; the position belongs to the organizational unit. The organizational unit has the passive relationship to the position; the organizational unit incorporates the position.

The relationship is formed by combining the passive (A) or active (B) indicator with the three-character number (nnn). The naming convention is

▶ Annn = passive relationship

▶ Bnnn = active relationship

Example

The code A002 is one relationship, which is "the line supervisor of." The 002 code on its own does not define the relationship. Rather, the combination of A plus 002 join to form A002, or the relationship when joined together. Similarly, the code B007 is another relationship, which is "describes." B plus 007 together define the relationship B007.

In these two instances, neither the A nor the B can stand alone, nor can the 002 or 007 function independently. The passive or aggressive indicator must be joined with the three-character code to make a relationship.

Additional settings can be made in the customizing views Relationship Characteristics and Additional Data on Relationships, shown in Figure 5.3. For relationships that are "weighted" relationships, you can control the response of the system if the 100% mark is exceeded. System responses include error, warning, and information messages. Similarly, you can show or hide the weighting percentage of a relationship and, if required, specify whether a recursiveness check should be active for your own relationships or not.

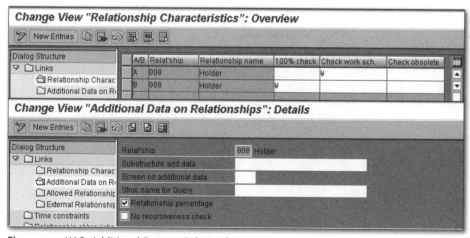

Figure 5.3 IMG: Additional Data on Relationships

5.1.2 Allowing Relationships between Objects

Relationships are further defined when they are assigned to different objects to permit their use with that object type. As shown in Figure 5.4, the further relationship IMG view Allowed Relationships defines the two objects that will be related, and the active or passive relationship that is allowed to join them together in the system.

Example

Work centers (A) and positions (S) are restricted to the passive relationship A008 Holder, which in layman's terms means a work center or position "may be held by" another object. The aggressive relationship B008 is restricted to the object types business partner (BP), central person (CP), person (P), and user (US). These are the only object types that are linked to an individual, meaning that someone "is the holder of" the work center or position.

To access this customizing view, you first select the relationship type in the Links view, and then select the Allowed Relationships view. In this case, relationship 008 is selected.

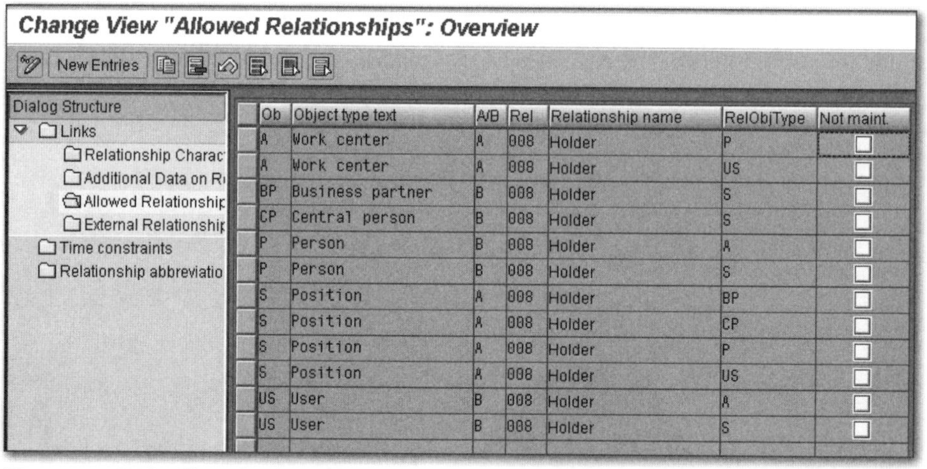

Change View "Allowed Relationships": Overview

Ob	Object type text	A/B	Rel	Relationship name	RelObjType	Not maint.
A	Work center	A	008	Holder	P	☐
A	Work center	A	008	Holder	US	☐
BP	Business partner	B	008	Holder	S	☐
CP	Central person	B	008	Holder	S	☐
P	Person	B	008	Holder	A	☐
P	Person	B	008	Holder	S	☐
S	Position	A	008	Holder	BP	☐
S	Position	A	008	Holder	CP	☐
S	Position	A	008	Holder	P	☐
S	Position	A	008	Holder	US	☐
US	User	B	008	Holder	A	☐
US	User	B	008	Holder	S	☐

Dialog Structure:
- Links
  - Relationship Charac
  - Additional Data on Ri
  - Allowed Relationship
  - External Relationship
- Time constraints
- Relationship abbreviatio

Figure 5.4 IMG: Allowed Relationships

Objects can be linked to other objects through any relationship as defined in this IMG task. The standard syntax used to identify a relationship is A/B 000. The parts form the reciprocal relationship, and are vital in holding the relationship together. Be aware that not all relationships are defined with both A and B parts. A relationship can be one-sided. For example, a relationship between the object O – organizational unit and an external object type K – a cost center in controlling has only one direction and so is one-sided.

In addition to selecting specific relationships in the IMG by selecting the Allowed Relationships view, you can use a standard report delivered by SAP to view the allowed relationships. Report RHRLAT0 (Allowed Relationships of Object Types) reports on the relationships permitted or allowed for particular objects.

5.1.3 Relationship to External Objects

As previously mentioned, objects in OM can be either internal or external. The designation of internal or external depends on where the master data information for the object is stored in the SAP database. Internal object types have their master data records stored in database tables belonging to SAP ERP HCM. External object types have their master data records stored in database tables that belong to other application areas.

> **Example**
>
> A cost center is an example of an external object. Cost center master data is stored in database tables belonging to the SAP ERP Financials. You can relate a cost center to an organizational unit to depict where the personnel-related costs associated with the organizational unit are to be charged.

When OM objects are related to external objects, the relationships are unidirectional. Relationship data is only stored from the perspective of the OM data object. Because the database tables in the non-OM component are not built the same way as those in OM, the relationship data cannot be stored in the same manner. Therefore, to present the non-OM data properly, external objects usually require special handling.

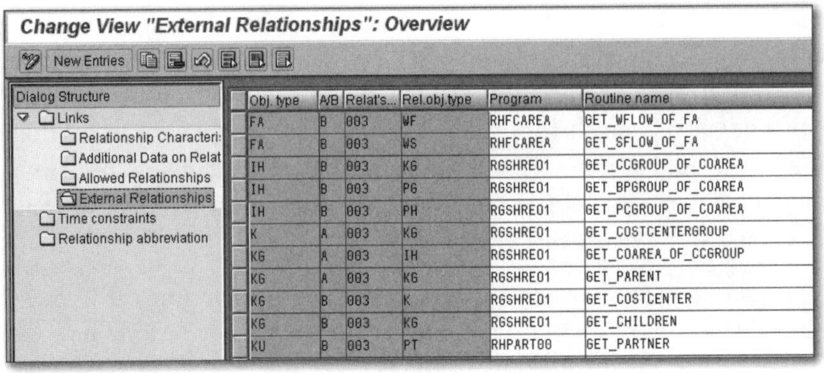

Obj. type	A/B	Relat's...	Rel.obj.type	Program	Routine name
FA	B	003	WF	RHFCAREA	GET_WFLOW_OF_FA
FA	B	003	WS	RHFCAREA	GET_SFLOW_OF_FA
IH	B	003	KG	RGSHRE01	GET_CCGROUP_OF_COAREA
IH	B	003	PG	RGSHRE01	GET_BPGROUP_OF_COAREA
IH	B	003	PH	RGSHRE01	GET_PCGROUP_OF_COAREA
K	A	003	KG	RGSHRE01	GET_COSTCENTERGROUP
KG	A	003	IH	RGSHRE01	GET_COAREA_OF_CCGROUP
KG	A	003	KG	RGSHRE01	GET_PARENT
KG	B	003	K	RGSHRE01	GET_COSTCENTER
KG	B	003	KG	RGSHRE01	GET_CHILDREN
KU	B	003	PT	RHPART00	GET_PARTNER

Figure 5.5 IMG: External Relationship Programs and Routines

SAP-delivered programs are provided to support the necessary data interface between components. As you can see in Figure 5.5, the Program and Routine name are listed for the external object that is to be used. The interface programs in the system read the data from the other application areas and provide the necessary information on the external object, as well as any data that may be related to that object in the other application area, as provided by the routine.

5.1.4 Relationship Time Constraints

Relationships have time constraints attached in their configuration definitions. These relationship time constraints can be defined generically using the wildcard character * to represent any or all objects, as shown in Figure 5.6, or they can be defined by the specific object type.

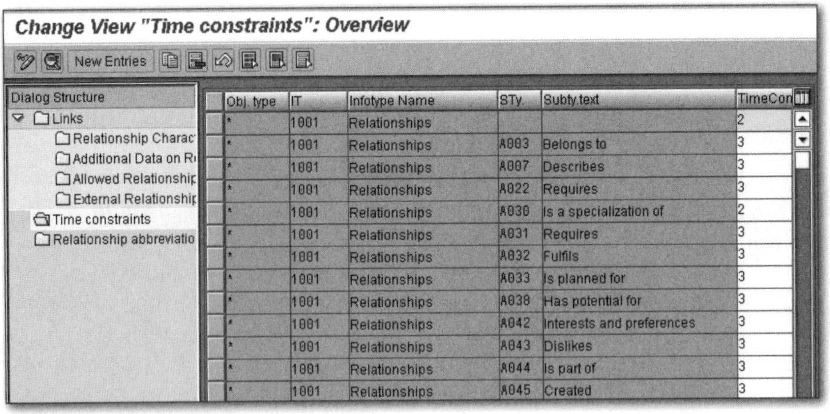

Obj. type	IT	Infotype Name	STy.	Subty.text	TimeCon
*	1001	Relationships			2
*	1001	Relationships	A003	Belongs to	3
*	1001	Relationships	A007	Describes	3
*	1001	Relationships	A022	Requires	3
*	1001	Relationships	A030	Is a specialization of	2
*	1001	Relationships	A031	Requires	3
*	1001	Relationships	A032	Fulfils	3
*	1001	Relationships	A033	Is planned for	3
*	1001	Relationships	A038	Has potential for	3
*	1001	Relationships	A042	Interests and preferences	3
*	1001	Relationships	A043	Dislikes	3
*	1001	Relationships	A044	Is part of	3
*	1001	Relationships	A045	Created	3

Figure 5.6 IMG: Relationship Time Constraints

The time-constraint principles explained in Section 4.1.5 for infotypes apply to relationships as well. Relationships can exist once or multiple times, with gaps or no gaps, depending on the time constraint setting. See Table 5.1 for details.

Value	Time Constraint Setting
0	A maximum of one relationship record of the same type and for the same objects can exist in the same period of time. No changes can be made to the record.
1	A maximum of one relationship record of the same type and for the same objects can exist in the same period of time. No gaps can exist between the records. Some changes can be made to the attributes of the record.
2	A maximum of one relationship record of the same type and for the same objects can exist in the same period of time. Gaps can exist between valid records.
3	Multiple relationship records of the same type and for the same objects can exist in the same period of time. Gaps can exist between valid records.

Table 5.1   Time Constraint Options for Relationships

Most basic object relationships are meant to exist multiple times, so they have time constraint 3. Relationships that should exist only one time have time constraint 2.

Example

An organizational unit typically has multiple positions reporting to it. For example, a staffing organization in a large enterprise may have 15 or more staffing consultants. This relationship A/B 003 (belongs to / includes) between position and organizational unit object types has time constraint 3. On the other hand, a position usually only has to be defined by one job at any particular time, so that relationship, A/B 007 (describes / is described by), has time constraint 2. The 15 positions in the staffing organization are defined by a single job: recruiter.

5.1.5   Relationship Abbreviations in Reporting

When viewing and displaying relationships, usually the system simply reflects either the bottom-up or top-down relationship description configured in the IMG.

In some specific instances, however, an alternate abbreviation for the description is used. Abbreviations or aliases are used in some standard reports to describe the relationship. The Semantic Abbreviation (Sem.abbr.) codes are called by SAP standard reports. The relationship alias is used as a direct description of the relationship code Annn or Bnnn. By having this alias readily available, the system can access it more quickly when needed.

Tip

If you decide to change the semantic abbreviations, aim to keep the general meaning of the abbreviation the same. For example, you may rename the description for PPWAY O-P "Internal Persons of an Organizational Unit" to "Employees of an Organizational Unit." Replacing the term *Internal Person* with *Employee* is appropriate because it keeps the intended meaning the same.

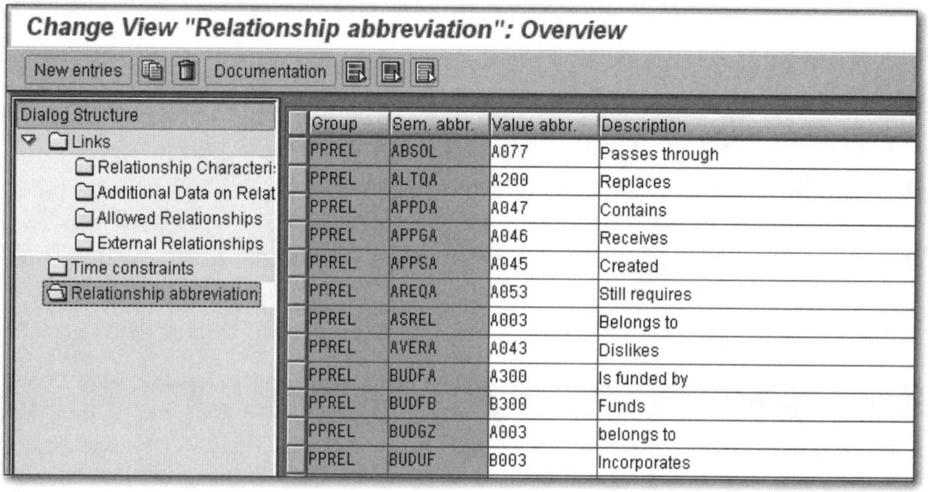

Change View "Relationship abbreviation": Overview

New entries | Documentation

Dialog Structure	Group	Sem. abbr.	Value abbr.	Description
▽ ☐ Links	PPREL	ABSOL	A077	Passes through
☐ Relationship Characteri:	PPREL	ALTQA	A200	Replaces
☐ Additional Data on Relat	PPREL	APPDA	A047	Contains
☐ Allowed Relationships	PPREL	APPGA	A046	Receives
☐ External Relationships	PPREL	APPSA	A045	Created
☐ Time constraints	PPREL	AREQA	A053	Still requires
☐ Relationship abbreviation	PPREL	ASREL	A003	Belongs to
	PPREL	AVERA	A043	Dislikes
	PPREL	BUDFA	A300	Is funded by
	PPREL	BUDFB	B300	Funds
	PPREL	BUDGZ	A003	belongs to
	PPREL	BUDUF	B003	Incorporates

Figure 5.7 IMG: Relationship Abbreviations

Figure 5.7 shows some examples of relationship abbreviation customizing. For group PPREL and PPWAY, you can specify an alternate description for the relationship, but SAP recommends that you only change these if absolutely necessary. Many standard reports rely on the delivered abbreviations, so changing the description may have unwanted effects on reporting output.

Now that you have an understanding of what OM relationships are and how they are created, let's examine a key principle that relationships support.

5.2   Inheritance Principle

You can save time in both implementation and ongoing maintenance by understanding the inheritance principle before you begin creating organizational relationships. Inheritance is when an object automatically receives the attributes of another object by virtue of their hierarchical relationship.

Example

The top-level organizational unit in a hierarchy can be assigned an address that represents the company's office location. All subordinate organizational units inherit this address by virtue of their reporting relationship to the higher-level organization. Because of this inheritance, there's no need to replicate the address information for all organizational units.

Inheritance is one of the most powerful benefits of the relationship between organizational objects. In particular, inheritance is a significant time saver when working with a large number of objects in the organizational plan. When you set up your organizational plan, many of the objects will share similar information, but setting up this similar information for each object can take significant time.

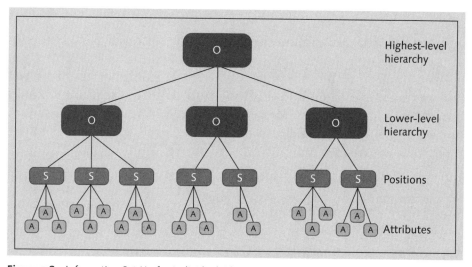

Figure 5.8 Information Set Up for Individual Objects

For example, in Figure 5.8, setting multiple instances of similar attributes would result in many individual records being created. In an enterprise where you can potentially have thousands of organizational units, jobs, and positions, mainte-nance of separate attributes for each organizational object would result in an expo-nential number of records. Such a maintenance workload would become daunting. Thankfully, inheritance does this work for you.

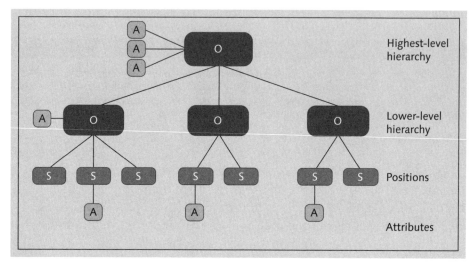

Figure 5.9 Organizational Plan Set Up Using Inheritance

By utilizing the relationship between the subordinate object and the higher object, you can set up attributes or characteristics once, and the lower-level objects can use them. With inheritance, the system can search for information that was set up once and use it for multiple objects. Figure 5.9 shows the simplified data model using the inheritance principle. Most attributes are maintained at the highest level. At lower levels, additional attributes can be added where appropriate, but these are done on an exception basis.

Let's look now at how relationships are used to build the organizational plan and the basic relationships you'll use most frequently.

5.3   Basic Relationships in OM

You can create hundreds of different relationships in OM. There are, however, some basic relationships that you should become familiar with when designing and implementing your organizational plan in OM. These relationships bring together the basic organizational plan objects:

- Organizational unit
- Position
- Job
- Person

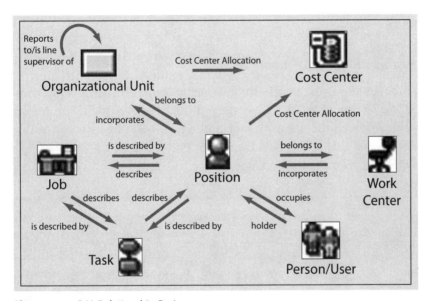

Figure 5.10 OM Relationship Basics

The core organizational plan objects and relationships are depicted graphically in Figure 5.10. We'll explore these core relationships in the next sections as we discuss how to build the organizational plan in OM.

5.3.1 Building the Organizational Hierarchy

One of the key principles in the relationship structure is that of hierarchy. For example, the relationship between a senior position in an organizational unit and another position in that same unit is hierarchical. The senior position (B 002) is the line supervisor to the lower-placed position (A 002), which reports to the position above. Similarly, the relationship between a senior organizational unit in an organizational unit and another organizational unit in that same unit is hierarchical.

The senior organizational unit (B 002) is the line supervisor to the lower-placed organizational unit (A 002), which reports to the organizational unit above.

This hierarchical representation of the object relationships is what builds the hierarchical depiction of the organization. This hierarchy is achieved through the use of three object relationships:

▶ Organizational unit to organizational unit

▶ Organizational unit to position

▶ Position to position

5.3.2 Organizational Unit Hierarchy

The organizational unit to organizational unit relationship is by far the most commonly used mechanism to build the hierarchical organizational plan. This hierarchy is achieved through the use of the relationship A/B 002 (reports to / is line supervisor of). Figure 5.11 shows how the relationship is created from the perspective of the higher-level organizational unit.

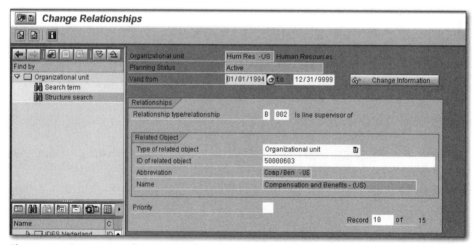

Figure 5.11 Organizational Unit Hierarchy Relationship (Top-Down)

In this case, the organizational unit Human Resources is the superior object. The relationship record from its perspective is aggressive: It supervises the Compensation and Benefits – (US) organization. From this perspective, the B 002 relationship is created.

In the grand scheme of the organizational plan, however, the Human Resources organizational unit is not the top organization. It too is a subordinate organization in this plan. As shown in Figure 5.12, Human Resources also has an A 002 relationship to organizational unit 00000300 US Exec. This relationship is a passive relationship from Human Resources' perspective: It reports to a higher-level organization.

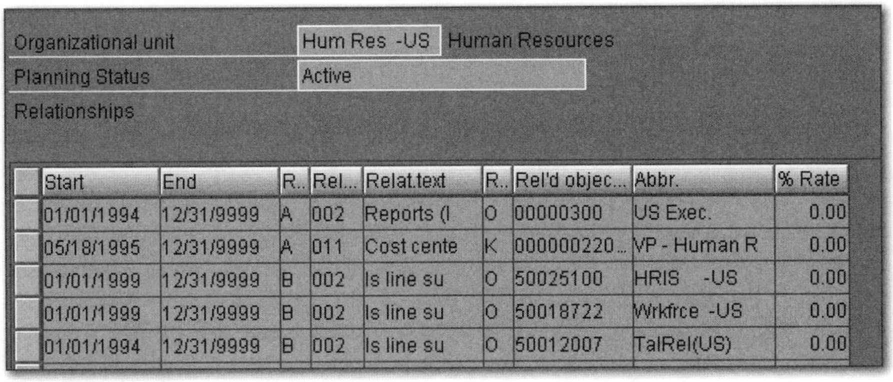

Organizational unit	Hum Res -US	Human Resources						
Planning Status	Active							
Relationships								

	Start	End	R.	Rel...	Relat.text	R..	Rel'd objec...	Abbr.	% Rate
	01/01/1994	12/31/9999	A	002	Reports (I	O	00000300	US Exec.	0.00
	05/18/1995	12/31/9999	A	011	Cost cente	K	000000220...	VP - Human R	0.00
	01/01/1999	12/31/9999	B	002	Is line su	O	50025100	HRIS -US	0.00
	01/01/1999	12/31/9999	B	002	Is line su	O	50018722	Wrkfrce -US	0.00
	01/01/1994	12/31/9999	B	002	Is line su	O	50012007	TalRel(US)	0.00

Figure 5.12 Organizational Unit Hierarchy Relationships (Bidirectional)

As organizational units are connected through the A/B 002 relationship, the overall enterprise reporting structure is formed.

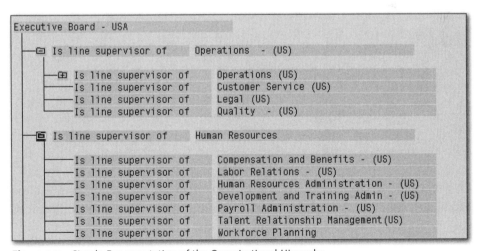

Figure 5.13 Simple Representation of the Organizational Hierarchy

You can see in Figure 5.13 how the SAP system graphically represents the organization hierarchy. Viewed in a different OM transaction, the same organizational hierarchy is also presented as a more graphical representation in Figure 5.14.

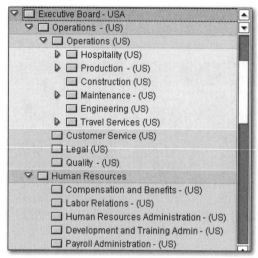

Figure 5.14 Graphical Representation of the Organizational Hierarchy

5.3.3 Staffing Assignments

The assignment of positions to organizational units creates what is called the staff assignment structure in OM. For every organizational unit in your organizational plan, you must create the relevant staff assignments. As we mentioned in Chapter 3, positions represent concrete instances of jobs that can be occupied by people in the organization. Staff assignments take the form of positions that are allocated to the organizational unit.

Positions are assigned to the organizational hierarchy through the use of the relationship A/B 002 (reports to / is line supervisor of). Figure 5.15 shows how the relationship between organizational units and positions is graphically displayed. In this view, the positions displayed each have a reporting relationship to the organizational unit under which they are displayed. The Executive Assistant position at the top of the list belongs to the organizational unit USA Company. Similarly, the Chief Executive Officer position also belongs to the same organizational unit—USA Company.

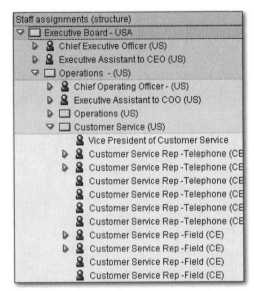

Figure 5.15 Organizational Hierarchy with Position Assignments

This independent assignment of the position to the organizational unit is important to note, because there is no inherent relationship between the two positions to identify one as superior or subordinate to the other. At this point in the organizational unit, all positions are created equal and are considered peers.

Example

In Figure 5.15 the Executive Assistant and Chief Executive Officer both report to the Executive Board – USA organizational unit. The positions are assigned to the organizational unit separately, and so have no relationship to one another in the form of hierarchy. At this point, the positions are peers.

5.3.4 Position-Based Reporting Structures

The reporting structure is mostly determined by the organizational structure. There are two additional identification settings that you can make at the position level to put more hierarchical information in your organizational plan.

The first is to utilize the Chief position indicator. As mentioned in Section 3.5.3, a position can be defined as a Chief position in the organizational hierarchy. This setting is made in the position details, and is indicated by a checkbox in the position basic data, as shown in Figure 5.16.

Details for Position Chief Executive Officer (US)
Basic data
Address
Cost distribution
Work schedule
Qualification
Tasks
Position
CEO - US
Chief Executive Officer (US)
Job
Executive (US)
Valid On
03/03/2008
Head of own organizational unit
No periods
Vacancy occupied or put on hold
Persnl Officer
Staff
Line manager
Holder
Icon
Holder
Percentage
Assigned as ...
Mrs Debbie Davis
100.00
10/01/1998
Description
Subtyp
General description

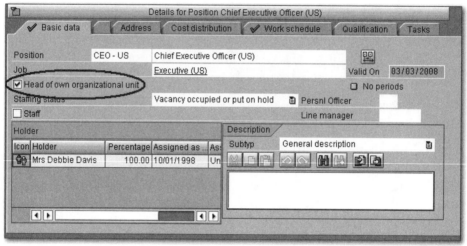

Figure 5.16 Chief Assignment Indicator for a Position

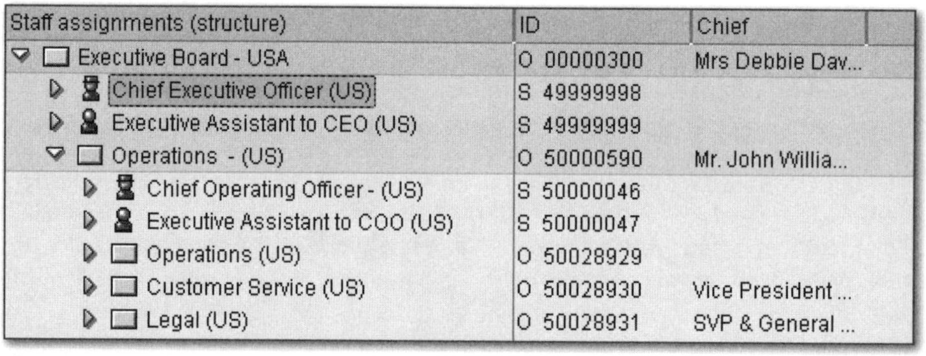

Staff assignments (structure)
ID
Chief
Executive Board - USA
O 00000300
Mrs Debbie Dav...
Chief Executive Officer (US)
S 49999998
Executive Assistant to CEO (US)
S 49999999
Operations - (US)
O 50000590
Mr. John Willia...
Chief Operating Officer - (US)
S 50000046
Executive Assistant to COO (US)
S 50000047
Operations (US)
O 50028929
Customer Service (US)
O 50028930
Vice President ...
Legal (US)
O 50028931
SVP & General ...

Figure 5.17 Chief Positions in the Staff Assignment Structure

When utilized, the Head of own organizational unit setting automatically creates relationship A/B 012 (Manages / is managed by) between the position and the organizational unit. When this relationship exists, the assumption is that any positions not similarly related will report to that head position. In addition to the relationship, as shown in Figure 5.17, the system also graphically provides two indications of the chief position: first, the change of icon for the position to one with a hat and, second, the display of the position title in the Chief data column. Only head positions display in this manner.

Example

As shown in Figure 5.17, the Chief Executive Officer in our top-level organization is now identified as the Chief position. The system assumption is that all other positions in the same organization report to the Chief position. This provides the mechanism for determining that the Executive Assistant to the CEO is a subordinate position and no longer a peer.

Depending on the complexity of your organizational reporting hierarchy, the use of the head position may provide sufficient information to identify managers of employees in the organization. Use of the Chief position indicator is by far the simplest mechanism to represent a manager position in the organization. For some organizations, however, this may not be sufficient. The organizational structure may have been created such that there are multiple managers in one organizational unit. In this case, you can create and view a position-based reporting structure that deviates from the organizational structure. To create a position reporting hierarchy, positions are connected to one another via relationship A/B 002 (reports to / is line supervisor of).

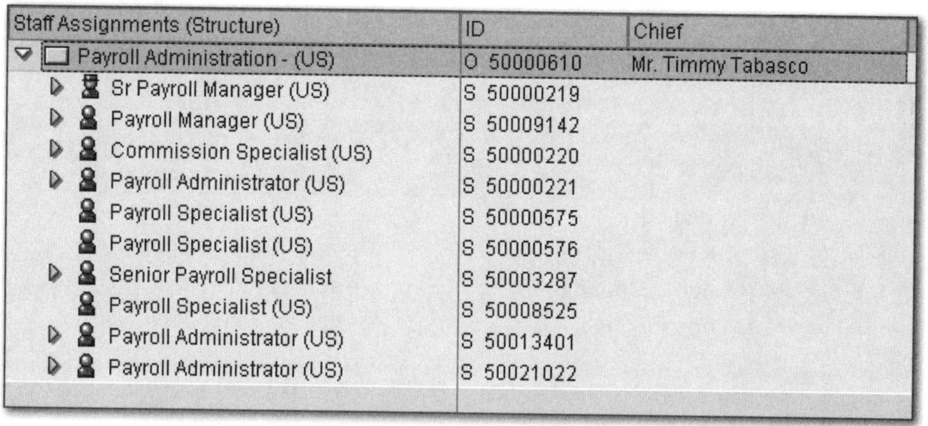

Staff Assignments (Structure)	ID	Chief
▽ ☐ Payroll Administration - (US)	O 50000610	Mr. Timmy Tabasco
▷ 🧑 Sr Payroll Manager (US)	S 50000219	
▷ 🧑 Payroll Manager (US)	S 50009142	
▷ 🧑 Commission Specialist (US)	S 50000220	
▷ 🧑 Payroll Administrator (US)	S 50000221	
🧑 Payroll Specialist (US)	S 50000575	
🧑 Payroll Specialist (US)	S 50000576	
▷ 🧑 Senior Payroll Specialist	S 50003287	
🧑 Payroll Specialist (US)	S 50008525	
▷ 🧑 Payroll Administrator (US)	S 50013401	
▷ 🧑 Payroll Administrator (US)	S 50021022	

Figure 5.18 Staff Assignment Structure with Multiple Managers

97

Example

The Payroll Administration – US organizational unit shown in Figure 5.18 shows how position-based reporting is useful. There are two management positions: the Sr Payroll Manager (US) and Payroll Manager (US). With the chief indicator set at the Sr Payroll Manager position, the system assumes that all positions in the same organization report to it. Unfortunately, this does not account for any positions that may report to the second Payroll Manager position.

To clarify the actual reporting structure, additional A/B 002 relationships are created between the manager positions and the specialist and administrator positions. In this example, the specialist positions report to the Sr Payroll Manager, and the administrator positions report to the Payroll Manager. By selecting an alternate view of the data, the position-based reporting hierarchy is clear. This is illustrated in Figure 5.19 for both manager positions. All positions still belong to the same organizational unit, but the reporting structure is altered.

Reporting Structure	Belongs to Organizational Unit
▽ Sr Payroll Manager (US)	Payroll Administration - (US)
Mr. Timmy Tabasco	
▷ Commission Specialist (US)	Payroll Administration - (US)
Payroll Specialist (US)	Payroll Administration - (US)
Payroll Specialist (US)	Payroll Administration - (US)
▷ Senior Payroll Specialist	Payroll Administration - (US)
Payroll Specialist (US)	Payroll Administration - (US)

Reporting Structure	Belongs to Organizational Unit
▽ Payroll Manager (US)	Payroll Administration - (US)
Mr. Samuel Marks	
▷ Payroll Administrator (US)	Payroll Administration - (US)
▷ Payroll Administrator (US)	Payroll Administration - (US)
▷ Payroll Administrator (US)	Payroll Administration - (US)

Figure 5.19   Position-Based Reporting Hierarchy

The reporting relationships between positions indicate that whereas two management positions exist in the organizational unit Human Resources, there is one top position to which the other reports. Entering and maintaining this type of relationship is very labor intensive, because each position must be linked to the managing position to which it reports, in addition to being assigned to the relevant organizational unit. This virtually doubles the amount of relationships that must be created in the organizational plan. The resulting reporting hierarchy, however, is unmistakable.

The position-based reporting hierarchy depicted above uses both position-to-position relationships and the chief indicator. The Chief icon is particularly useful in graphical depictions of the organizational structure, because the visual clue leaves little question about who is the head of the organization. Choosing this type of position-to-position reporting hierarchy is a double-edged sword. Whereas it provides absolute clarity on the reporting hierarchy, it requires absolute diligence in creating the initial structure properly and keeping it accurate on an ongoing basis.

5.3.5 Position Management Hierarchy Best Practices

Although there are a few different ways to achieve the position management hierarchy structure in OM, the implementation best practice is to follow two basic design principles:

1. Create separate organizational units at the manager or supervisor level. Organizational units can represent any type of structure in the organization. As such, it's useful to create organizational units at every reporting level so that you can truly represent the organizational hierarchy of the enterprise.

2. Use the chief indicator and relationship to indicate who the head of each organization is. Using the Chief position indicator saves valuable time and energy for maintaining position information. Leverage the position-to-organizational unit relationships to build the reporting hierarchy. SAP by default uses the Chief position to identify organizational unit leaders, so you should too.

5.3.6 Relating Jobs and Positions

Jobs usually only appear once in the organizational plan. A position represents a specific instance of the job, and so appears multiple times in the organizational plan. Positions are related to jobs through relationship A/B 007 (describes / is described by). When you create positions, the basic entry screen provides a field to specify the related job, as shown in Figure 5.20. The relationship to the job is automatically created in the organizational plan via a background process when the job is selected. This method is useful when you are creating one position at a time.

Details for Position New position
Basic data
Account assignment
Address
Cost distribution
Work schedule
Qualification
Tasks
Position
New position
New position
Job
Not assigned
Valid from
01/01/2008

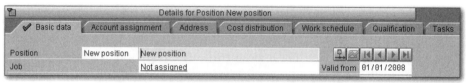

Figure 5.20 Creating a New Position

When creating the initial organizational plan in implementation, you may find it useful to create multiple positions at once. For example, if in your Staffing department you have a job Recruiter, you may need to create 15 positions for the enterprise. Rather than create these individually, you can use Report RHMULT00 to duplicate the objects at once.

Alternatively, if you work in the simple maintenance transaction, which we'll cover in Chapter 8, you can create multiple positions from jobs as well. Once created, the position-to-job relationship is stored like other relationships, as shown in Figure 5.21.

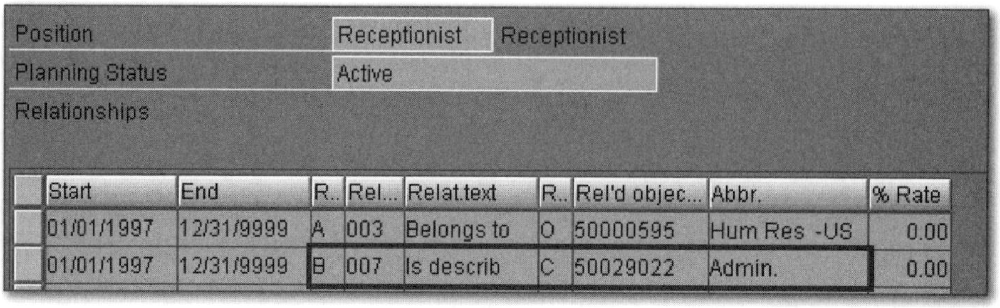

Position
Receptionist
Receptionist
Planning Status
Active
Relationships
Start
End
R..
Rel...
Relat.text
R..
Rel'd objec...
Abbr.
% Rate
01/01/1997
12/31/9999
A
003
Belongs to
O
50000595
Hum Res -US
0.00
01/01/1997
12/31/9999
B
007
Is describ
C
50029022
Admin.
0.00

Figure 5.21 Position-to-Job Relationship Assignment

5.3.7 People in Staff Assignments

Persons (object type P) or Users (object type US) can be holders of a position in the organizational plan. This assignment is achieved through the use of the relationship A/B 008 (Holder). The relationship to either person or user object is stored in the same manner from the perspective of the position, and is depicted in Figure 5.22.

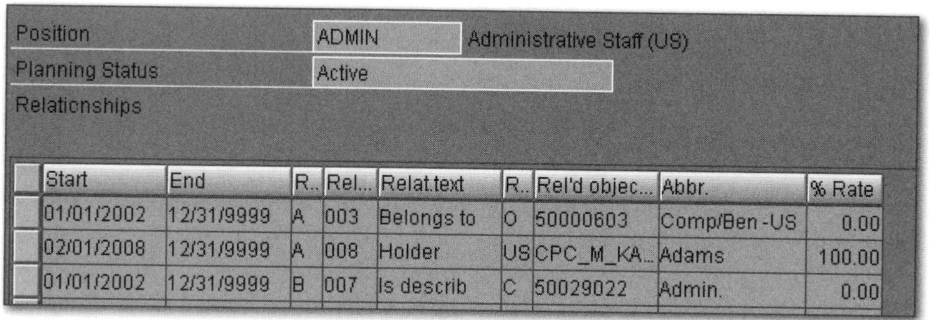

	Start	End	R..	Rel...	Relat.text	R..	Rel'd objec...	Abbr.	% Rate
	01/01/2002	12/31/9999	A	003	Belongs to	O	50000603	Comp/Ben -US	0.00
	02/01/2008	12/31/9999	A	008	Holder	US	CPC_M_KA..	Adams	100.00
	01/01/2002	12/31/9999	B	007	Is describ	C	50029022	Admin.	0.00

Position: ADMIN — Administrative Staff (US)
Planning Status: Active
Relationships

Figure 5.22 Position-to-User Relationship Assignment

In the example in Figure 5.22, the position is assigned to a user (US). Here, the system user ID CPC_M_KA... and the name associated with the user ID, Adams, is displayed. User Adams is the full-time holder of this position and so is allocated at 100%.

For person assignment, as shown in Figure 5.23, the object type P refers to the personnel number assigned to Felix in the Personnel Administration (PA) component of SAP ERP HCM.

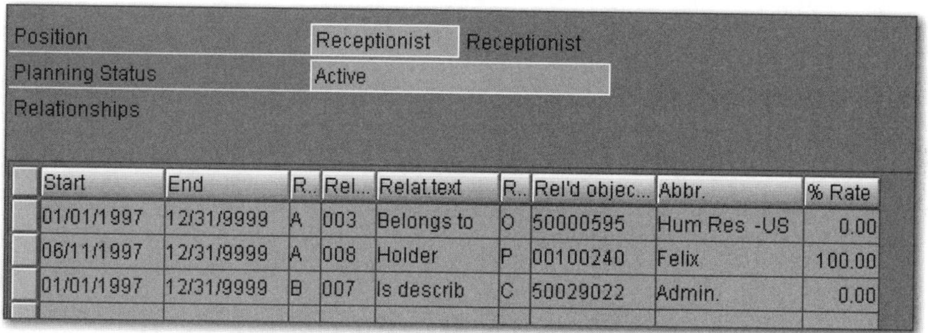

Position: Receptionist — Receptionist
Planning Status: Active
Relationships

	Start	End	R..	Rel...	Relat.text	R..	Rel'd objec...	Abbr.	% Rate
	01/01/1997	12/31/9999	A	003	Belongs to	O	50000595	Hum Res -US	0.00
	06/11/1997	12/31/9999	A	008	Holder	P	00100240	Felix	100.00
	01/01/1997	12/31/9999	B	007	Is describ	C	50029022	Admin.	0.00

Figure 5.23 Position-to-Person Relationship Assignment

While positions can be related to either persons or users, the assignment to either object is made very differently. Assignment to users is very simple, and may be maintained from within the organizational plan maintenance screens. The user object is related directly to the position, and the relationship infotype record created at the point the information is saved.

The assignment to persons takes place from the PA component, and should not be made directly from OM. In PA, the assignment of a person to a position occurs through the use of two infotypes. Infotype 0000 Actions is used first to record the personnel transaction that occurs for the employee.

> **Example**
>
> You can use personnel actions to hire an employee, transfer him to another part of the organization, promote him to another role, or document when he leaves the company. You decide which actions to record.

Figure 5.24 shows how the relationship is created from the perspective of the Person. The Actions infotype is actually a combination view of two infotypes. If you look at Figure 5.24, you can see that the top two screen areas Personnel action and Status belong to the Infotype 0000 Actions. The lower section, Organizational assignment, is actually another infotype: 0001 Organizational Assignment.

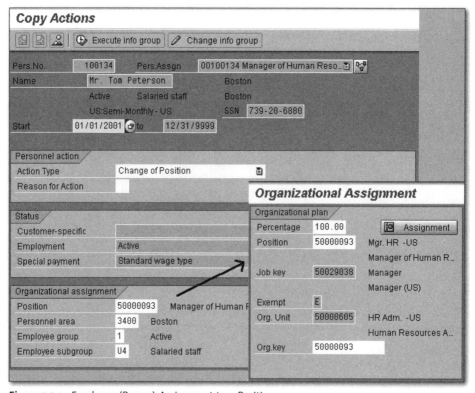

Figure 5.24 Employee (Person) Assignment to a Position

The Actions infotype provides an entry point for the assignment of key personnel information, including the position. When saved, the information is carried forward to Infotype 0001 Organizational Assignment, where the points of integration to OM are stored. The relationship to the position is created when this infotype is saved. In the process, the SAP system also evaluates the relationships of the position and carries forward (display mode only) the related organizational unit, job, and cost center assignment for that position.

Any other information related to the position or job that may be useful in Infotype 0001 Organizational Assignment can also be brought to the infotype for consistency checks. This can include, for example, personnel area, employee group, and employee subgroup.

Multiple Staff Assignments

When persons are allocated to multiple positions at a <100% percentage basis, the assignment information in both OM and PA differs. In OM, the position has multiple relationship records to multiple holders. Each relationship record has a specific percentage applied, which when totaled should not exceed 100%, as in Figure 5.25.

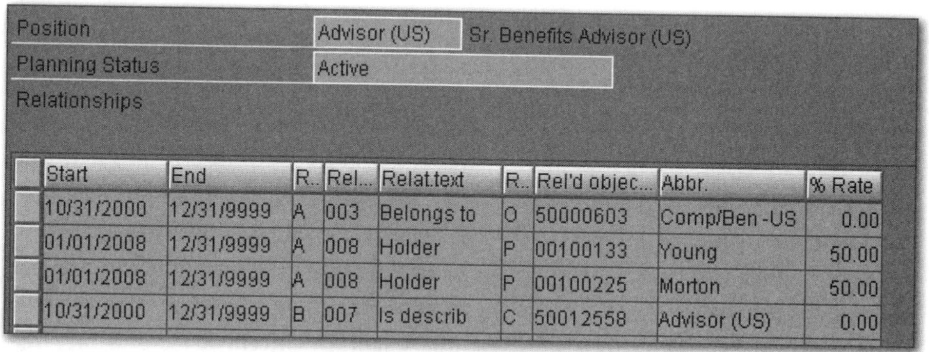

Position		Advisor (US)	Sr. Benefits Advisor (US)				
Planning Status		Active					
Relationships							

Start	End	R..	Rel...	Relat.text	R..	Rel'd objec...	Abbr.	% Rate
10/31/2000	12/31/9999	A	003	Belongs to	O	50000603	Comp/Ben -US	0.00
01/01/2008	12/31/9999	A	008	Holder	P	00100133	Young	50.00
01/01/2008	12/31/9999	A	008	Holder	P	00100225	Morton	50.00
10/31/2000	12/31/9999	B	007	Is describ	C	50012558	Advisor (US)	0.00

Figure 5.25 Multiple Person Assignments to One Position

Similarly, the employee personnel record will also show multiple positions. In Infotype 0001, the Assignment [🖹 Assignment] button provides a view to the employees' multiple position assignments, as shown in Figure 5.26.

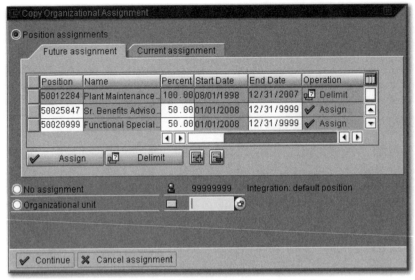

Figure 5.26 Multiple Positions in Infotype 0001 Organizational Assignment

Incomplete Staff Assignments

In some circumstances, personnel records can be created with no assignment to a position in the organizational plan. This can occur during implementation and testing, when the position function is perhaps not necessary for the process being designed and tested. Alternatively, a position may not yet be approved in the organizational plan and be unavailable for assignment to the person. In any case, the situation may arise where a personnel record is saved with no position assigned. In this case, the SAP system provides a means to assign the employee to the organizational unit only. A default position 99999999 serves as a placeholder for the organizational assignment. This is also shown in Figure 5.26. Similarly, if a person is not affiliated with either a position or an organizational unit, you can elect identify "no assignment," in which case the default position is used and the organizational unit is left blank.

> **Note**
>
> Keep in mind that the integration of positions and persons is one of the more compelling integration points throughout SAP ERP HCM and will enable you to take full advantage of all SAP ERP HCM functions. Use of the default position in the SAP system should be kept to a minimum, though, to ensure the best use of the SAP ERP HCM functions.

5.3.8 Cost Center Assignments

The last element of the basic organizational plan design is the cost center assignment. The assignment of a cost center to an organizational object is the most common method of indicating the financial origin of costs. By assigning a cost center to an organizational object, you are indicating where the costs incurred by that organization are to be charged. Cost centers are typically assigned to the organizational unit, and the assignment is inherited by any subordinate organizational units or positions. Exceptions can, of course, be made at the position level, if you want to charge specific positions to alternate cost centers in Controlling.

Cost center assignment can occur one of two ways. As shown in Figure 5.27, an organizational object can be assigned a direct cost center through the Account Assignment area. The cost centers are determined by a combination of information. The Controlling Area is directly associated with the cost centers, and by that assignment will also be displayed in OM. This helps prevent people from choosing inappropriate combinations of cost elements. If enterprise organization is active in a controlling area, you can only maintain an organizational unit's cost center and company code assignments in Controlling.

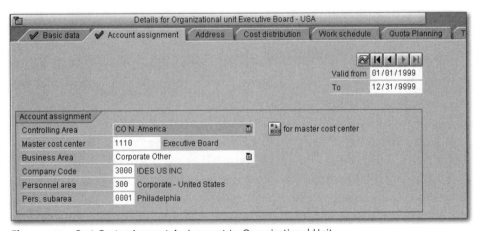

Figure 5.27 Cost Center Account Assignment to Organizational Unit

When the cost center assignment is saved, two infotype records are created. A relationship from the organizational unit (or position) to the cost center is created in Infotype 1001. This is achieved through relationship A011 (cost center assignment). A record is also created in Infotype 1008 Account Assignment. No percentage assignment is made in Infotype 1008, because the system assumes that all costs (100%) will be allocated to the master cost center.

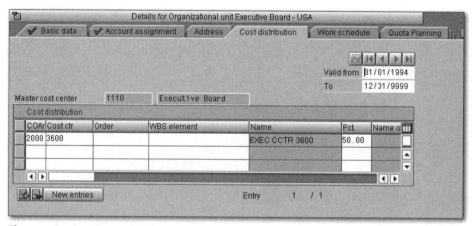

Figure 5.28 Cost Center Distribution

The second way to assign costs is to distribute a percentage allocation over multiple cost centers. This is done through Infotype 1018 Cost Distribution, shown in Figure 5.28. Here, a cost center and percentage record for the cost center assignment is entered. If a master cost center is directly related to the object, the additional cost center percentage allocation doesn't have to equal 100%. The system automatically allocates any remaining percentage to the master cost center. If, however, no master cost center exists, the total percentage must equal 100% allocation. The system reconciles to percentage allocations before you can save your data.

Up to now we've discussed how to create the basic organizational plan elements. The organizational structure, staffing assignments, reporting hierarchy, and account assignments are all created using relationships. The explanations have all focused on the use of standard relationships that SAP provides. But what if you have requirements that are not met by the standard relationships? The next section focuses on creating custom relationships to answer that question.

5.4 Creating New Relationships for Your Objects

SAP typically delivers relationships that will fit most every need. However, if you cannot utilize a standard relationship delivered by SAP to relate the OM objects in your organizational plan, you can create your own relationships. The IMG activities provide the steps necessary to enhance the existing data model with custom relationships. There are six primary steps in the process:

1. Access the IMG via Transaction SPRO

2. In the section **Personnel Management • Organizational Management**, expand the sections **Data Model Enhancement • Relationship Maintenance**. Select Relationship Maintenance (Figure 5.29).

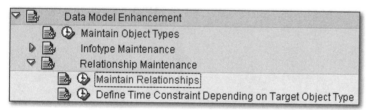

Figure 5.29 IMG: Maintain Relationships

3. Click on the New Entries button to get a blank entry screen.

4. Enter the three-character ID (AAA-ZZZ) for your new relationship (Figure 5.30) and a passive and aggressive description. Save your entry.

	Relat'ship	Relationship bottom up	Relationship top down	
Dialog Structure	Z01	Works for project	Includes project member	
▽ ▢ Links	Z02			
▢ Relationship Charac	Z03			
▢ Additional Data on Re				
▢ Allowed Relationship				
▢ External Relationship				
▢ Time constraints				

Figure 5.30 IMG: New Relationship Creation

5. Select the new relationship, and select the Allowed Relationships view (Figure 5.31).
6. Enter the objects, passive and/or aggressive indicator, and relationship number that you want to use in the system.

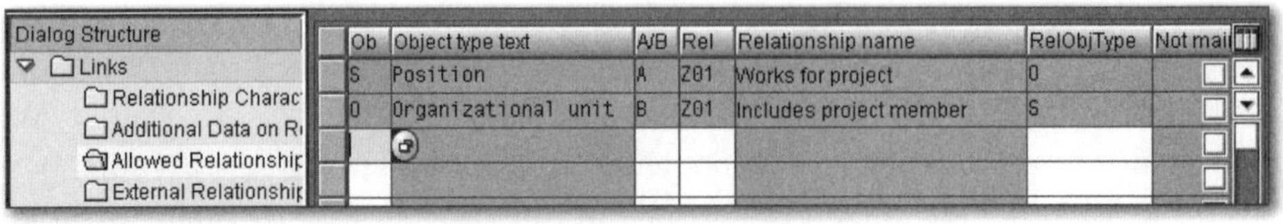

Dialog Structure
Links
Relationship Charac
Additional Data on R
Allowed Relationshi
External Relationshi
Ob
Object type text
A/B
Rel
Relationship name
RelObjType
Not mai
S
Position
A
Z01
Works for project
O
O
Organizational unit
B
Z01
Includes project member
S

Figure 5.31 IMG: New Allowed Relationships

Note

By default, your relationship will have time constraint 2: Only one relationship will be allowed at a time for the objects chosen. If this is appropriate, you can stop at this point. If you want to change this to another time constraint value, continue to the next step.

7. Navigate back to the IMG and select the Infotype Maintenance folder if it not already open. Select Maintain Subtypes. Select the New Entries button to get a blank entry screen and add the bottom-up and top-down relationships as shown in Figure 5.32.

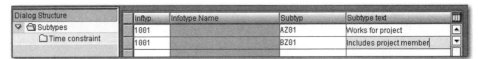

Dialog Structure
Subtypes
Time constraint
Inftyp.
Infotype Name
Subtyp
Subtype text
1001
AZ01
Works for project
1001
BZ01
Includes project member

Figure 5.32 IMG: New Infotype Subtypes

8. Navigate back to the IMG and select Relationship Maintenance. Select the Time constraints view and choose New Entries. You may either enter the allowed objects individually or use the * wildcard character (Figure 5.33). Enter the appropriate time constraint value for each relationship subtype (A and B).

Tip

Unless you have a specific need to control the time constraint by object type, we advise that you always use the wildcard character * so that all object types are handled appropriately.

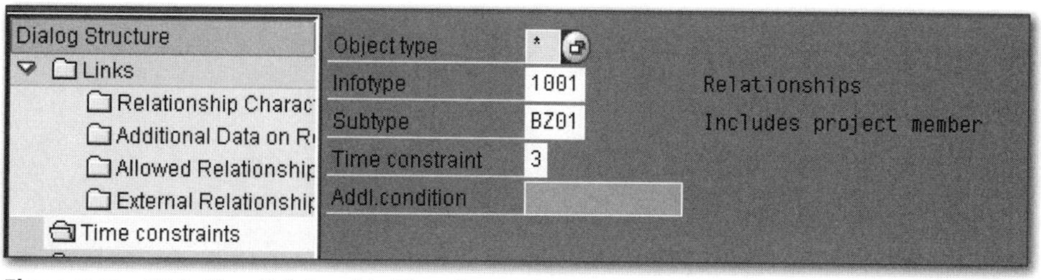

Figure 5.33 IMG: New Relationship Time Constraints

9. Save your entries. Your relationships are now ready to be used.

Creating your own relationships is a creative way to get more functionality out of OM. You can set up virtually any type of hierarchy structure, or relate custom characteristics to your organizational objects. Because the relationship information is driven by table configuration, you don't have to create custom code to use it.

5.5 Conclusion

In this chapter, we've examined how relationships are used to tie together the objects in the organizational plan. Relationships are the key to creating a hierarchical depiction of the enterprise in the SAP software, allowing you to create multiple dimensions in the organization. Now that you have an understanding of how relationships work, let's take this concept to the next level and discuss how relationships are used in reporting on the organizational data. The next chapter will focus on evaluation paths, which use relationships to connect seemingly unrelated information.

Getting data back out of the system can be more complicated than putting data into it. So, good reporting is an important part of any implementation, and evaluation paths provide the means to achieve complex reporting between the objects in your organizational plan.

6   Reporting with Evaluation Paths

As we learned in the previous chapters, objects and the data associated with them form the basis of the organizational plan. Each object's infotype data, for example, an organization's cost center assignment, is stored in an individual infotype record. At first glance, the data appear to be fairly independent. Given how the data is stored, you may wonder how the SAP software navigates through all of the objects and infotype data to display an entire organizational structure, and, more importantly, how you can report on the various plan elements yourself.

6.1   What are Evaluation Paths?

In organizational reporting, evaluation paths are the key to finding and displaying what you're looking for. Evaluation paths provide instructions to the programs and user interfaces on which object types are to be included in searches. They use the relationships between objects to navigate through the organizational plan and select data along the way for display.

Evaluation paths can be very simple, defined by the relationship between one object and another. For example, an evaluation path may simply show the positions that are assigned to an organizational unit. In this case, the singular relationship between these two objects may be all that is needed to find the link and display the two object types. However, evaluation paths can also be quite complex, using multiple objects and relationships to connect the dots along the way.

> **Example**
>
> Displaying the manager of a particular person may require multiple object connections:
> - Person assigned to a position
> - Position assigned to an organizational unit
> - Organizational unit assignment to chief position
> - Person linked to the chief position

From single-level list displays to hierarchical structures, evaluation paths use relationships to find the connections between objects and display them so that the user sees and understands how the data is linked together.

Evaluation paths are the key element of the OM component that will enable you to do organizational reporting. Without evaluation paths, all you would have are lists of objects and their individual infotype information. With evaluation paths, you can report on information collectively and display the information that is linked via relationships.

6.2   How Evaluation Paths Are Defined in OM

In this section, we'll explain how evaluation paths are defined and configured in OM.

6.2.1   Evaluation Path Configuration

To understand how to use evaluation paths, let's examine how they are built. Evaluation paths are defined by an up-to-eight-character alphanumeric code. A lengthy text description is available to accompany the code to help users choose the right evaluation path to use for their search. SAP provides several hundred evaluation paths for immediate use.

Figure 6.1 shows some of the simpler evaluation paths that are defined in the IMG. You can access this table via the IMG path **Personnel Management · Organizational Management · Basic Settings · Data Model Enhancement · Maintain Evaluation Paths** or directly via Transaction Code OOAW.

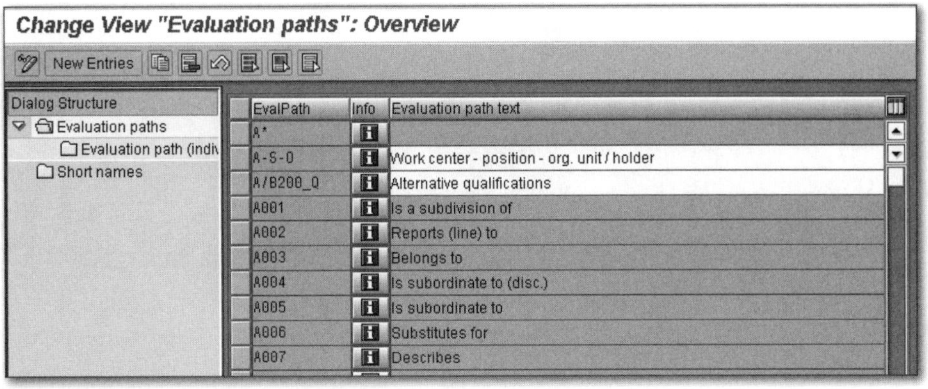

Figure 6.1 IMG: Evaluation Paths

Many evaluation paths mirror the relationship that is used between objects. For example, evaluation path A002 displays objects that are connected via the single relationship A002. This is a relatively simple evaluation path, for which the results are very straightforward. The SAP system provides an evaluation path for each relationship it delivers in the standard system. This is true for both passive (Annn) and active (Bnnn) relationships.

Many more complex evaluation paths are also provided in this IMG table. The naming convention for the evaluation path is typically alphabetical, although you can create alphanumeric codes as well. If you choose to create your own evaluation paths, keep in mind that customer-defined paths should be in the Z* name range.

Tip

SAP does not recommend changing any of the delivered evaluation paths, because many standard SAP reports and functions rely on evaluation paths as delivered in the IMG. Changing these evaluation paths can affect all programs and reports that use those evaluation paths and lead to problems.

In the second IMG view, the details of the evaluation path are specified. Figure 6.2 provides an example of a commonly used evaluation path that is more complex in both name and design.

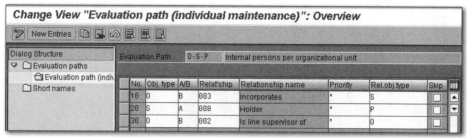

Figure 6.2 IMG: Evaluation Path Details

The evaluation path O-S-P can be used to display the organizational plan structure with the organizational units in a hierarchy, including positions and their holders. Let's examine the evaluation path configuration more closely, explaining each part.

Sequential Number

Evaluation paths are defined by one or more lines of instructions. The sequential number defines the order in which the path between objects is searched.

Seq	Obj	A/B	Relationship	Priority	Rel Obj	Skip
10	O	B	003	*	S	
20	S	A	008	*	P	
30	O	B	002	*	O	

The evaluation path searches the object information in the sequential order provided until the resulting object (or no result) is found. The system starts with the lowest numbered step and performs the steps in order. Because the sequence number is a two-character field, up to 99 types of search instructions can be used in a single evaluation path.

The sequence of the relationships included in the evaluation path also determines how the results of the evaluation are displayed. The objects that are higher in the sequential order are displayed first.

Object

The object code specifies the object type being evaluated. Most evaluation paths specify a particular object type in the evaluation path. If you want to evaluate all

objects to search for a specific relationship, you can use the wildcard character *
in place of a specific object type.

Seq	Obj	A/B	Relationship	Priority	Rel Obj	Skip
10	O	B	003	*	S	
20	S	A	008	*	P	
30	O	B	002	*	O	

A/B and Relationship

The A/B and Relationship fields identify the bottom-up (passive) or top-down
(active) indicator and relationship code to use in the search. The evaluation paths
delivered can describe either single relationships (Axxx or Bxxx) or a combination
or relationships (paths). The more specific the search, the more relationships are
generally used.

Seq	Obj	A/B	Relationship	Priority	Rel Obj	Skip
10	O	B	003	*	S	
20	S	A	008	*	P	
30	O	B	002	*	O	

One or more relationships can be used in the path, but only one relationship type
is specified on each line of instruction in the evaluation path configuration.

Priority

The Priority field is used when you want to restrict the evaluation search to objects
that have been assigned a certain priority number. The priority field is in Infotype
1000 Object. This field is typically not used in evaluation paths, so most contain
the wildcard character * to utilize all entries.

Seq	Obj	A/B	Relationship	Priority	Rel Obj	Skip
10	O	B	003	*	S	
20	S	A	008	*	P	
30	O	B	002	*	O	

Related Object

The related object is the object type in the relationship being evaluated. If you specify an object type, only those objects related to the initial object via the relationship A/B and code are selected. If you want all objects related to the initial object by the relationship, you can use the wildcard * character to search all object types.

Seq	Obj	A/B	Relationship	Priority	Rel Obj	Skip
10	O	B	003	*	S	
20	S	A	008	*	P	
30	O	B	002	*	O	

Skip

The skip indicator is used to indicate that you want the relationship to be evaluated in the search but don't want the related object to be displayed as part of the search results.

Seq	Obj	A/B	Relationship	Priority	Rel Obj	Skip
10	O	B	003	*	S	
20	S	A	008	*	P	
30	O	B	002	*	O	

If you indicate skip, the last object is used in the search but not displayed in the results. This option may be useful in complex searches where multiple steps are required to get from one object to another, but where you only want to display the final object information.

The Result

In the example used above, evaluation path O-S-P:

▶ Line 10 looks at the root organizational unit and finds all positions related by relationship B 003 Incorporates.

▶ Line 20 looks at the positions found in line 10 and finds all persons related by relationship A 008 Holder.

▶ Line 30 looks at the subordinate organizational units related to the root organization by relationship B 002 Is line supervisor of.

Figure 6.3 provides an example of the results of a report run with evaluation path O-S-P. Here, the report is run with organizational unit Executive Board-USA as the root organization specified in the selection criteria.

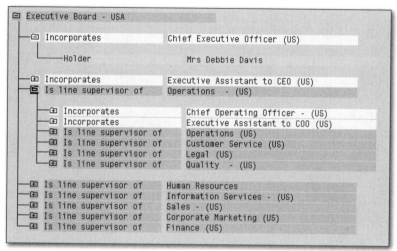

Figure 6.3 Results of Evaluation Path O-S-P

The result of this evaluation path is a display of the root organizational unit, its positions (object S) and the people (object P) who hold that position, and all subordinate organizational units and their positions and people. We'll explore more about how to use evaluation paths in reporting in the next section.

6.3   Evaluation Paths in Organizational Plan Reporting

Similar to relationships delivered in the SAP system, hundreds of evaluation paths are provided as well. Evaluation paths are used in most standard reports delivered in OM. In some cases, the evaluation paths are preset by the report. In other cases, you can choose the evaluation path to use in the report. Figure 6.4 provides a sampling of the report options available in OM.

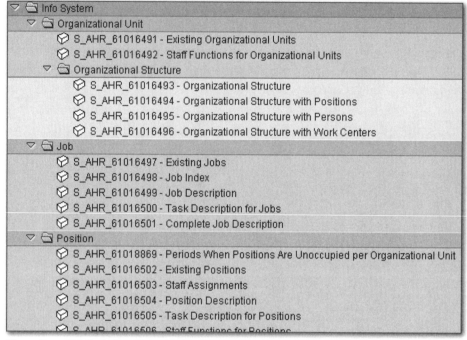

Figure 6.4 OM Reporting Menu Options

Many of the standard SAP reports allow you to specify the evaluation path as part of the report selection criteria. Choosing the right root object and evaluation path will help ensure that you display the correct report results the first time, and may reduce how long it takes your report to run.

Example

Figure 6.5 shows a sample report selection screen where the evaluation path is entered among other selection criteria. The root organizational unit 300 is selected in plan version 01. This restricts the selection of organizational units to only organizational unit 300 and those organizational units that report to it. The reporting period is today, which restricts objects to those whose validity period spans today's date. The evaluation path O-S-P is selected to choose and display the positions and holders along the organizational hierarchy. Only objects in status 1 (Approved) are selected, so any planned or submitted objects are not selected. This is a typical selection set for organizational structure reports.

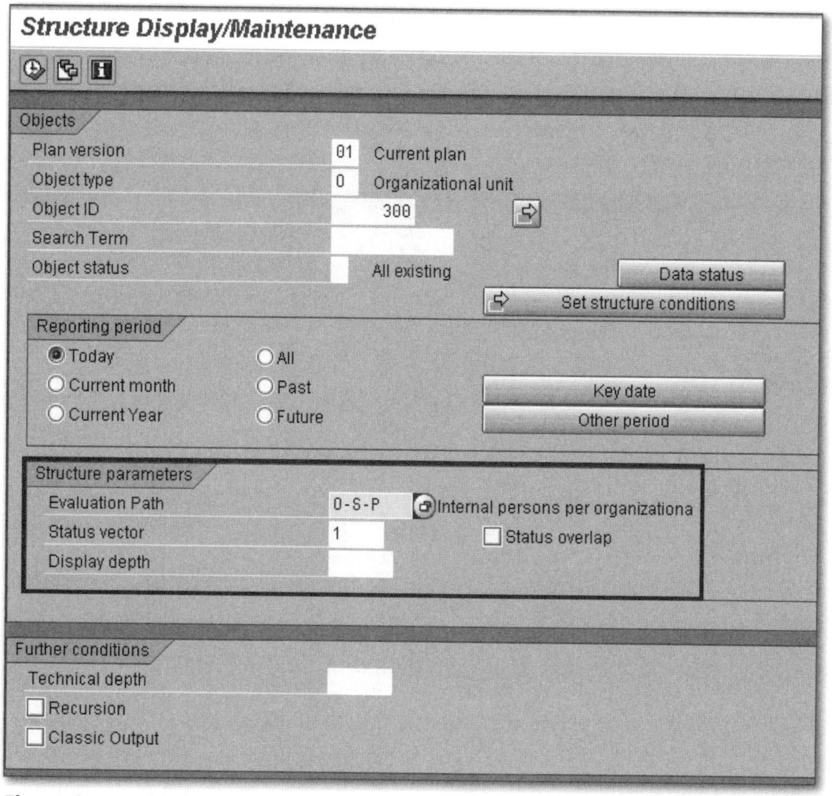

Structure Display/Maintenance

Objects

Plan version	01	Current plan
Object type	0	Organizational unit
Object ID	300	
Search Term		
Object status		All existing

Data status

Set structure conditions

Reporting period

- ⦿ Today
- ○ All
- ○ Current month
- ○ Past
- ○ Current Year
- ○ Future

Key date

Other period

Structure parameters

Evaluation Path	0-S-P	⦿ Internal persons per organizationa
Status vector	1	☐ Status overlap
Display depth		

Further conditions

Technical depth

- ☐ Recursion
- ☐ Classic Output

Figure 6.5 OM Report Selection Screen

Given that SAP provides several hundred evaluation paths to choose from, choosing the right one can be a daunting task. One way to choose the correct path is to look at how the evaluation paths are configured in the IMG. This is the most comprehensive means for determining which objects and relationships are utilized in the evaluation path. Given the sheer volume of evaluation paths, this is likely unrealistic to undertake. Fortunately, SAP also provides another mechanism for narrowing down your choices.

When choosing an evaluation path to use in your report, you have three options:

- ▶ Typing in the evaluation path name directly
- ▶ Choosing from a list of all evaluation path choices
- ▶ Specifying the objects included in the path and choosing from a list

The first two options rely on the user knowing the right evaluation path to use. The latter option provides the mechanism for narrowing down the choice of evaluation paths to only those that will find the objects and relationships you need. Figure 6.6 provides a view of how this is achieved.

Figure 6.6 Evaluation Path Selection Prompt

In the evaluation path selection window, users can specify a starting, middle, and ending object type to narrow down the evaluation path choices. By specifying one or all of these elements, only those evaluation paths that utilize these object types in the evaluation path configuration are presented to the user as choices.

In the example in Figure 6.6, we're looking for an evaluation path where the starting point for the search is object type O, organizational unit. The ending point for the evaluation path is object type P, person. We want to get from the organizational unit to the person via object type S, position. The results of this search are presented in Figure 6.7.

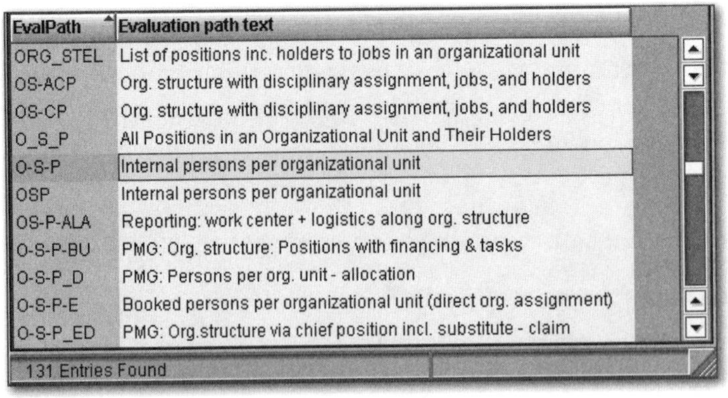

EvalPath	Evaluation path text
ORG_STEL	List of positions inc. holders to jobs in an organizational unit
OS-ACP	Org. structure with disciplinary assignment, jobs, and holders
OS-CP	Org. structure with disciplinary assignment, jobs, and holders
O_S_P	All Positions in an Organizational Unit and Their Holders
O-S-P	Internal persons per organizational unit
OSP	Internal persons per organizational unit
OS-P-ALA	Reporting: work center + logistics along org. structure
O-S-P-BU	PMG: Org. structure: Positions with financing & tasks
O-S-P_D	PMG: Persons per org. unit - allocation
O-S-P-E	Booked persons per organizational unit (direct org. assignment)
O-S-P_ED	PMG: Org.structure via chief position incl. substitute - claim

131 Entries Found

Figure 6.7 Evaluation Path Selection Results

With the object types specified, the system searches through the evaluation path configuration information and only selects those evaluation paths that meet this criteria. Rather than a list of all possible evaluation paths, specifying the objects O, S, and P has narrowed the choices to 131 entries. Although this is still a large list from which to select a value, it's far less daunting that the entire list of nearly 900 evaluation paths.

> **Tip**
>
> Because a large number of evaluation paths use similar information, namely objects O, S, and P, it's important to become familiar with this subset of evaluation paths, and to closely examine and potentially revise the text description of these evaluation paths so that you and other users truly understand the information the evaluation path will return.

For example, there are subtle differences between the evaluation paths:

- O-O-S-P: Staff assignments along organizational structure
- O-P: Internal persons of an organizational unit
- O-S-P: Internal persons per organizational unit

Close examination of the configuration for these three evaluation paths reveals that whereas they use the same objects and relationships, the order in which the relationships are searched is different, and in one case the positions are skipped in the display. This is not readily apparent from the descriptive text associated with the evaluation path, so you may find it useful to rename the path to something your users will find more descriptive.

> **Example**
>
> Evaluation path O-P is named "Internal persons of an organizational unit." You can choose to call this "Positions and Holders of the selected Organization" to better represent the results that a user may see when he chooses the evaluation path. Similarly, evaluation path BOSSONLY is named "Chief and Organizational assignment." This may be better termed "Chief positions and holders in the selected Org Units."

6.3.1   Additional Reporting Selections

In addition to the evaluation path itself, standard reports also provide a number of additional selection criteria that are useful in further narrowing down data in organizational reporting. Depending on the actual report run, some or all of the parameters shown in Figure 6.8 may be present for use.

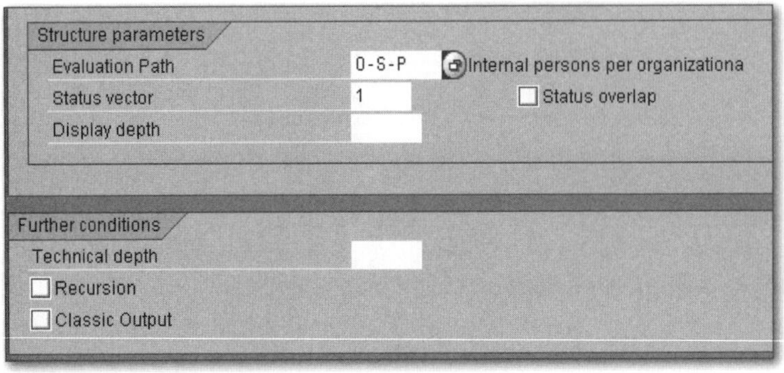

Structure parameters		
Evaluation Path	0-S-P	⊙ Internal persons per organizationa
Status vector	1	☐ Status overlap
Display depth		

Further conditions	
Technical depth	
☐ Recursion	
☐ Classic Output	

Figure 6.8 OM Reporting Standard Selection Screen Parameters

Structure Parameters

The Status Vector and Status Overlap fields are used in conjunction with one another. Because organizational plan data may be created in multiple status values, it can be useful to narrow down reporting to only the active status (value 1) for reporting on actual data in productive use, or on other status values (for example, 2 for planned) for reporting on proposed data. The default value for reports is value 1 for active data only.

Using the Status overlap function allows you to run a simulation of data, showing the results of activating planned or proposed relationship data. With this option, you can choose one or all non-active status values, and the report will display data in this status as if it were active. This temporary display of proposed or planned object information may be useful in verifying the consequences of planned organizational changes.

> **Example**
>
> If you are looking to reorganize a department, you may want to display both the current (active) and planned versions of the organizational hierarchy concurrently so that you can visualize the proposed changes. Selecting both active and planned status values in the selection criteria provides object data in both statuses.

The Display depth for the structure determines how much data is displayed in the report results. Many enterprise structures can contain significant levels in the organization. In situations where you may want to only display the highest levels of the organization, this parameter is very useful. The report or program processes all data in the organizational plan; however, only the number of levels of data specified in this field are actually shown.

Further Conditions

The Technical Depth field is similar to the Display Depth parameter, in that it limits the depth of the organizational plan evaluation. The key difference is that this parameter limits the number of records that are processed in the evaluation path, not simply those that are displayed. Beginning with the root object, the evaluation path is processed down to the number of levels specified. Because the entire organizational plan is not evaluated, this option can save significant time in report processing if your organizational plan is very large and you only need to see a specific number of levels down from the root object.

The Recursion option is used to check whether objects are related in such a way that they form an endless loop. This is similar to a circular reference in an Excel formula. Using this option checks for such occurrences.

Finally, the option Classic Output alters the display of the report results to the "classic" or simple view of data display. This option doesn't alter the data selected for evaluation but simply changes the data view.

6.4   Creating New Evaluation Paths

Similar to relationships, SAP delivers evaluation paths that will suit most needs. The IMG activities provide the steps necessary to enhance the existing data model with custom evaluation paths should the need arise. There are four steps in the process:

1. Access the IMG via Transaction SPRO

2. In the section **Personnel Management •Organizational Management**, expand the section **Basic Settings**. Choose **Maintain Evaluation Paths** as shown in Figure 6.9. Alternatively, you can access the view directly using Transaction Code OOAW.

Basic Settings
Maintain Number Ranges
Data Model Enhancement
Maintain Evaluation Paths

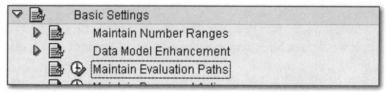

Figure 6.9 IMG: Maintain Evaluation Paths

3. Click on the New Entries button to get a blank entry screen. Enter the evaluation path code and description. Save your entry.

Figure 6.10 shows a sample evaluation path being created.

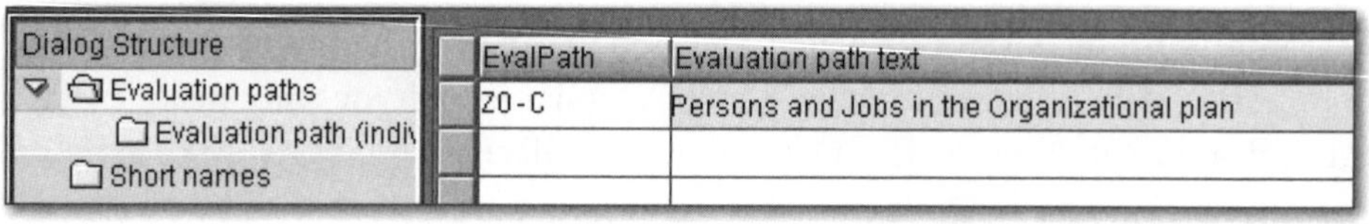

Dialog Structure
Evaluation paths
Evaluation path (indiv
Short names
EvalPath
Evaluation path text
ZO-C
Persons and Jobs in the Organizational plan

Figure 6.10 IMG: New Evaluation Path

4. Select your entry and select the Evaluation Path (individual maintenance) view. Again, select New Entries, and enter the evaluation path details (Figure 6.11). Save when complete.

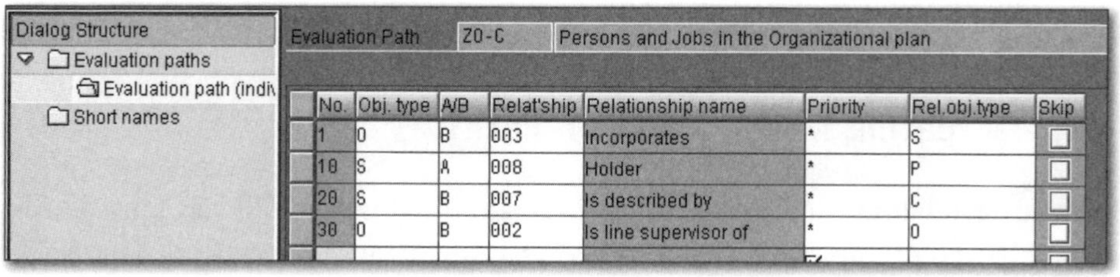

Dialog Structure
Evaluation paths
Evaluation path (indiv
Short names
Evaluation Path
ZO-C
Persons and Jobs in the Organizational plan
No. | Obj. type | A/B | Relat'ship | Relationship name | Priority | Rel.obj.type | Skip
1 | O | B | 003 | Incorporates | * | S
10 | S | A | 008 | Holder | * | P
20 | S | B | 007 | Is described by | * | C
30 | O | B | 002 | Is line supervisor of | * | O

Figure 6.11 IMG: New Evaluation Path Details

Report RHSTRU00 Structure Display/Maintenance can be used to test your evaluation path. This report allows any object and evaluation path to be reported on. Figure 6.12 provides a sample result of the evaluation path created in these instructions.

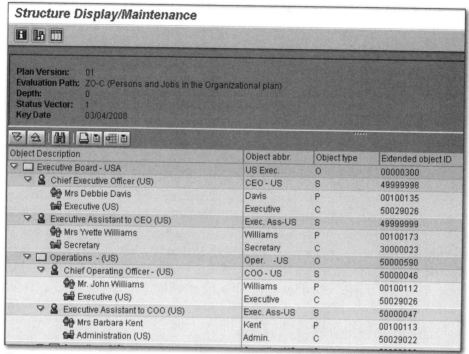

Figure 6.12 Report RHSTRU00: Using the New Evaluation Path

Now that you've seen how evaluation paths can be used in organizational reporting selection criteria, let's take a closer look at all the reporting options.

6.5   Organizational Plan Reporting

Efficient and effective organizational management requires that you have the most up-to-date information on the enterprise at any given time. The SAP system offers a variety of reporting and analysis options to provide you with the information you require. In addition to reports delivered in each of the SAP components, tools are available that enable you to create your own reports with little or no programming experience required. These various options work together to give you the information you need to support your business decision-making processes. In each of the following sections, we'll take a high-level look at the reporting options, and look at a few commonly used reports.

6.5.1 SAP ERP HCM Reporting Options

Multiple reporting options are available in SAP ERP HCM, each with its own pros and cons. The information in this section is meant to give you some general guidance about the options available and how they might best be used to meet your reporting needs. Depending on the needs of your users and organization, multiple or all options may be required to fulfill your reporting requirements.

Standard Reports

With SAP ERP HCM, you get standard reports for most frequent reporting needs. Evaluation paths and data displayed are predetermined by the report design. Reports are accessed the same way for all SAP ERP HCM components. They can be found in the Information System menu for a particular component, as well as in the Information System menu for SAP ERP HCM as a whole. There are approximately 40 standard reports for direct OM data reporting. Reports in the OM Information System menu are grouped by object type. There are standard reports for organizational units, jobs, positions, work centers, and tasks. In addition, there are general reports that can be used for any object type.

Running a standard report typically involves entering the appropriate selection criteria and clicking on the Execute button. The report output is displayed on screen, at which point you can print or save the results in a local file.

Example

The Structure Display/Maintenance general report is widely used to display OM information. This report was used to explain the selection criteria in Section 1.3. Upon choosing the root organizational unit and evaluation path, the resulting report output is shown in Figure 6.13.

▶ **Pros:** Immediately available to use, these require no programming to run. Most reports provide data in a list format and have options to save data in an external file format, such as Excel.

▶ **Cons:** Standard reports are limited in their flexibility because data output cannot be controlled or affected by the user. Users may have the option of changing object types displayed, but fields and the format of reports are usually fixed. Casual users may require extended support to run standard reports.

With over 200 reports available for the entire SAP ERP HCM component suite, you have a solid foundation for your informational reporting.

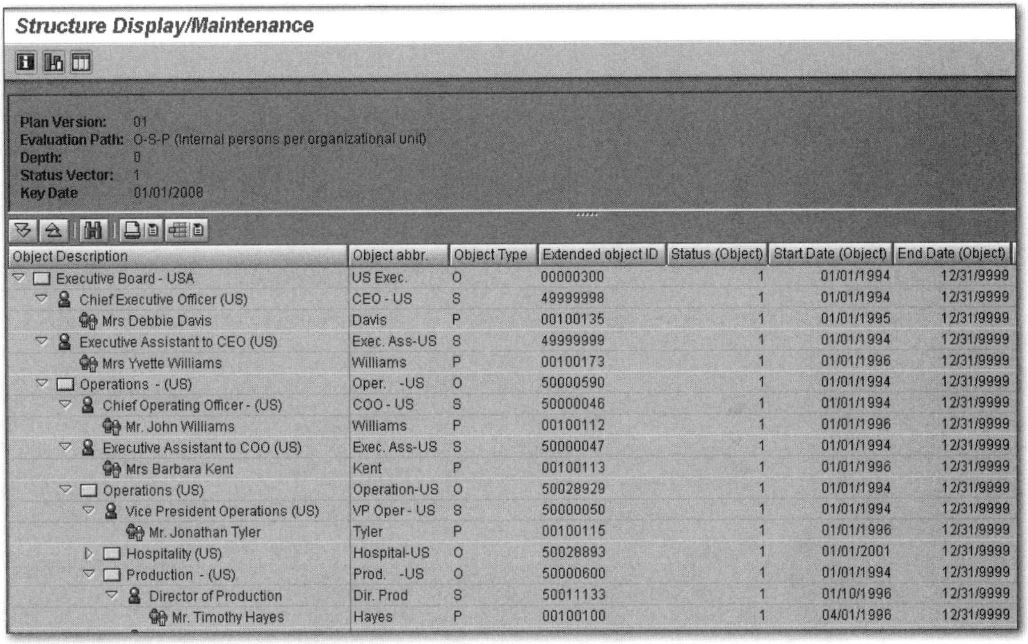
Structure Display/Maintenance

Plan Version: 01
Evaluation Path: O-S-P (Internal persons per organizational unit)
Depth: 0
Status Vector: 1
Key Date 01/01/2008

Object Description	Object abbr.	Object Type	Extended object ID	Status (Object)	Start Date (Object)	End Date (Object)
Executive Board - USA	US Exec.	O	00000300	1	01/01/1994	12/31/9999
Chief Executive Officer (US)	CEO - US	S	49999998	1	01/01/1994	12/31/9999
Mrs Debbie Davis	Davis	P	00100135	1	01/01/1995	12/31/9999
Executive Assistant to CEO (US)	Exec. Ass-US	S	49999999	1	01/01/1994	12/31/9999
Mrs Yvette Williams	Williams	P	00100173	1	01/01/1996	12/31/9999
Operations - (US)	Oper. -US	O	50000590	1	01/01/1994	12/31/9999
Chief Operating Officer - (US)	COO - US	S	50000046	1	01/01/1994	12/31/9999
Mr. John Williams	Williams	P	00100112	1	01/01/1996	12/31/9999
Executive Assistant to COO (US)	Exec. Ass-US	S	50000047	1	01/01/1994	12/31/9999
Mrs Barbara Kent	Kent	P	00100113	1	01/01/1996	12/31/9999
Operations (US)	Operation-US	O	50028929	1	01/01/1994	12/31/9999
Vice President Operations (US)	VP Oper - US	S	50000050	1	01/01/1994	12/31/9999
Mr. Jonathan Tyler	Tyler	P	00100115	1	01/01/1996	12/31/9999
Hospitality (US)	Hospital-US	O	50028893	1	01/01/2001	12/31/9999
Production - (US)	Prod. -US	O	50000600	1	01/01/1994	12/31/9999
Director of Production	Dir. Prod	S	50011133	1	01/10/1996	12/31/9999
Mr. Timothy Hayes	Hayes	P	00100100	1	04/01/1996	12/31/9999

Figure 6.13 Structure Display/Maintenance Standard Report Output

HIS: Human Resources Information System

The Human Resources Information System (HIS) is a mechanism for running personnel-based reports from the organizational plan hierarchy. The HIS is more a tool for person-related reporting than for OM data reporting. Typically, the standard reports that are available for personnel reporting contain selection criteria based on Personnel Administration (PA) infotypes. For example, the fields Personnel Area, Personnel Subarea, Employe Group, and Employee Subgroup are widely used in PA standard reports. These fields come from PA Infotype 0001 Organizational Assignment. Because these fields typically do not correspond to the organizational hierarchy, it can be difficult to report on employees as they are grouped in the organizational plan. While some standard reports include a means to select the organizational structure as part of the selection criteria, many do not. The HIS solves this problem.

The HIS transaction begins by asking you to specify the organizational plan elements to display graphically. You can choose to view organizational units alone, with positions, with persons, or with both positions and persons. You then specify the root organizational object, the display depth, and the validity period.

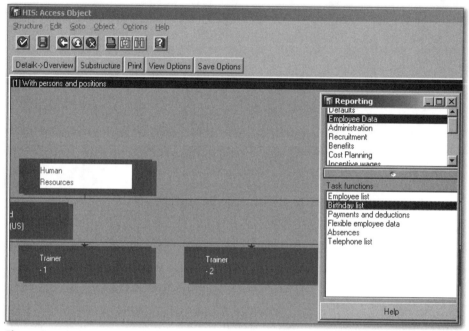

Figure 6.14 HIS Reporting Interface

You are then presented with a structural display of the OM hierarchy (Figure 6.14). From the hierarchy display, you can select one or more organizational objects. From this selection, you can then run a variety of standard reports from a reporting window. The reporting window contains all the SAP ERP HCM component reports available. The HIS uses the organizational elements you selected and passes these on to the standard report.

The ability to preselect portions of the organizational plan enables you to run the various SAP ERP HCM standard reports using the organizational data as selection criteria.

▶ **Pros:** Same pros as standard reports. It is questionable whether this is a slightly more user-friendly method of running standard reports for a section or selection of the organization.

▶ **Cons:** Same cons as standard reports. Navigating the structural hierarchy is a bit difficult for novice users. It is hard to see any level of detail when viewing the entire organizational structure, which makes selecting a particular subset of the organization difficult.

InfoSet Query

Also referred to as Ad Hoc Query, InfoSet Query is a tool that enables you to create custom reports on the fly (Figure 6.15). Users pick and choose fields to use for selection and display, and can save the reports for reuse.

▶ **Pros:** Very simple user interface. Graphical interface elements and drag-and-drop features make this tool easy to use. All query information, such as selection criteria and fields for output, is available on a single screen. Data output is immediate and can be refreshed as users add, change, or remove fields or selection options. Data may be printed or output to file formats such as Excel.

▶ **Cons:** Configuration of InfoSets and User Groups is required before users can use the tool. There is no display option for multiline lists, meaning you are restricted to one line of output for data. There is no selection of data along the organizational hierarchy. For example, users have to know the organizational unit codes to select departments. It's not possible to combine databases: OM, PA and applicant data must be reported on separately. Users can cause heavy use of system resources by not narrowing selection criteria or by choosing too many output fields.

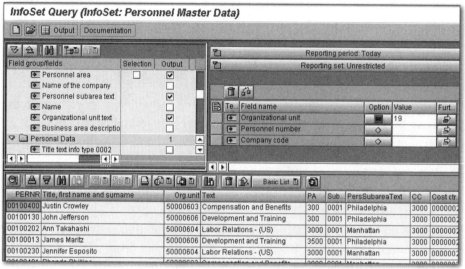

Figure 6.15 SAP InfoSet or Ad Hoc Query of HR Information

SAP Query

Similar to InfoSet Query, SAP Query is a more advanced reporting tool for users to create custom ad hoc reports. SAP Query (Figure 6.16) has more compex options such as the ability to create statistics and ranked lists. Once created, SAP Query reports are run like standard reports, with a selection screen.

▶ **Pros:** You can use InfoSet queries as a basis for creating an advanced query. It has more customizing options for selection and output criteria. Multiline lists are allowed, and it can perform calculations and insert code snippets for custom fields or formulas. It also enables you to make a basic data template and save multiple versions of statistics or ranked lists of the output. Similar to standard reports, you can select data along the organizational hierarchy when the report is run.

▶ **Cons:** It requires more training than the other reporting options. It has the same cons as InfoSet query concerning combining databases and causing heavy use of system.

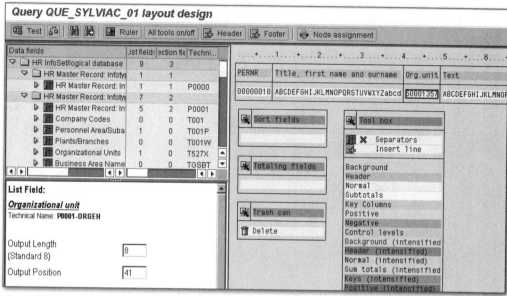

Figure 6.16 Creating an SAP Query Report

Business Intelligence/Business Warehouse

SAP NetWeaver Business Intelligence (BI), referred to as SAP Business Warehouse (BW) prior to release 7.0, is an independent analytical reporting solution used for information and decision-making purposes. SAP NetWeaver BI (Figure 6.17) includes detailed business content such as HR extractors, InfoCubes, key figures (key performance indicators), and standard queries. SAP NetWeaver BI provides the ability to do time series comparisons, which allows you to perform trend analysis, strategy measurement, and strategic planning for future needs.

▶ **Pros:** It's extremely flexible and easy to use, and allows you to report on SAP and non-SAP data together. It facilitates complex calculations and reporting needs. It's made available via web browser for ease of use.

▶ **Cons:** It uses a data extraction method, so real-time data is not accessed. Sold as a separate SAP component, SAP NetWeaver BI requires a full implementation effort to utilize its functions.

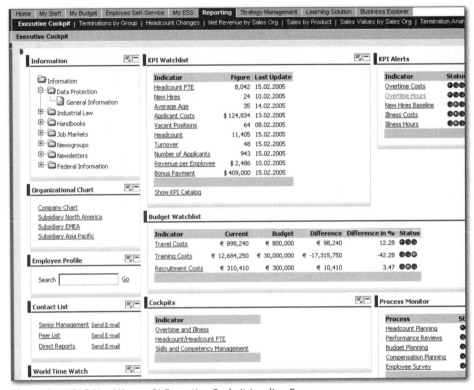

Figure 6.17 SAP NewWeaver BI Executive Cockpit Landing Page

Custom Reports

As with any SAP component, there's always the option of creating custom reports using the ABAP/4 development language. The ABAP Workbench offers all tools needed by ABAP developers to design, develop, deploy, manage, and update ABAP-based reports, as well as business applications.

▶ **Pros:** The ABAP Workbench provides complete freedom and flexibility in report design. Developers can use queries or SAP standard reports as a basis for creating custom reports. Once developed, custom reports can be inserted into the SAP menu through custom transactions or published as Web services for access via a web browser or enterprise portal.

▶ **Cons:** Expert programming resources are required to build reports.

ABAP development is very labor intensive. Care and attention must be paid throughout the report development process. Completely understanding the target audience and purpose of the custom report ensures that you gather comprehensive report requirements for data selection, data processing, field output, and the resulting format of the report data.

6.5.2 Variant Management

Most of the reporting options result in the utilization of a selection screen when the report is run. If you regularly use the same report using complex selection criteria, you can save time by using report variants. Variants enable you to save and reuse selection criteria under a user-defined name. Every time you access the report, the variant is available for you to use. When you select the variant, the system automatically populates the values stored in the variant to the individual selection fields.

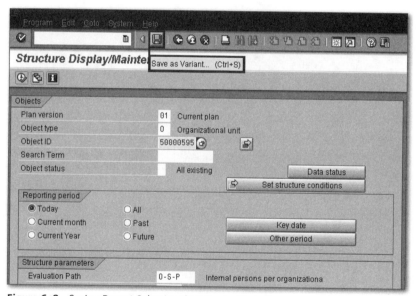

Figure 6.18 Saving Report Selection Criteria as a Variant

To create a variant, customize the report to meet your requirements. This includes identifying the following elements on the selection screen:

▶ Enter the required values for selection fields.

▶ Use the Organizational Structure or other search helps to make data selections.

▶ Enter any necessary sort criteria.

▶ Specify data processing limitations, such as number of records or structure depth levels to be processed.

You then save the variant using the Save function on the selection screen (Figure 6.18), at which time you assign it a name.

In addition to saving the selection and processing criteria, you can specify processing criteria for your variant. For example, you can protect variant field values from being overwritten, hide the selections from users, and make field selection criteria required.

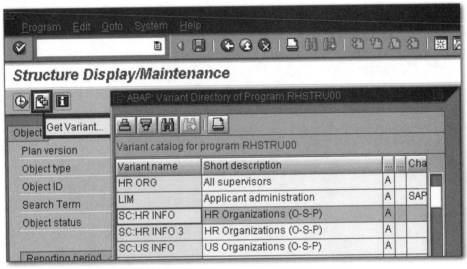

Figure 6.19 Report Variant Selection

When you later reuse the report, any variants you have saved are available for selection. As shown in Figure 6.19, when selecting variants, you may select variants that you have created yourself or any variant that any user has saved for the report. This allows you to set up variants for department or enterprise use, or simply to share variants among colleagues.

Now that we've described the various reporting tools available in the SAP system, let's take a look at how to determine which tool is right for your reporting needs.

6.6 Choosing the Right Reporting Tool

When deciding on the right reporting tool, you need to keep in mind both the report data and the person using the report. The ultimate goal is to provide users with the reporting tool that will most effectively provide sound data for business decision making. How the information is accessed, formatted, summarized, and secured, and how up-to-date it needs to be will steer you to one reporting solution or another. As you evaluate each of the tools, it may be useful to keep in mind the criteria in Table 6.1.

Goal/Purpose	Appropriate Reporting Option
Run a report where selection and output are predefined	Standard reports, HIS
Report on hierarchical structures	HIS
Create a custom list of data from one database	InfoSet or Ad Hoc Query
Create a statistical list, color formatted report, or multi-line output or perform field calculations	SAP Query
Report on key figures or execute time series comparisons	SAP NewWeaver BI
Combine information from multiple SAP ERP HCM components where no SAP-delivered report is offered	Custom ABAP reporting

Table 6.1 Criteria for Choosing a Reporting Option

6.7 Preparing and Using Organizational Charts

Before closing out this chapter on reporting, it's important to mention organizational chart reporting. Organizational charts are traditionally used to display reporting relationships between individuals. However, other information is also valuable when displayed hierarchically, such as the person's name, title, cost center, or global location. Although many of the OM organizational plan user interfaces and structural graphics reports provide a hierarchical display of information, the format is not in a typical organizational chart format.

The structural graphics user interface is also not very user friendly (see Chapter 8, Section 8.6.1 for more information on structural graphics). Most enterprises want position-based organizational chart reporting that not only shows the hierarchical reporting relationship between positions, but can also incorporate extensive position detail, vacant or planned positions, dotted line relationships, shared positions, and multiple-manager reporting.

Because organizational chart reporting is an important function in most enterprises, SAP provides certified interfaces to several third-party organizational chart software packages. The interface allows a third-party vendor's application to extract organizational plan objects, relationships, and attribute data from OM and PA components. Extracted data are displayed in a graphic presentation in the third-party application. A few of the solutions currently available include:

- OrgChart® by Nakisa (sold directly as well as through SAP)
- OrgPublisher® by Aquire Inc. (formerly TimeVision)
- OrgPlus® by Human Concepts
- org.manager® by Ingentis

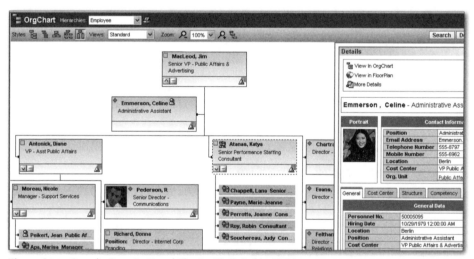

Figure 6.20 Sample Organizational Chart with Detail by Nakisa

An example of the organizational chart solution by Nakisa OrgChart is displayed in Figure 6.20, and one by HumanConcepts OrgPlus in Figure 6.21.

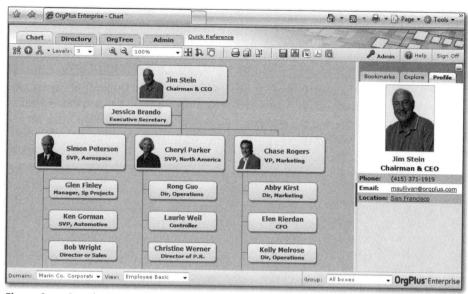

Figure 6.21 Sample Organizational Chart with Detail by HumanConcepts

Most of these products allow you to pick and choose the organizational plan and person-related attributes that are displayed on the organizational chart. The format and style of the organizational chart itself, however, are usually not very customizable. Because these products are separate from the SAP ERP solution suite, they typically require a user or enterprise license fee of their own. Because these fees can range from a few hundred to several thousand dollars, and many companies already have enterprise Microsoft Office licenses, some SAP customers have turned to Microsoft Visio to create organizational charts that can be periodically updated or run as needed.

The Microsoft Visio Solution Center provides a how-to article for creating organizational charts by uploading from a data file: *http://office.microsoft.com/en-us/visio/HA010774641033.aspx*. A simple SAP Query can easily generate the data file with all the object types, relationships, and attributes needed to create an organizational chart. The Microsoft article describes how to structure your data file, run the Visio organizational chart wizard, and create an organizational chart from the command line using macros.

6.8 Conclusion

In this chapter we've explained how evaluation paths use relationships to navigate the enterprise hierarchy. By connecting objects via their relationships and selecting data along the way, organizational management reporting and hierarchical data displays become possible. We've also reviewed the various options that SAP provides for OM reporting. In the next chapter, we'll focus on OM infotypes, which store attribute data for the object types in the organization.

The infotypes used in OM play a critical role in creating and managing your organizational plan. By choosing the right infotypes, you'll determine how much detailed information is required to set up object types and maintain them for the life of your SAP ERP HCM solution. This chapter will review the infotypes commonly used in OM.

7   Choosing and Using Infotypes in OM

Initially described in Chapter 4, an infotype is a collection of fields or attributes related to a particular type of content. Infotypes are defined by a four-character number and are used throughout the SAP ERP HCM component for employee or business information. Users enter information into infotypes to create corresponding database records, and they can then create, modify, copy, delimit, or delete data using infotypes.

7.1   Infotypes Used in Organizational Management

Numerous infotypes are used in the OM component, each with a particular set of details or characteristics for an object. Because nearly 150 different infotypes are used throughout OM, this chapter will provide a detailed explanation of only some of the more commonly used infotypes in the organizational plan.

Where possible, we'll outline how the infotype is designed to be used and outline best practices for incorporating specific infotypes into your organizational plan. In addition to an explanation of the infotype and its use, this chapter also includes information on customizing activities and options for specific infotypes where appropriate. In some cases, general infotype configuration such as subtype creation will have been explained in an earlier chapter. In this case a reference to the previous section will simply be noted.

7.2   Infotype 1000 Object

The Object infotype (Figure 7.1) defines the existence of an organizational object. As soon as you create an object with this infotype, you can then add other infotype information for the object. When an object is created, it is typically given an eight-digit identifying object ID number using the number range configuration in the system. When you create a new object, the validity period that is used to create Infotype 1000 automatically limits the validity period for any other infotype. Other infotype records can't begin or end after the validity period of the Object infotype.

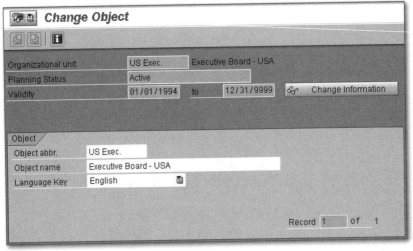

Figure 7.1   1000 Object Infotype

The object is defined by both a short name, or abbreviation, and a long name. Transactions and reports use either the abbreviation or the long name or both when displaying objects in OM, so it's helpful to use an abbreviated name that is easily identifiable. The names are stored with a language key. This allows you to create multiple versions of the Object infotype in multiple languages.

Keep in mind that the validity periods of all records are tied to one another, and so will limit the creation of new language versions to the overall object validity period. You can change the name of the object over time as your enterprise functions change by creating new Object infotype records with a new starting validity date. Using the delimit function ends the validity period of the old name as of the day before the new name.

You can use the delete function with the Object infotype, but this should be used carefully and only when an object is created in error. Deleting the Object infotype causes the system to delete all other infotypes for that object, thereby erasing all evidence of that object's existence.

7.3 Infotype 1001 Relationships

The Relationships infotype (Figure 7.2) is used to define relationships between different objects. Creating and maintaining relationship records is a vital part of setting up the OM component. Without relationships, all you have are isolated pieces of information in objects and infotype records. Relationships between the various organizational units form the organizational hierarchy structure in your enterprise. Relationships between organizational units, positions, and persons depict the organizational plan in OM.

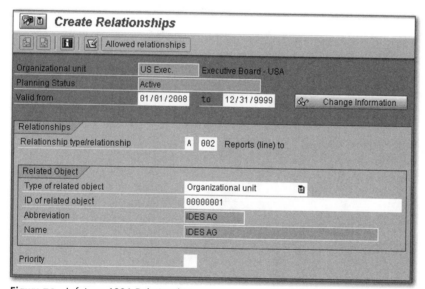

Figure 7.2 Infotype 1001 Relationships

Many different types of relationships are possible between objects; some relationships are only valid for certain object types. Each relationship is a subtype of Infotype 1001. You can create and edit multiple relationships for each object in the organizational plan.

The Relationships infotype is the primary vehicle for integration between OM components and between SAP ERP HCM components in SAP. By relating persons and positions, you carry out integration between PA and OM. You must carefully determine which relationships are required in your organizational structure, because keeping up the integrity of the relationships ultimately results in better reporting. A key benefit of relationships lies in the reporting results you obtain when you report on certain relationships in your organizational plan. Relationship reporting is done via evaluation paths.

7.4 Infotype 1002 Description

The Description infotype (Figure 7.3) is primarily reference information for the various objects that you create in OM. The description is a free-form text area into which you can enter any information you deem relevant in describing the object you have created.

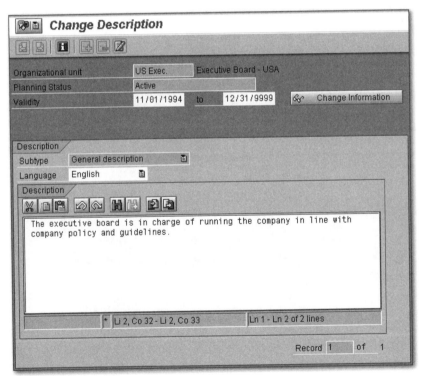

Figure 7.3 Infotype 1002 Description

Multiple descriptions can be entered by using the infotype subtype characteristic. You can also enter descriptions in multiple languages, which is useful if your enterprise operates in many countries. SAP does not recommend using this infotype for job descriptions, because the reporting options for the descriptions are very limited. Many customers do use the infotype in this manner, however, and rely on custom reporting to display the descriptions where needed.

7.5 Infotype 1003 Department/Staff

The Department/Staff infotype (Figure 7.4) is used to indicate to which organizational units or positions you can assign staff, or to indicate which organizational units are departments. This infotype is usually considered optional.

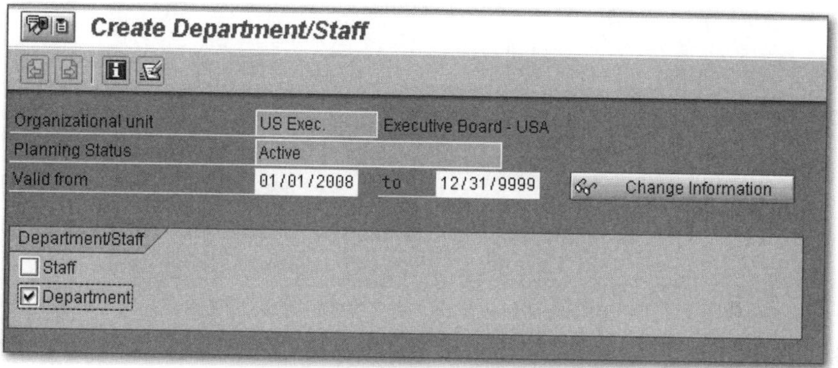

Figure 7.4 Infotype 1003 Department/Staff

The Staff flag indicates that an organizational unit or position is not part of the normal reporting structure at your company, but rather reports directly to a high-level position or organizational unit. This type of use is rare.

> **Note**
>
> The Staff flag only affects the display of the objects in the Structural Graphics display, which is discussed in Chapter 8, Section 8.6.1. Positions or organizations marked with the Staff flag appear beside their higher-level organizational unit, rather than below it.

The Department flag is used when integration between PA and OM is active. Some organizational units can be created that do not have assigned positions; you may not want employees to be assigned to these organizations. Flagging an organizational unit as a department allows only flagged data records from OM to be written to PA. If you use the Department flag, you must maintain the entries PPABT PPABT in the integration Table T77S0 for the flags to operate properly.

7.6 Infotype 1007 Vacancy

The Vacancy infotype is used to identify position vacancies. The infotype can indicate a current or future vacancy, as shown in Figure 7.5, or can be a historical record of a previous vacancy as in Figure 7.6.

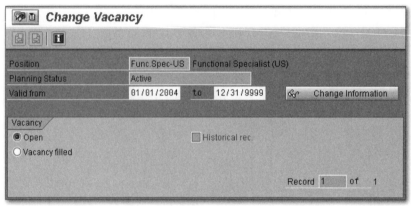

Figure 7.5 Infotype 1007 Vacancy – Open Vacancy

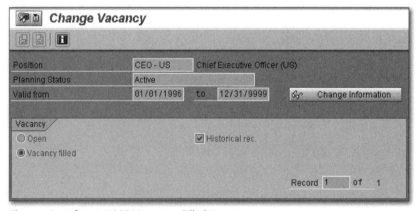

Figure 7.6 Infotype 1007 Vacancy – Filled Vacancy

When a vacancy is filled or marked historical, you can no longer edit the information. Whether you choose to use the vacancy infotype depends on how you view unoccupied positions. When a position is vacant, you can either consider it automatically available to be occupied, or you may have to specifically identify an unoccupied position as one that can be occupied. If any unoccupied position is considered eligible for someone to occupy, you don't need the vacancy infotype. If, however, you require positions to be specifically marked as vacant and eligible to be occupied, then you need to mark the positions as vacant with the creation of this infotype.

Example

You may require position requisitions to be open and approved before a vacancy can be created for a position. In this case, any unoccupied position cannot automatically be considered vacant. Instead, you would create a vacancy record only when the requisition is approved.

Three customizing settings are relevant for vacancy management. The customizing table is accessible via the IMG path **Organizational Management • Infotype Settings • Activate/Deactivate "Vacancy" infotype**. The customizing table is shown in Figure 7.7.

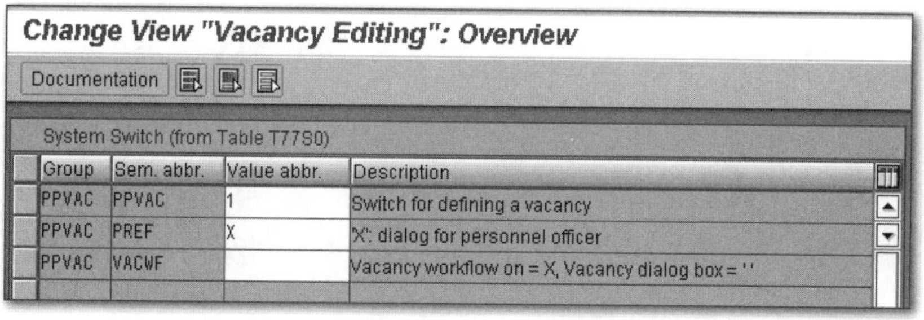
Change View "Vacancy Editing": Overview
Documentation
System Switch (from Table T77S0)
Group
Sem. abbr.
Value abbr.
Description
PPVAC PPVAC 1 Switch for defining a vacancy
PPVAC PREF X 'X': dialog for personnel officer
PPVAC VACWF Vacancy workflow on = X, Vacancy dialog box = ''

Figure 7.7 IMG: Vacancy Infotype Settings

In the IMG table, the following options are available:

- **PPVAC PPVAC:** When this is set to "1," the Vacancy infotype will be created when a position is vacant. When this is set to "0," all unoccupied positions are considered vacant.
- **PPVAC PREF:** When this is set to "X," the system will prompt you to enter the personnel officer and line manager responsible for managing the vacancy. This is only used in Recruitment vacancy functions.

▶ **PPVAC VACWF:** When this is set to "X," a workflow is generated with each vacancy creation to the personnel officer previously assigned to the employee occupying the position.

In addition to marking positions as vacant for PA integration, the vacancy infotype is used in other SAP ERP HCM components. Recruitment uses vacancies to reference when open positions are filled by either external or internal candidates. Personnel Cost Planning can take vacancies into consideration when projecting personnel costs. Career and Succession Planning can use vacancies to suggest potential future positions for employees.

7.7 Infotype 1008 Account Assignment Features

The Account Assignment Features infotype (Figure 7.8) has a dual purpose. It is used to define cost center assignments for organizational units and positions. It is also used to define personnel administration defaults. The creation of an account assignment infotype creates a Relationships infotype record A 011 "cost center assignment" between the objects.

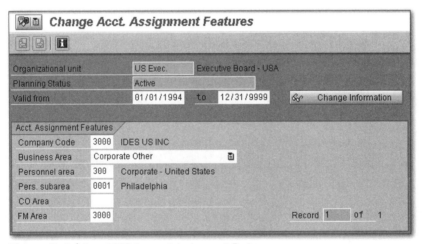

Figure 7.8 Infotype 1008 Account Assignment Features

The cost center assignment is likely the most often used function of this infotype. By assigning a cost center to an organizational unit or position, you provide the default cost center that is assigned to the holder via the inheritance principle. Setting the cost center assignment to the organizational unit ensures that any persons assigned to positions in that organization are all given the same cost center. This eliminates the need to assign individual people to a cost center, reducing data entry errors. Position overrides can be made by assigning a cost center to the position.

The personnel structure defaults for personnel area and personnel subarea can also be assigned in the account assignment infotype. By defining these fields at the organization or position, you can also reduce data entry and eliminate errors associated with these fields. The personnel structure and cost center fields are defaulted on the employee's Infotype 0001 Organizational Assignment in PA.

To effectively assign the account assignment defaults, two integration settings must be made in customizing. The first customizing table is accessible via the IMG path **Organizational Management • Basic Settings • Activate Inheritance of Account Assignment Features** (Figure 7.9).

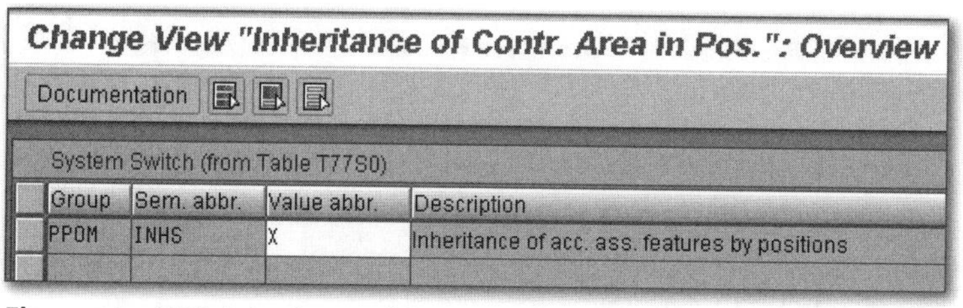
Change View "Inheritance of Contr. Area in Pos.": Overview

Documentation

System Switch (from Table T77S0)

Group	Sem. abbr.	Value abbr.	Description
PPOM	INHS	X	Inheritance of acc. ass. features by positions

Figure 7.9 IMG: Inheritance of Account Assignment Features

The second customizing table is accessible via the IMG path **Organizational Management • Integration • Integration with Personnel Administration • Set Up Integration with Cost Accounting** (Figure 7.10).

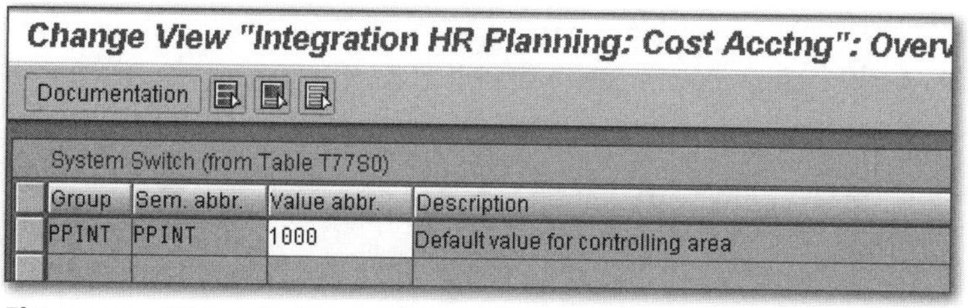
Change View "Integration HR Planning: Cost Acctng": Overv

Documentation

System Switch (from Table T77S0)

Group	Sem. abbr.	Value abbr.	Description
PPINT	PPINT	1000	Default value for controlling area

Figure 7.10 IMG: Inheritance of Controlling Area

The customizing options are:

- **PPOM INHS:** This entry must be set to "X" for the personnel area and subarea to be inherited to PA. This setting does not affect cost center assignment, which is inherited by general integration settings.

- **PPINT PPINT:** This entry defines the default controlling area used in Infotype 1008. The controlling area narrows down the cost center search and selection. If you use multiple controlling areas in your enterprise, you may want to leave this entry blank.

Two additional customizing settings are available in the system control Table T77S0 that affect the Account Assignment Features infotype. The customizing settings are only necessary when multiple company codes or controlling areas are set up in your SAP system. There is no IMG activity in OM for these settings, so you can access the table directly via Transaction Code SM30. The settings relate to cost center assignment in the infotype.

> **Example**
>
> Only one controlling area and company code can be assigned to an organization. When the top-level organization is assigned a cost center, the system assumes that all lower-level organizations will inherit that cost center, and thereby also inherit the related company code and controlling area of that cost center. If you have multiple company codes, you'll want to assign a different company code and controlling area. In ECC 6.0, both the Company Code and Controlling Area fields are grayed out when the system is installed. This prevents data entry in the two fields, even if you select a cost center in a different company code or controlling area.

The following customizing settings open the fields for data entry:

- **PPOM INHIC:** Set this entry to "X" to remove the obligatory inheritance of Company Code from the cost center.

- **PPOM INHIH:** Set this entry to "X" to remove the obligatory inheritance of Controlling Area from the cost center.

SAP also provides Note 1009742 in the service marketplace (*service.sap.com*), which describes additional corrections needed for code fixes to allow entry of these fields.

The Account Assignment infotype integration to PA is quite useful and can save data entry keystrokes as well as reduce data entry errors. Keeping this data up to date is a very important task in the maintenance of the organizational plan.

Because organizations and cost centers change frequently in large enterprises, it can be difficult to stay on top of the changes. This is something to keep in mind as you design the master data management structure for your organization. Whether you keep data entry tasks central or decide to decentralize responsibility for keeping data updated, this is a key data component that must be current.

7.8 Infotype 1018 Cost Distribution

The Cost Distribution infotype works with the Account Assignment infotype to distribute costs across multiple cost centers. Costs incurred by an organizational object are usually charged back to the master cost center assigned to the organizational unit or inherited from a higher-level organizational unit. If you want to distribute costs across multiple cost centers, you specify the additional cost centers in Infotype 1018. When you create a cost distribution infotype record, the system creates a Relationships infotype record A 014 "cost distribution" between the objects.

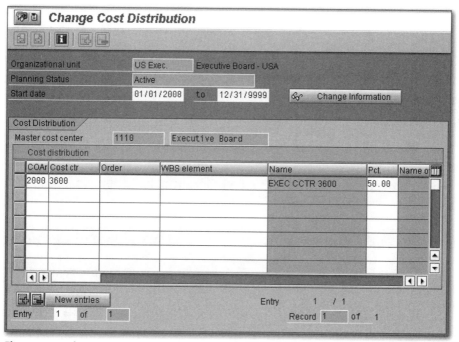

Figure 7.11 Infotype 1018 Cost Distribution

In the Cost Distribution infotype, the master cost center from Infotype 1008 is displayed for reference if one exists. Any additional cost centers are entered in the infotype and are assigned a percentage for cost assignment. For example, Figure 7.11 identifies one additional cost center to charge 50% of costs incurred by the organizational unit. Any remaining percentage is charged to the master cost center. If no master cost center is directly assigned to the organizational object, you can simply enter multiple cost centers in the cost distribution infotype. In either case, the system checks that the percentage allocation over all cost centers does not exceed 100%.

The Cost Distribution infotype does provide some slight flexibility over the Account Assignment infotype in that in addition to cost centers you can assign orders or work breakdown structure (WBS) elements as defaults for cost assignment. These fields are not available on the Account Assignment infotype.

One customizing setting has to be maintained when using the cost distribution infotype. The customizing table is accessible via the IMG path **Organizational Management · Integration · Integration with Personnel Administration · Set Up Integration for Cost Distribution** (Figure 7.12).

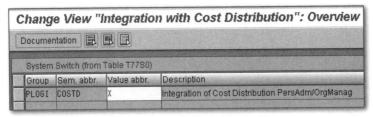

Figure 7.12   IMG: Set Up Integration for Cost Distribution

The customizing value must be "X" in order for the cost distribution information in OM to integrate with PA.

> **Note**
>
> A similar cost distribution record may be created in the employee master via PA Infotype 0027 Cost Distribution. When payroll looks for cost distribution information to pass on costs to SAP ERP Financials, it takes any cost center assignments it finds from Infotype 0027. If this infotype is not present, information from the position or organizational unit Infotype 1018 will be used to distribute costs.

7.9   Infotype 1013 Employee Group/Subgroup

The Employee Group/Subgroup infotype (Figure 7.13) is an optional infotype you can create for positions. Similar to the Account Assignment infotype that provided information for personnel area and subarea, this infotype provides a place to record the employee group and subgroup for the position. However, unlike the Account Assignment infotype, this information is not used to default data to the employee's Organizational Assignment Infotype 0001. The employee group and subgroup are only used to check or validate the data entry made in PA. If the employee group or subgroup entered is inconsistent with that in OM, a warning message appears. The user can either correct the data entry or proceed with inconsistent information.

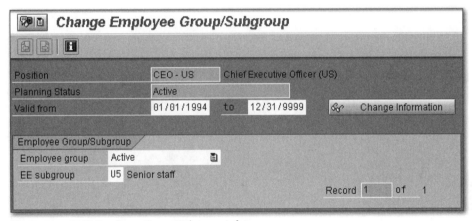

Figure 7.13   1013 Employee Group/Subgroup Infotype

The employee group and subgroup are also used with Infotype 1011 Work Schedule. This integration is described later in this chapter.

7.10   Infotype 1028 Address

The Address infotype is used to store addresses of companies or external participants, as well as information on the location of organizational objects and resources. The information is largely used for reference in the Training and Event

Management (TEM) component, but can be used for general reference and reporting in any component.

You can take advantage of the infotype subtype to set up different types of addresses, such as physical location or mailing address. Addresses can be created and assigned to objects manually or they can be table driven. Examples of both of these options are provided in Figures 7.14 and 7.15. If created manually, fields for address entry are provided for the user to complete. The layout of the address fields is not specific to any particular country requirements. Alternatively, you can create building types in customizing that the user can select from a drop-down list, as shown in Figure 7.15. In this case, the address information is preset in the table and is auto-filled in the infotype.

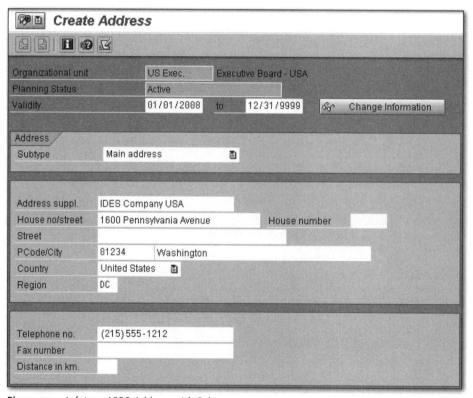

Figure 7.14 Infotype 1028 Address with Subtype

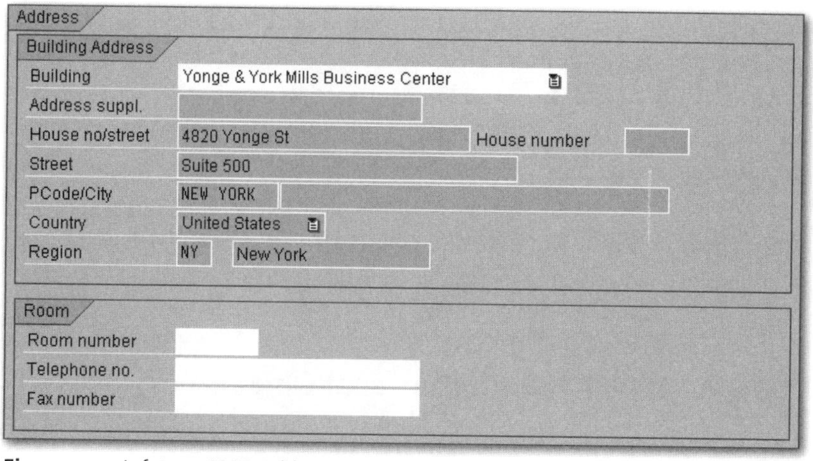

Figure 7.15 Infotype 1028 Address with Building

Two customizing settings are required for using preset building information. The first customizing table is accessible via the IMG path **Organizational Management · Infotype Settings · Set Up Check Values for Buildings** (Figure 7.16). The building information entered here is displayed in the Address infotype when the building is selected.

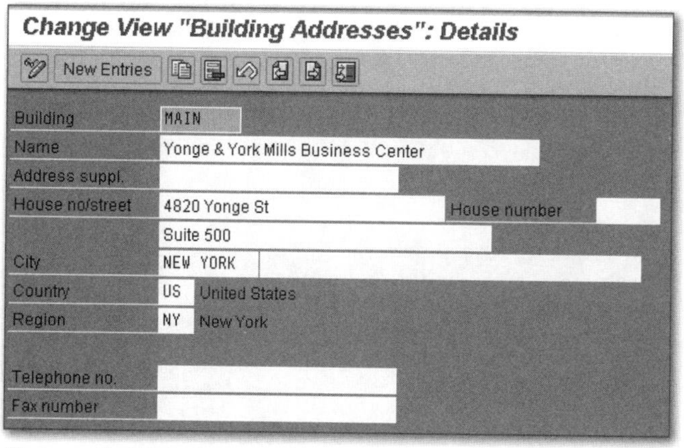

Figure 7.16 IMG: Create Building Address Information

The second customizing table is the Infotypes per Object Type view previously reviewed in Chapter 4, Section 4.1.2 (see Figure 4.3 for reference). In this view, for Infotype 1028 Address, you must indicate alternate screen number 2100 for the object types that you want to use building presets.

Building addresses are an all or nothing customizing setting for a given object type. You either use building presets for an object type or you enter your own addresses. When the customizing setting for the alternate screen number is set, building addresses are turned on for that object type, and the subtypes are no longer available. Similarly, when the alternate screen setting is removed, buildings are no longer available. Because this customizing is so absolute, you should determine carefully whether buildings are right for your enterprise, because you'll have to configure and transport new buildings to production each time a new entry is required.

7.11   Infotype 1208 SAP Organizational Object

The SAP Organizational Object infotype is used to maintain relationships between SAP organizational objects and OM objects. SAP organizational objects are defined in the Business Object Repository. Typically, an SAP organizational object is assigned to an organizational unit in OM; however, you can also assign it to positions or work centers.

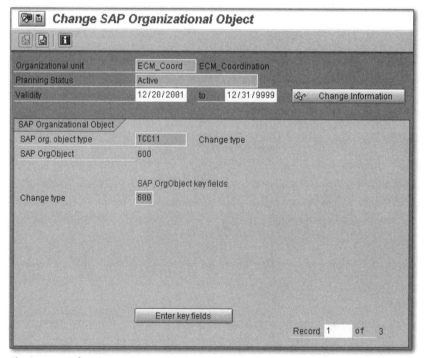

Figure 7.17   Infotype 1208 SAP Organizational Object

These relationships are relevant only for SAP Business Workflow customers who are using rules to identify agents for the individual steps in a workflow (Figure 7.17). The fields in the OM infotype are display-only fields. You can't enter data directly to assign the organizational object; the Enter key fields function can be used to select the appropriate organizational objects. The process flow for this function is multistep, as shown in Figure 7.18.

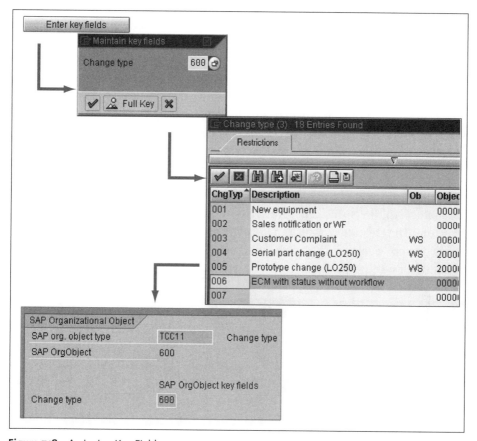

Figure 7.18 Assigning Key Fields

It is generally not advised to create the SAP organizational object assignment directly in Infotype 1208. Rather, the Business Workflow menu provides transactions to create the organizational object assignments: **Tools • Business Workflow • Development • Definition tools • Organizational Management • SAP Org. Objects • Create Assignments**. From this transaction, you can proceed to select the OM organizational unit, position, or work center that should be assigned to an SAP organizational object.

The Business Workflow assignment of OM objects to SAP organizational objects primarily serves to limit task execution. For example, if you want to restrict the task of purchasing certain hazardous materials to a specific organizational unit, then creating the assignment between a purchasing group (an SAP organizational object) and an OM organizational unit will achieve the restriction. This function provides a great deal of control in managing workflow responsibilities.

7.12 Infotype 1222 General Attribute Maintenance

The infotypes described up to now provide fields and table checks for very specific types of use. If none of the infotypes provided by SAP meet your needs for the object characteristics that you want to store, you have two choices: Create a custom infotype of your own, or use the General Attribute Maintenance infotype.

Creation of a custom infotype will certainly meet your needs, because the fields and values will be specifically prescribed by you when you create the infotype structure. The creation of a custom infotype requires both technical and functional resources, however, which can prove to be an overhead burden that some enterprises don't want to bear.

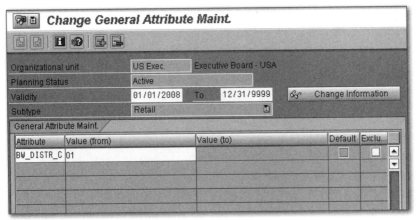

Figure 7.19 Infotype 1222 General Attribute Maintenance

In this case, SAP provides the General Attribute Maintenance infotype to store general information that's primarily user defined, as shown in Figure 7.19. Created initially for use with SAP Customer Relationship Management, the General Attribute Maintenance infotype allows you to store data generally in the form of attributes and values (Figure 7.20). Values can be individual or can be stored as a range. Data can be divided by the use of the infotype subtype.

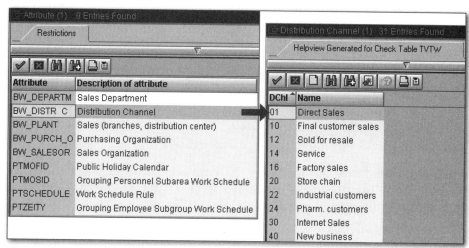

Figure 7.20 General Attribute Selections and Values

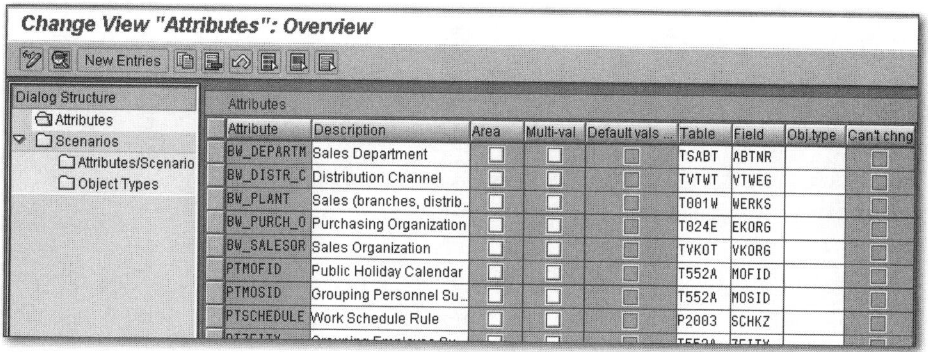

Figure 7.21 Customizing View T77OMATTR Attributes

There's no standard IMG path that can be used to access the customizing activities necessary for the General Attributes infotype, so customizing activities should be carried out using Transaction Code OOATTRCUST (view for the customizing Table T770MATTR, Figure 7.21).

From this view, there are four customizing activities that require maintenance. The first activity is to create the infotype attributes, shown in Figure 7.21. Attributes are defined with specific characteristics, and are given an up-to-10-character code and a long text description. You can determine whether the attribute can be restricted to a single value (the default behavior), a range of values, or multiple values with or without default values allowed.

The attribute is typically defined by a link to a table and field as defined in the SAP Data Dictionary, but may also be referenced to an SAP organizational object defined in the business workflow object repository. When you choose a table and field combination, the inherent check table values for that field are used in the general attribute field assignment as well. This allows you to assign virtually any table value to an OM object in the organizational plan.

Once you have created the attributes, you must assign them to a scenario in the infotype, which is equivalent to the infotype subtype. You can segregate your attributes in as many or as few scenarios as you want, but you must define at least one scenario for the infotype (Figure 7.22).

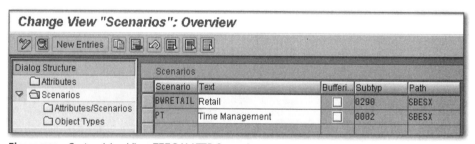

Figure 7.22 Customizing View T77OMATTR Scenarios

Note that in the scenario definition, you must assign it to a subtype. This subtype must be created separately. Infotype subtypes were previously reviewed in Chapter 4, Section 4.3.

Upon creating the scenario, you must then associate the attributes with it so they can be assigned in the infotype. This is done in the following two views. You first assign the attribute to the scenario, as in Figure 7.23. Here you define how the attribute is to be inherited along the evaluation path used in the scenario. You also define attribute behavior such as the sort order, whether it is visible or hidden on the screen, if the attribute is optional or required, and help or check function modules that may be utilized.

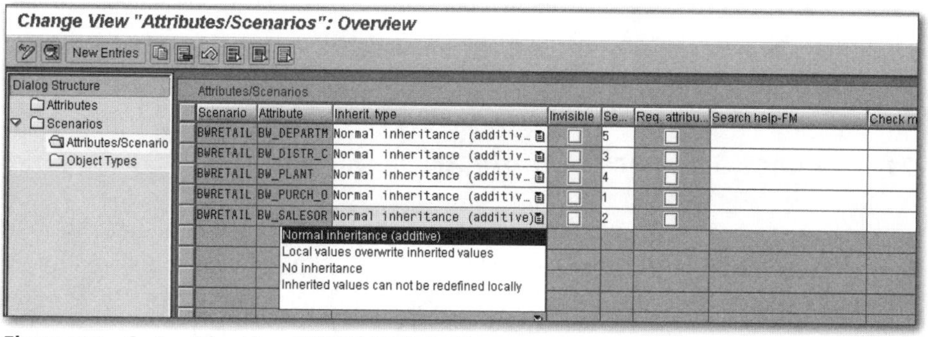

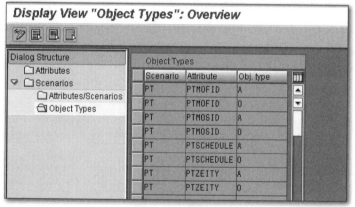

Figure 7.23 Customizing View T77OMATTR Attributes per Scenario

Figure 7.24 Customizing View T77OMATTR Object Types per Scenario

In the final view, you specify the object types that can be assigned the attributes in each scenario. This allows you to set up a scenario generally but control which object types use certain attributes.

> **Note**
>
> Unlike other customizing tables, you cannot use the wildcard character to represent all object types (Figure 7.24). Each object type must be identified specifically for each attribute you want to maintain.
>
> Also, in addition to the infotype customizing, you must ensure that Infotype 1222 is allowed for the object type. This customizing activity was reviewed in Section 4.2.

7.13   Function-Specific Infotypes

The infotypes discussed up to this point have been rather generic, meaning that they can be and are used by multiple objects, for multiple components, and for all countries. Some infotypes are specifically reserved for certain SAP ERP HCM components and country functions. These are explained in the following sections.

7.13.1   Infotype 1016 Standard Profiles

The Standard Profiles infotype is one of two infotypes used with authorization administration in SAP systems (Figure 7.25). With the Standard Profiles infotype, you can assign authorization profiles to positions, jobs, tasks, or organizational units. Authorization profiles are used throughout SAP components to control the functions and activities that the user can carry out in the system.

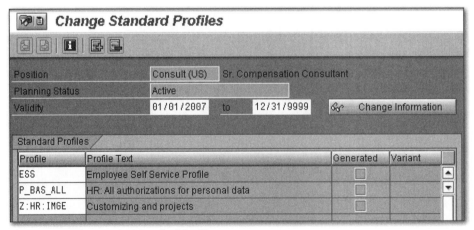

Figure 7.25   Infotype 1016 Standard Profiles

An authorization profile is a list of authorizations that control access to different areas of the system. For example, within SAP ERP HCM, authorizations can prescribe the types of objects and infotypes that users work with in the system. Traditionally, authorization profiles are assigned directly to users. This places a heavy burden on user administrators, who must constantly maintain and update user authorizations as people enter and exit the company and as people change roles and positions in the enterprise. By using the Standard Profiles infotype, you don't have to assign authorizations to users individually. Rather, you can assign authorizations to organizational units, jobs, positions, or tasks in the organizational plan. When holders are assigned to these organizational objects, they can inherit the assigned authorizations with the use of Report RHPROFL0 Generate User Authorizations.

> **Example**
>
> All administrators and analysts in the benefits organization should have access to some basic employee data and all benefits enrollment records to help answer any questions employees may have about their benefits. You set up the authorization profile Benefits Administrator to allow read access to some basic personnel infotypes (for example 0001 Organizational Assignment and 0002 Personal Data) and to all benefits infotypes. You assign the authorization profile to the organizational unit Benefits so that all employees in the organization can inherit the profile.

Report RHPROFL0 searches all objects in the organizational plan to determine those with Infotype 1016 records. Using the evaluation path PROFL0, the system then determines the holders in the plan (P Persons or US Users) and assigns the relevant profiles to those user IDs. For Persons, the PA Infotype 0105 Communication is used to determine the employee's system user ID. Because changes in the organizational plan occur every day, many customers schedule a nightly job to run Report RHPROFL0, ensuring that the authorizations are kept up to date.

7.13.2 Infotype 1017 PD Profiles

The PD Profiles infotype is also used in authorization administration, but is specifically designed to administer structural authorizations. Structural authorizations limit or control which objects a user can access or maintain along the organizational structure. The system uses an intersection of standard profiles and structural profiles to create the overall user access controls. More information on structural authorizations is provided in Chapter 10.

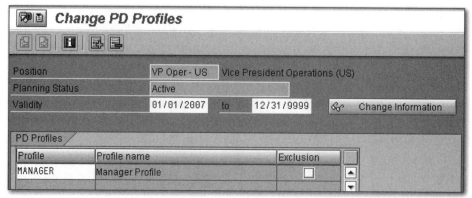

Figure 7.26 Infotype 1017 PD Profiles

Example

A manager should be limited to only see those employees in his part of the organization that report up to him. This is managed via profile MANAGER in Figure 7.26. Report RH-PROFL0 also searches for Infotype 1017 records when assigning authorization profiles to user IDs.

7.13.3 Infotype 1004 Character

The Character infotype is an optional infotype that is used to categorize the various Tasks that you use in Business Workflow. This infotype is only used for object type Task (TS) or Standard Task (TS) (Figure 7.27). With the Character infotype, you can categorize a task according to rank, phase, and purpose.

▶ *Rank* is used to classify a task as a planning, completion, or control task.

▶ *Phase* is used to classify how the task fits into the business process.

▶ *Purpose* identifies how the task contributes to the products or services that the company provides.

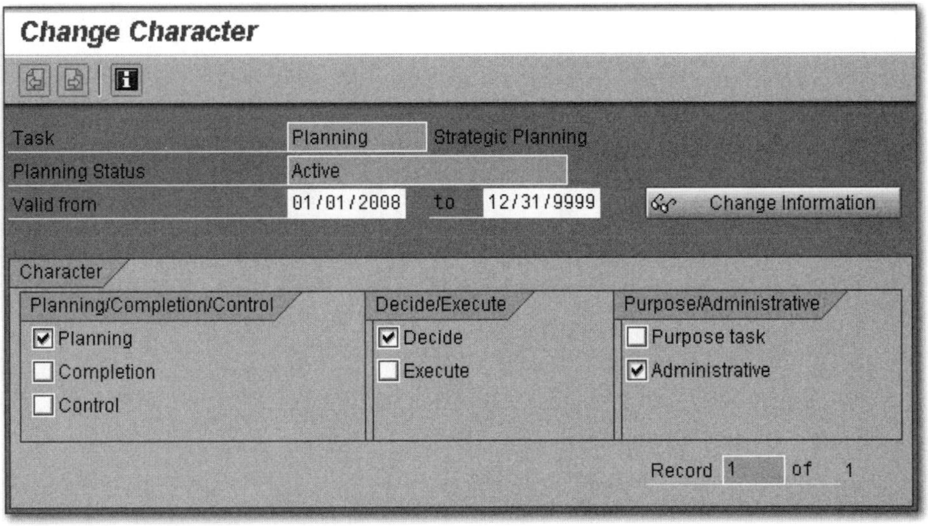

Figure 7.27 Infotype 1004 Character

The various classifications are provided via checkboxes in the infotype. The meanings of the options are largely user defined, meaning you can interpret the categories as you see fit for your organization. You can determine whether to use some or all of the categorizations as well, because none are mandatory.

7.13.4 Infotype 1006 Restrictions

The Restrictions infotype is used to identify any constraints that may be placed on work centers in the organizational plan (Figure 7.28).

> **Example**
>
> You may have an Operations Associate position in a shipping and receiving facility. Among the many position requirements, you may require the employee to be able to push loads requiring 60 pounds of force and lift up to 50 pounds. These requirements can be entered as physical restrictions, with the push and lift requirements as reasons.
>
> Similarly, you may have a Chemist position that requires employees to be exposed to hazardous materials. This position is not suitable for pregnant women due to the risk of birth defects. This should be entered as a restriction on the position as well.

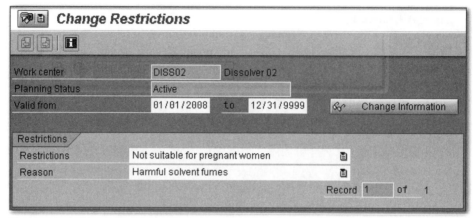

Figure 7.28 Infotype 1006 Restrictions

Restrictions and the reasons for restrictions are the two IMG activities have to be maintained to use this infotype (Figure 7.29). The customizing activities are separate in the IMG because the two fields are not directly related to one another: You can use any reason with any restriction.

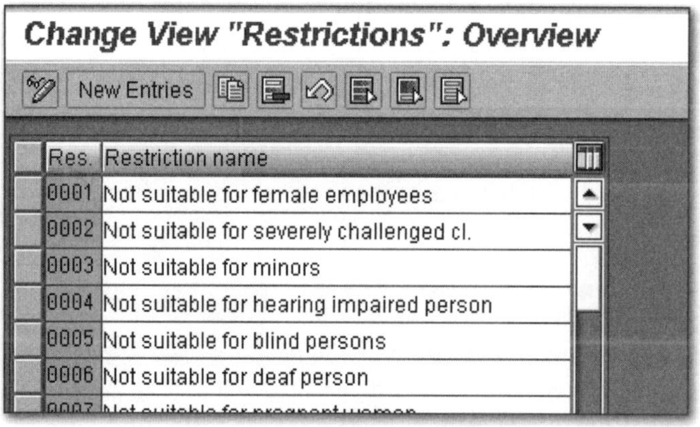

Figure 7.29 IMG: Set Up Check Values for Restrictions

Restrictions and reasons are defined by both a four-character code and a long text description (Figure 7.30).

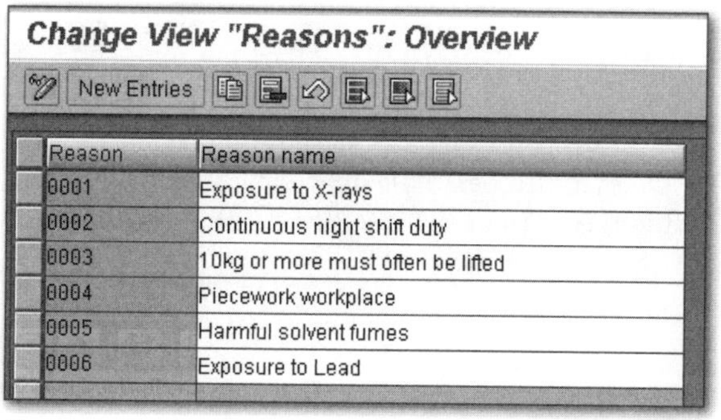

Figure 7.30 IMG: Set Up Check Values for Restriction Reasons

7.13.5   Infotype 1009 Health Examinations

Similar to the Restrictions infotype, the Health Examinations infotype is used to record health-related prerequisites and restrictions for work centers.

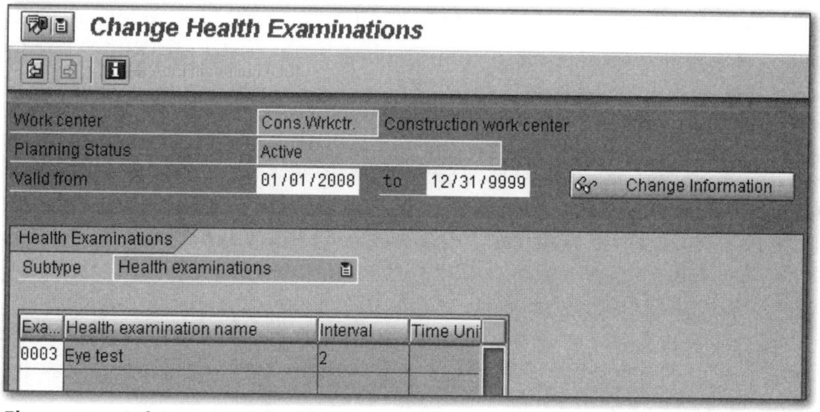

Figure 7.31 Infotype 1009 Health Examinations

The Health Examinations infotype (Figure 7.31) uses a subtype to distinguish required health examinations in order to be assigned to a work center, as well as restrictions resulting from health examinations. With health examinations, you can specify the examinations that are required in order to be assigned or continue to be assigned to a work center. You can add other subtypes as needed. The interval period identifies when periodic examinations are required.

Example

Process operators in the pharmaceutical industry are often required to have corrected or 20/30 vision to operate equipment in support of biopharmaceutical manufacturing. Vision may be tested annually to ensure that the operator is sufficiently able to view the equipment and instructions for operation. The vision test in this case would be stored as a health examination for the Process Operator position.

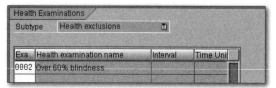

Figure 7.32 Infotype 1009 Subtype for Health Exclusions

Health exclusions identify when an employee or user is restricted from being assigned to a work center due to an ailment or the results from a health examination (Figure 7.32). Again, an interval can be used in conjunction with the exclusion, such as if a person has been exposed to an infectious disease within the past 6 months. In either an examination or exclusion, the time interval is an optional field.

Example

Following on the process operator example above, if employees can't pass vision tests with a certain percentage, for example, over 60% blindness, they can no longer perform the manufacturing process activities. The vision requirement in this case would be stored as a health exclusion for the Process Operator position.

Change View "Health Examinations": Overview

New Entries

STy.	Subtype text	Exam. type	Health examination name
0001	Health exclusions	0001	TB
0001	Health exclusions	0002	Over 60% blindness
0001	Health exclusions	0003	Over 40% deafness
0002	Health examinations	0001	Silicosis
0002	Health examinations	0002	Asbestos
0002	Health examinations	0003	Eye test
0002	Health examinations	0004	Preventive med. checkup
0002	Health examinations	0005	Lead Level Test
0002	Health examinations	0006	Audiometric Test

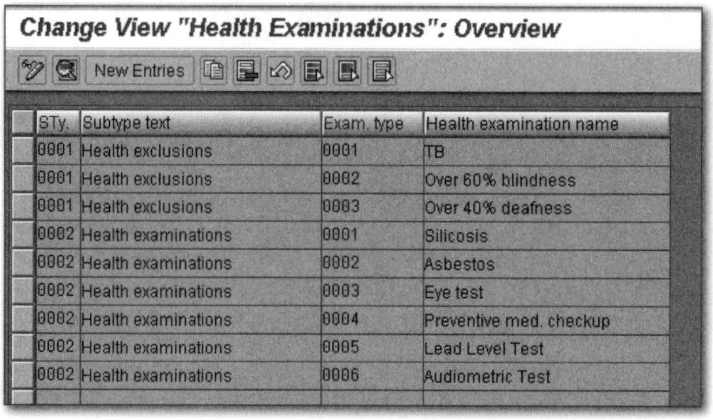

Figure 7.33 IMG: Set Up Check Values for Health Examinations

Examinations and exclusions are configuration activities in the same IMG activity (Figure 7.33). You identify a four-character code and description for each exam type to be used with either the exclusion or examination.

7.13.6 Infotype 1010 Authorities and Resources

The Authorities and Resources infotype is used to identify the authorities and resources that are granted to certain positions or work centers in the organization (Figure 7.34). Authorities may represent purchasing approval limits, contract signature valuations, and legal representations, for example. Resources can include office and technology equipment, company cars, and other assets you can assign to personnel.

The Authorities and Resources infotype uses a subtype to distinguish between types of authorities and resources. For example, you can have a separate subtype for purchasing authorities and contract approvals. You can create multiple subtypes to segregate information as you want, or you can put all authorities and resources under one subtype.

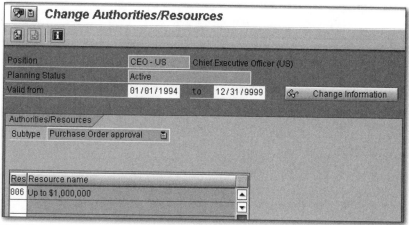

Figure 7.34 Infotype 1010 Authorities and Resources

The Resource Category field is used to identify the specific type of authority or resource that is assigned to the position. The Resource field is also used to identify specific equipment or other resources assigned to or made available to the position, which can eliminate guesswork and ease the onboarding process for new personnel.

Example

You can have multiple purchasing limits in your enterprise. Various levels of the organizational hierarchy can approve certain limits. For example, managers can approve up to $25,000, directors up to $100,000, vice presidents up to $500,000, and executives up to $1,000,000. Each dollar-value purchasing limit can be a separate resource type. Once created, the purchasing limit resource types are assigned to jobs and positions in the reporting hierarchy.

The category values can be used to determine how workflow tasks are routed to various positions. Comparing the task value to the resource limit defined in the Resource field is one mechanism to route workflow effectively.

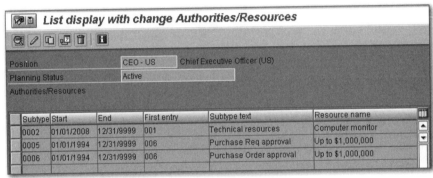

Figure 7.35 Infotype 1010 Authorities and Resources List View

Figure 7.35 provides a list view of the multiple records that exist in Infotype 1010 for a position. It's useful to note that the list view for the infotype only displays the first resource type entry. Because the infotype may have multiple resources associated with it, it's important to note that the list view won't definitively show all information.

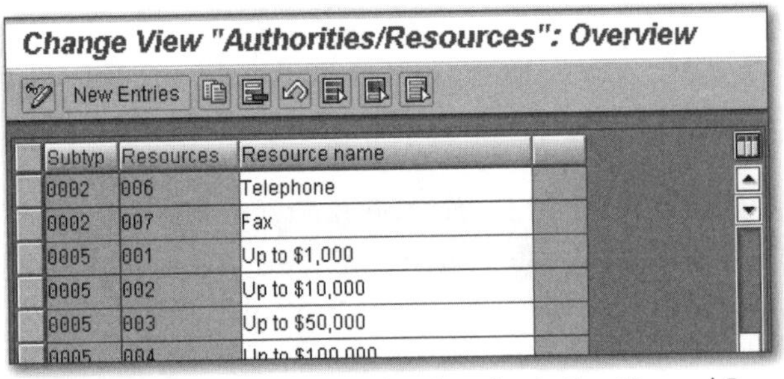

Figure 7.36 IMG: Set Up Check Values for Authorities and Resources

Configuration for the Authorities and Resources infotype consists of setting a subtype and a resource categorization. The resource is a three-character field with a long text description (Figure 7.36).

7.13.7 Infotype 1014 Obsolete

The Obsolete infotype is used to identify positions that are no longer required as a result of reorganization, but are still occupied. This enables you to recognize instantly if any action is required for the holders of such positions (Figure 7.37). The Recruitment component checks the system for positions that have been flagged as obsolete so that new positions can be found for the holders of the obsolete positions. If the holder of an obsolete position is assigned to a new position or leaves the company, the user will be prompted to delimit the validity period of the obsolete position.

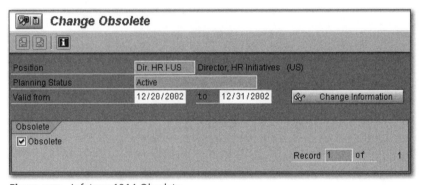

Figure 7.37 Infotype 1014 Obsolete

7.13.8 Infotype 1019 Required Positions/Quota Planning

The Required Positions infotype, also known as Quota Planning, is used to plan how many positions or how many full-time equivalents (FTEs) you will need in the future for a particular organizational unit. The planning is typically based on the particular jobs that are available in the organizational unit (Figure 7.38). You can plan how many positions, defined based on these jobs, or FTEs the organizational unit will need in the future.

A full-time equivalent is the required capacity expressed in terms of full-time positions. This is calculated by considering the working time of the position as a fraction of the working time of the organizational unit to which the position is assigned. For example, a position required at 20 hours per week in an organization with a 40-hour work week can be represented as 0.5 FTE.

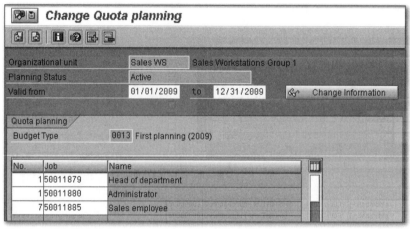

Figure 7.38 Infotype 1019 Quota Planning

Because workforce planning is generally iterative, multiple versions of the plan are modeled and considered before the final plan is approved. When setting up quota planning, you can use the Budget Type to identify these iterations (Figure 7.39).

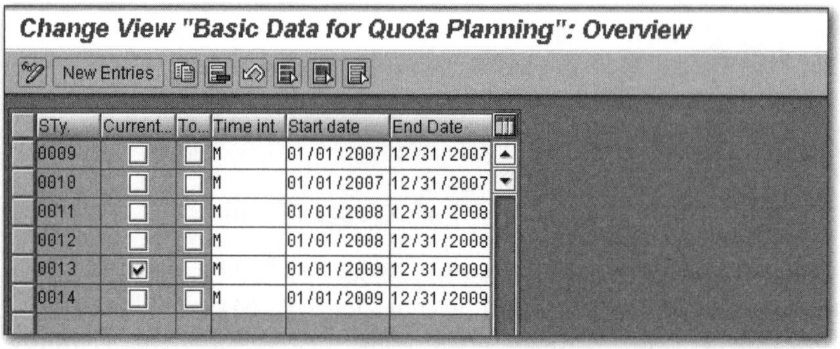

Figure 7.39 IMG: Define Quota Planning Types and Period

Three IMG customizing activities are required for using the Quota Planning infotype. First, create the infotype subtype. Once the subtype is created, it is associated with the planning period. You can define a planning period with any time interval; yearly planning is most commonly used. Only one planning period can be the current period at any time.

If you choose to complete planning in FTEs, two additional customizing settings are required (Figure 7.40). The integration settings are:

▶ WORKT FTEP: Set to "X" to determine the value of an FTE with relation to the staffing percentage of the position, taking into account the capacity utilization level of the employee (person).

▶ WORKT FTEQ: Set to "X" to specify that you want to carry out quota planning in FTE instead of in positions.

The FTEP setting is particularly useful for the calculation of existing required positions in FTE, where the actual hours worked by an employee (person) in the position are important. For example, a part-time employee working 20 hours per week in an organization with a 40-hour standard work week would be planned at 0.5 FTE.

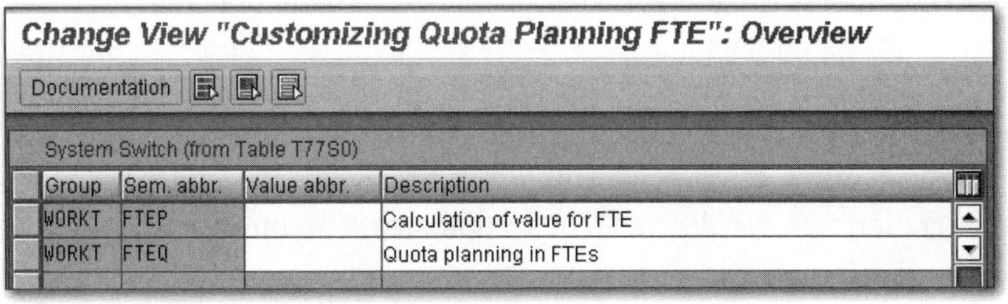

Change View "Customizing Quota Planning FTE": Overview

Documentation

System Switch (from Table T77S0)

	Group	Sem. abbr.	Value abbr.	Description	
	WORKT	FTEP		Calculation of value for FTE	▲
	WORKT	FTEQ		Quota planning in FTEs	▼

Figure 7.40 IMG: Define Calculation in FTEs

7.13.9 Infotype 1032 Mail Address

The Mail Address infotype is used to store email addresses and other relevant mail information for the TEM component and the SAP mail system. TEM uses the infotype to email correspondence or notifications to attendees or instructors (Figure 7.41). In this scenario, the attendees (persons, users, external persons, etc.) have the infotype maintained with their SAP or Internet email address, which TEM uses to send manual or automatic correspondence output. The SAP mail system can also generically use this infotype information to send email correspondence to specific email addresses or to distribution lists.

The format of the email address to be entered will vary according to the subtype used. For the Internet Mail subtype, a full Internet email address (SMTP) must be entered. For SAP Mail subtypes, the entry is validated against users or distribution lists that have been created in the SAP system.

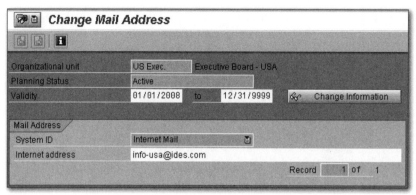

Figure 7.41 Infotype 1031 Mail Address

7.13.10 Infotype 1011 Work Schedule

The Work Schedule infotype is used to define scheduled work hours for organizational units, positions, and work centers. Work schedules are defined in the Time Management component of SAP ERP HCM and assigned to an organizational plan object to reflect the projected volume of work per object. This work time projection is subsequently used in cost planning and budgeting; this planned work schedule integration was also described in Section 7.13.8 on Infotype 1019 Quota Planning.

In the PA component, the work schedule assigned to the organization or position that an employee occupies is checked against the work schedule assigned to the employee in his Infotype 0007 Work Schedule. Although the work schedule information stored in the organizational plan does not provide defaults to assign data to the employee, it is useful for data entry checks. If an inconsistency is present, the user is prompted with a warning message to correct the inconsistency.

Work schedules can be assigned in OM based on system-wide defaults. You can create enterprise work schedule rules that are automatically assigned to all organizational objects. As a best practice, you should assign a work schedule infotype to the root organizational unit in your organizational plan and mark it as the standard working time; this work schedule is inherited by all subordinate organizations. You can then create Infotype 1011 records where the specific organizational units or positions do not follow the default. This reduces the amount of data entry necessary.

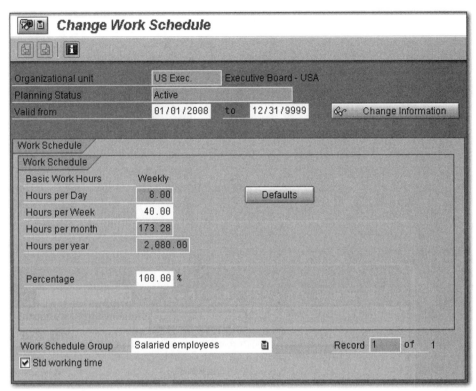

Figure 7.42 Infotype 1011 Work Schedule

The Work Schedule infotype (Figure 7.42) includes a work schedule group that is defined as a subtype of Infotype 1011 (see Section 4.1.3) in the IMG. Work schedule groups are assigned based on the employee group/subgroup stored in Infotype 1013 (see Section 7.9). Work schedule groups are essentially optional, because they don't drive the work hours assignment.

The customizing activities for the working time infotype are accessible via the IMG path **Organizational Management • Infotype Settings • Working Time**. The two customizing tables are shown in Figures 7.43 and 7.44. In the first activity, the work schedule groups that have been defined as subtypes of Infotype 1011 are assigned to the relevant employee group and subgroup. As in the first table entry, you can use the wildcard character * for all groups.

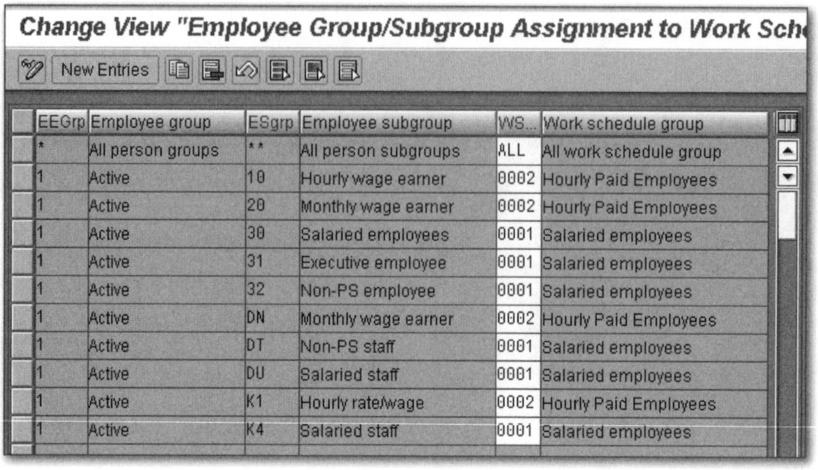

Change View "Employee Group/Subgroup Assignment to Work Sch

New Entries

EEGrp	Employee group	ESgrp	Employee subgroup	WS...	Work schedule group
*	All person groups	**	All person subgroups	ALL	All work schedule group
1	Active	10	Hourly wage earner	0002	Hourly Paid Employees
1	Active	20	Monthly wage earner	0002	Hourly Paid Employees
1	Active	30	Salaried employees	0001	Salaried employees
1	Active	31	Executive employee	0001	Salaried employees
1	Active	32	Non-PS employee	0001	Salaried employees
1	Active	DN	Monthly wage earner	0002	Hourly Paid Employees
1	Active	DT	Non-PS staff	0001	Salaried employees
1	Active	DU	Salaried staff	0001	Salaried employees
1	Active	K1	Hourly rate/wage	0002	Hourly Paid Employees
1	Active	K4	Salaried staff	0001	Salaried employees

Figure 7.43 IMG: Maintain Working Time Groups

In the second customizing activity (Figure 7.44), a variety of system rules set the general behavior of the working time infotype for the enterprise. Each rule either controls a specific working time field on the infotype, or is used to manage system behavior that references the working time infotype. The settings are:

- WORKT DAILY: The average working time per day in hours.
- WORKT DAYMT: The average number of working days per month.
- WORKT DAYWK: The average number of working days per week.
- WORKT DAYYR: The average number of working days per year.
- WORKT DECNO: The number of decimal places for default working time. The default is two decimal places.
- WORKT FTEP: Set as "X" to determine the FTE value based on the staffing percentage of the position or holder, rather than planned working hours.
- WORKT FTEQ: Set as "X" to plan based on FTEs rather than positions.
- WORKT MAXHR: Maximum value allowed for working hours per day.
- WORKT MINHR: Minimum value allowed for working hours per day.
- WORKT PATHA: The evaluation path used to determine working time for a work center on the basis of its organizational unit.
- WORKT PATHO: The evaluation path used to determine working time for an organizational unit on the basis of its parent organizational unit.

▶ WORKT PATHS: The evaluation path used to determine working time for a position on the basis of its organizational unit.

▶ WORKT PERCK: Determines the work hours field that is open for data entry on the Work Schedule infotype. Only one field is open for entry; all other values are calculated based on this entry. D = Daily hours, W = weekly hours, M = monthly hours, and Y = yearly hours.

Change View "Work Schedule: Rule Values": Overview

Documentation

System Switch (from Table T77S0)

Group	Sem. abbr.	Value abbr.	Description
WORKT	DAILY	800	Average working time per day
WORKT	DAYMT	2166	Average number of working days per month
WORKT	DAYWK	500	Average number of working days per week
WORKT	DAYYR	26000	Average number of working days per year
WORKT	DECNO	2	Number of decimal places for default working time
WORKT	FTEP		Calculation of value for FTE
WORKT	FTEQ		Quota planning in FTEs
WORKT	MAXHR	2400	Maximum values for working hours per day
WORKT	MINHR	100	Minimum values for working hours per day
WORKT	PATHA	WRKT_AO	Evaluation path: work center / organizational unit
WORKT	PATHO	WRKT_O	Evaluation path: org.unit / org.unit
WORKT	PATHS	WRKT_SO	Evaluation path: position / organizational unit
WORKT	PERCK	W	Type of working hours check

Figure 7.44 IMG: Maintain Rule Values for Working Time

The working time units entered in customizing assume a two-character decimal place and so are entered without the decimal. For example, the WORKT DAILY entry 800 is read as 8.00 hours, and the entry WORKT DAYYR 26000 is read as 260.00.

7.13.11 Infotype 1039 Shift Group

The Shift Group infotype is used to define shift group assignments to organizational units, as shown in Figure 7.45. This infotype is used in the Shift Planning component. A shift group is a collection of different shifts. The group is user defined, so the meaning can vary according to your enterprise needs. By assigning a shift group to an organizational unit, you determine which shifts will be worked in that organization.

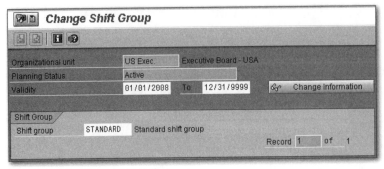

Figure 7.45 Infotype 1039 Shift Group

The characteristics of the shift group are passed on to the organization to which it is assigned. The system uses the shift group assignment and its characteristics in both Shift Planning and Capacity Planning to ensure that the shift plans you set up in those components include the correct shifts and requirement types for each organizational unit you use.

7.13.12 Infotype 1015 Cost Planning

The Cost Planning infotype is the infotype on which all the cost elements that form the basis of personnel costs can be stored and modeled. Personnel Cost Planning is a subcomponent of the Compensation Management function in SAP ERP HCM. Personnel Cost Planning focuses on all a company's personnel costs, wages, salaries, and employer contributions to social insurance, for example.

Cost planning allows you to design various scenarios for modeling and projecting personnel costs. These scenarios can subsequently be passed on to Controlling as input to the budgeting process. This component enables you to determine current personnel costs and experiment with and project future costs. You can also work with costs that are not directly related to personnel. For example, you can calculate education and training costs as well as the cost of providing leisure activities for employees.

The Cost Planning infotype uses wage elements to store the various pay or cost components for positions or jobs (Figure 7.46). It's also possible to create Cost Planning infotype records for organizational units and work centers, for example, if there are broad costs that cannot be allocated to specific jobs or positions. Wage elements represent the typical cost elements that are borne by the position or job. A maximum of seven wage elements can be created in a single infotype record.

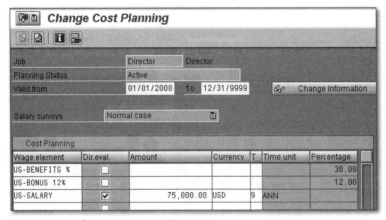

Figure 7.46 Infotype 1015 Cost Planning

Wage elements can be stored as a dollar figure or percentage, and can be derived from personnel information such as actual and projected payroll results. This infotype is automatically maintained when you use projected pay as the basis for your cost calculations. Programs in cost planning are used to derive the payroll result–related figures, and the results are stored in the Cost Planning infotype.

Because the configuration requirements for cost planning are quite involved, we won't outline them here. You can refer to the customizing guide for Compensation Management for detailed information on setup activities required for Personnel Cost Planning.

7.13.13 Infotype 1005 Planned Compensation

The Planned Compensation infotype is used to plan salary and pay scale compensation data at the job and position level. The system uses this information to propose compensation-related defaults to employee's Basic Pay Infotype 0008. Because jobs can be defined globally, the planned compensation infotype includes a country indicator as a key, allowing multiple versions of the infotype to exist for a particular job or position.

> **Example**
>
> The Job Manager may exist in an international company with operations in France and the United States. Because the position valuation and currency requirements are different, you need two planned compensation records for the position. In one record, the pay information is in U.S. dollars. In the other records, the pay information is in Euros.

Three options are available when maintaining planned compensation information, each represented by a different tab in the infotype. Only one tab can be maintained at any given time.

Let's look at the particulars of each planned compensation tab.

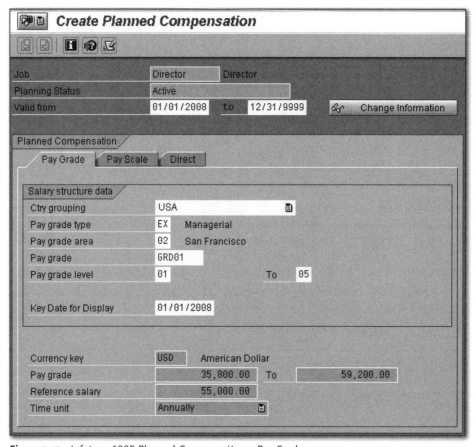

Figure 7.47 Infotype 1005 Planned Compensation – Pay Grade

On the Pay Grade tab, shown in Figure 7.47, you can store information from the salary structure, such as the pay grade type, area, grade, and level. In Compensation Management, you configure these elements to correspond to either a specific pay amount or a pay range. The system provides as reference the salary range that is the lowest and highest amount that will be paid for the job or position. A reference salary serves as an average of the range data.

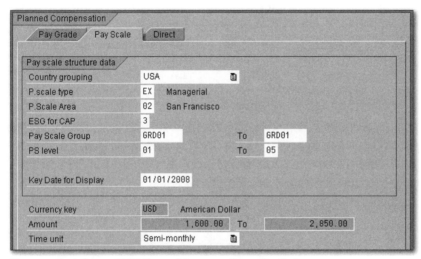

Figure 7.48 Infotype 1005 Planned Compensation – Pay Scale

On the Pay Scale tab, shown in Figure 7.48, you can store information from the pay scale structure, such as the pay scale area, type, group, and level. You can also specify the employee subgroup grouping for pay scales. This configuration is also made in Compensation Management. The system displays the minimum and maximum salary for the job or position. You can change the salary reference time period. No reference salary is calculated.

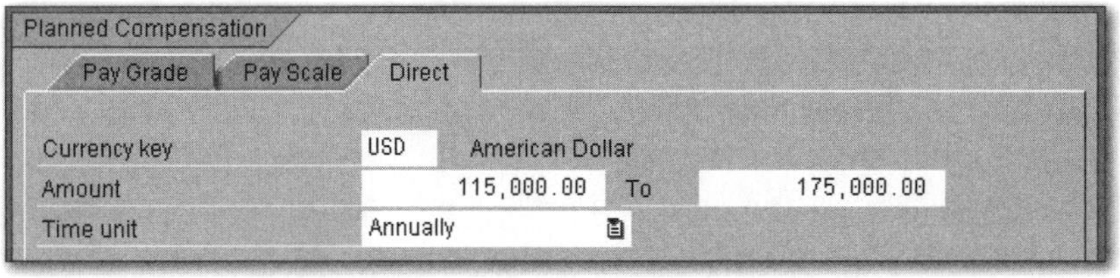

```
Planned Compensation
   Pay Grade | Pay Scale | Direct

   Currency key        USD     American Dollar
   Amount                   115,000.00   To        175,000.00
   Time unit           Annually          📋
```

Figure 7.49 Infotype 1005 Planned Compensation – Direct

Lastly, in the Direct tab, shown in Figure 7.49, you can enter the minimum and maximum amounts paid directly for a job and position. No pay structure information is used. The Direct salary option is generally used in enterprises where no pay structure is in place or for positions where salary ranges are position specific. One example of this is in executive compensation, where each officer role may have a specific salary range.

Because the configuration requirements for salary structures are quite extensive, we will not outline them here. You can refer to the customizing guides for Personnel Management and Compensation Management for detailed information on setup activities required for salary structures.

7.13.14 Infotype 1050 Job Evaluation Results

The Job Evaluation Results infotype is used to store the results of a job evaluation process for the jobs and positions in your organization. The job evaluation results can be used to store the relative worth of the job or position in points, and to indicate whether the job is a benchmark job (Figure 7.50).

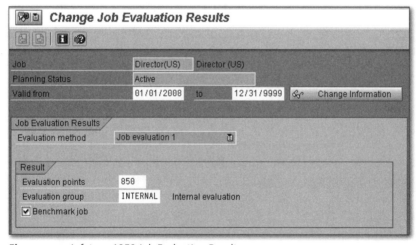

Figure 7.50 Infotype 1050 Job Evaluation Results

The configuration necessary for this infotype is the creation of the evaluation method, which is set up as a subtype of the infotype in the IMG. Additionally, an evaluation group may be created to segregate evaluation results and provide easier reporting of the evaluation results. The IMG activities are contained within the Compensation Management component configuration menu.

7.13.15 Infotype 1051 Salary Survey Results

The Salary Survey Results infotype is similar to the Job Evaluation Results infotype in that it is used to store the results of salary survey information on jobs and positions, which reflects market evaluations of these objects. Salary survey results include information such as average base salary and annual bonuses (Figure 7.51).

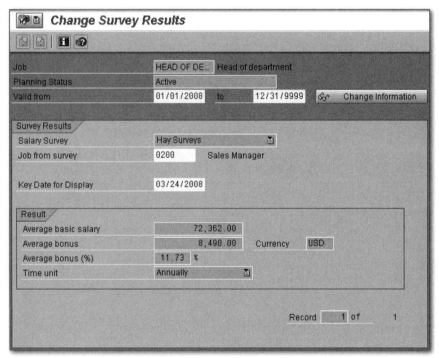

Figure 7.51 Infotype 1051 Salary Survey Results

The salary survey is configured as a subtype of the infotype. The other necessary configuration is the setup of the survey job codes and titles. These codes are typically provided by the firm conducting the salary survey, and are linked to your internal jobs to provide a point of comparison. The configuration activities are contained within the Compensation Management IMG menu.

7.14   U.S.-Specific Infotypes

This section provides an explanation of some infotypes in the organizational plan that are specific to the United States.

7.14.1   Infotype 1610 U.S. EEO/AAP Information

The EEO/AAP Information infotype allows you to maintain legally required data for jobs within U.S. organizations. In this infotype, you can specify the Equal Employment Opportunity (EEO) category, the Affirmative Action Plan (AAP) category, the Occupational Classification Category (OCC), and the Fair Labor Standards Act (FLSA) indicator for regulatory reporting (Figure 7.52).

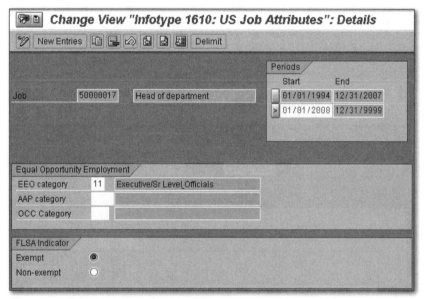

Figure 7.52   Infotype 1610 EEO/AAP Information

7.14.2   Infotypes 1612 & 1613 U.S. Workers Compensation Codes

Two infotypes are provided that allow you to store workers' compensation code information for U.S. organizations. Infotype 1612 is used to store information for organizational units (Figure 7.53), and Infotype 1613 is used to store information for positions (Figure 7.54).

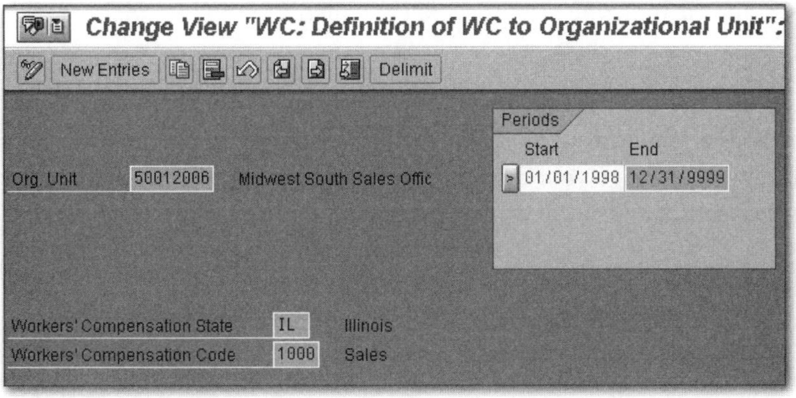

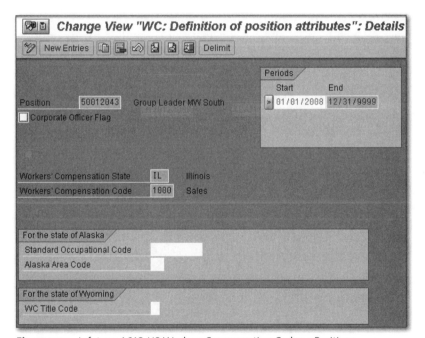

Figure 7.53 Infotype 1612 US Workers Compensation Codes – Organizational Units

Figure 7.54 Infotype 1613 US Workers Compensation Codes – Positions

In both infotypes, fields are provided to enter the workers' compensation state and code. The position Infotype 1613 contains additional fields to identify the position as a corporate officer, and contains state-specific fields for Alaska and Wyoming.

In both cases, the customizing activities are contained in the Personnel Management IMG.

We've just taken a look at many of the infotypes that are available for use in your organizational plan. In many cases, the infotypes and configuration activities are sufficient to manage your organizational plan. The next section discusses some additional settings that you may also find useful when managing your OM infotypes.

7.15 Customer-Specific Infotype Settings

As a final word on OM infotype options, it's useful to point out two customizing options available in the IMG path **Organizational Management • Basic Settings • Data Model Enhancement • Infotype Maintenance**. The first activity is used to make a number of customer-defined settings that can be applied to any infotype in OM.

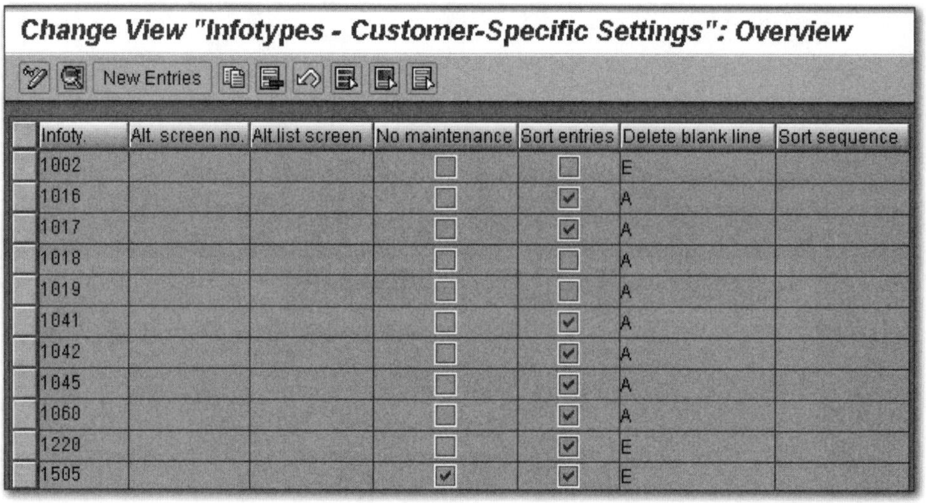

Change View "Infotypes - Customer-Specific Settings": Overview

New Entries

Infoty.	Alt. screen no.	Alt.list screen	No maintenance	Sort entries	Delete blank line	Sort sequence
1002			☐	☐	E	
1016			☐	✔	A	
1017			☐	✔	A	
1018			☐	☐	A	
1019			☐	☐	A	
1041			☐	✔	A	
1042			☐	✔	A	
1045			☐	✔	A	
1060			☐	✔	A	
1220			☐	✔	E	
1505			✔	✔	E	

Figure 7.55 IMG: Maintain User-Defined Settings for Infotypes

In the user-defined settings table (Figure 7.55), you can specify the following:

▶ Identify an alternate screen number for general maintenance and the list screen

- Indicate if no general maintenance is allowed for the infotype
- Sort entries that are stored in table infotypes; entries can be sorted in ascending or descending order by subtype and "from" date as identified in the sort sequence field
- Specify how blank lines in language-specific infotypes are to be processed (E = blank lines deleted at the end only, A = all blank lines are deleted, " " = blank lines are retained)

In the second customizing activity (Figure 7.56), you identify which infotypes are country specific. An entry in this customizing table determines whether an infotype is displayed via country settings in expert maintenance transactions (see Chapter 8, Section 8.4.5).

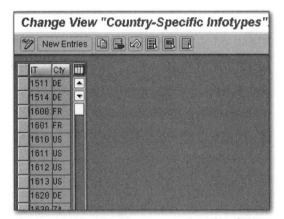

Figure 7.56 IMG: Maintain Country-Specific Infotypes

> **Note**
>
> The country-specific infotype settings are client independent, so any changes you make in the customizing table will affect all clients in your SAP system.

7.16 Conclusion

In this chapter we took a detailed look at the infotypes that store the organizational plan data you'll be creating in OM. We also looked at some specific infotypes that are used in the United States to meet some very specific regulatory requirements. With this knowledge of the infotypes and their functions, you should have the information necessary to carefully plan which infotypes you'll create and maintain in your organizational plan. Now that you've determined what information you want to maintain, the next chapter will focus on how to maintain the information. The various maintenance transactions available for organizational plan creation and management will be reviewed in detail.

Once you have defined the data you want to create and maintain, the question of how you'll keep the data up to date must be answered. Choosing the appropriate maintenance interface for your users will help keep your data current.

8 Maintaining Organizational Management Data

Up to now we've mostly discussed the various types of data that need to be created and maintained in the organizational plan. Now that the objects in your organizational plan are defined, infotypes identified, and relationships ready to use, the data is ready to be created. Creating the organizational plan data is one of the more difficult implementation tasks you'll face. Maintaining the data on an ongoing basis may be just as difficult, if not more so. You need to use an SAP transaction to perform this data maintenance.

8.1 Many Maintenance Options Exist

Just as there are many types of objects, infotypes, and data details to be maintained, there are just as many user transactions with which to maintain them. Most OM transactions are accessible using either of these two paths:

▶ **Human Resources • Organizational Management**

▶ **Tools • Business Workflow • Organizational Plan**

OM transactions are separated into two general categories:

▶ Organizational plan mode, where you can develop and model the organizational plan objects together

▶ Expert mode, where you can edit specific object types and their details in isolation

In implementation and in production use, you can utilize both transaction types. Each provides different options for creating and maintaining data, and situations may arise where one transaction is more appropriate than the other. The maintenance menu options are displayed in Figure 8.1.

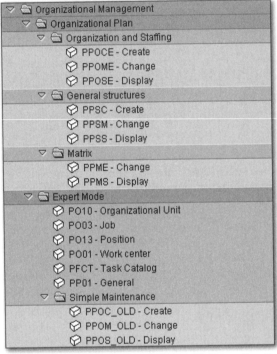

Figure 8.1 OM Maintenance Options with Transaction Code

8.2 The OM User Interface

Before we get into the specifics about how each maintenance interface works, let's review in general terms how the screens are laid out. The various OM user interfaces all follow the same design principle. Depending on the transaction you use to maintain data, the specific components will vary slightly. Some of the components may not be used or may not be available for use depending on the transaction used.

The OM user interface is divided into the four areas depicted in Figure 8.2. Let's take a look at each screen area and its functions.

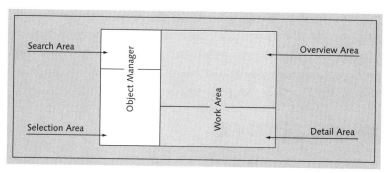

Figure 8.2 OM User Interface Areas

8.2.1 OM Object Manager

The Object Manager is made up of the search area and selection area. This area is shaded light in Figure 8.2. The Object Manager exists in all OM maintenance transactions.

Search Area

The search area is used to search for the objects that you want to display or maintain. Depending on which transaction you're in, the options to search will vary. In some transactions, there may be only one object to search for, with one or more methods of search. In other cases, you can search for multiple types of objects, again with one or more search methods.

The search methods for the objects are marked with the binoculars ![icon] icon. SAP delivers many types of search methods, and you can create your own as well using the customizing options outlined in Chapter 10. Figure 8.3 shows an example of the search area.

Figure 8.3 OM User Interface Search Area

The objects available to search are presented in a list. The object folder is expanded to reveal the different search methods available. You select a search method by clicking on the option. For some search methods, a dialog box will open with search parameters for you to narrow down the selections. For example, the Search Term option is shown in Figure 8.4.

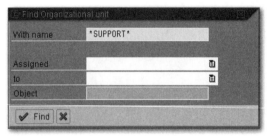

Figure 8.4 Search Term Entry Window

The Search Term function is used to find an object by name, abbreviation, or ID. Wildcard characters (*) can be used at the beginning and end of the entered description to find a relevant match. Other search options that can be used with the object you're working with will be listed and can be utilized in a similar manner. Another common search option is the Structure Search, which allows you to display an object according to its assignment in the object hierarchy.

At the top of the search area, a number of icons are presented that provide some additional functions that are worthwhile to note. After searching for more than one object in a session, you can navigate or scroll back and forth between searches with the ⇐ ⇒ icons.

In some search functions, you are presented with a selection screen pop-up that allows you to refine your search with a combination of search criteria. You can save these search criteria as a search variant so you can reuse it later. Search variants are managed using one of three icons ▦ ▦ ▦. The first icon allows you to create or save a variant, the second lists saved variants for you to reuse, and the third icon is used to delete search variants you no longer want.

Selection Area

The selection area is used to display the results of the search, and to subsequently select the objects that you then want to edit. Each time you enter an OM user interface, the last objects you edited are called up again for easy selection and access. Figure 8.5 provides an example of the selection list resulting from the Search Term method.

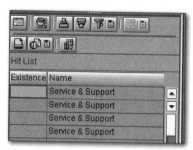

Figure 8.5 Search Results Displayed in the Selection Area

If your search results in a high number of hits, you can scroll up and down the list in the selection area. If a very high-volume result is obtained, your list may be limited to a maximum number of hits. You can search again or refine your search terms to select a new list.

With the Structure Search, the results are displayed in a hierarchy tree format. Figure 8.6 shows an example of this. You can expand and collapse the structure as necessary to find the objects you are looking for.

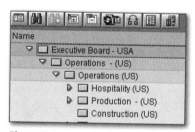

Figure 8.6 Structure Search Results Display

Once an object is listed in the selection area, you have two options:

▸ Double-click on the object to bring up details of that object for editing. The object will be displayed in the overview area, and its information will be displayed in the detail area. This is the most common function users choose.

▶ Click on it once to assign the object to another object using drag-and-drop. This option is only available in certain interfaces, which will be discussed in the following sections.

Configuration settings determine which fields are displayed in the selection area, but you can change the fields by using the ⊞. A dialog box opens, allowing you to select from the allowable fields.

Other icons in the header of the selection list allow other options. For example, you can increase or decrease the size of the selection list to show more or less data, sort the results of the search, or print the search results list. Available icon functions change depending on the object type that is searched.

8.2.2 OM Work Area

The work area is made up of the overview area and can also include the detail area. The detail area is not present in all OM transactions. The work area is shaded darker back in Figure 8.2.

Overview Area

In the overview area, the selected object is displayed. The display varies depending on the object type selected. At minimum, the object icon and text description are displayed. For objects in a hierarchy, the selected object is displayed as the topmost item, with subordinate related objects also displayed, as shown in Figure 8.7.

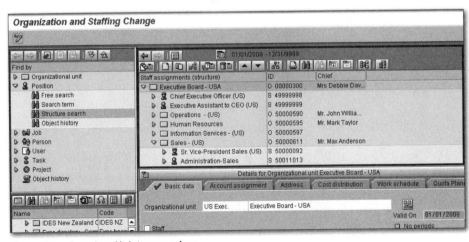

Figure 8.7 Overview Maintenance Area

Depending on the transaction you're in, the environment of the display can also be different. In all transactions, you have the option of editing, creating, changing, delimiting, or deleting objects, or of selecting other objects with which to work.

Detail Area

The detail area is used to display detailed characteristics of the object you have selected in the overview area. You can edit the characteristics that are presented, or add new records as needed. Infotype records for the objects are presented in a tabbed interface through which the user can navigate. Where data exists for an object, a check mark ✔ is present next to the tab description. Whereas most infotypes are presented in a separate tab, some infotype data is combined in one screen, as is the case for the Basic data tab. Here information from Infotypes 1000 Object, 1001 Relationships, 1002 Description, 1003 Department/Staff, and 1007 Vacancy are all presented in part in the same tab. How data is displayed in the tabs is controlled by configuration settings. Figure 8.8 outlines the detail area.

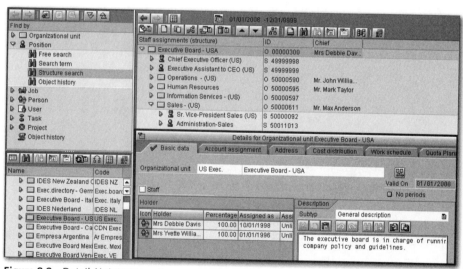

Figure 8.8 Detail Maintenance Area

In some transactions, you can hide the detail area using the 🗑 icon on the detail area header bar so that you can view more information in the overview area. You can display the detail area again using the 🗂 icon.

Now that you have a basic understanding of the maintenance interface components, let's review the available transactions in detail.

8.3　Organizational Plan Maintenance Transactions

As mentioned earlier, OM transactions are separated into two general categories: organizational plan and expert maintenance. With organizational plan maintenance transactions, you can maintain several organizational plan objects together. Multiple transactions are available and are listed in Table 8.1. Some of the transactions were depicted earlier in Figure 8.1.

Transaction	Organizational Plan Maintenance Transactions
PPOCE	Create Organization and Staffing
PPOME	Change Organization and Staffing
PPOSE	Display Organization and Staffing
PPSC	Create General Structures
PPSM	Change General Structures
PPSE	Display General Structures
PPME	Change Matrix Organization
PPMS	Display Matrix Organization
PPOC_OLD	Create Organizational Unit (Simple)
PPOM_OLD	Maintain Organizational Plan (Simple)
PPOS_OLD	Display Organizational Plan (Simple)
PPOCW	Create Organization and Staffing (WF)
PPOMW	Change Organization and Staffing (WF)
PPOSW	Display Organization and Staffing (WF)

Table 8.1　Simple Maintenance Transactions

The organizational plan transactions allow you to create organizational objects quickly and easily and relate them to an organizational hierarchy. Your organizational plan is presented in a tree structure, which enables you to maintain it according to your requirements.

8.3.1　Simple Maintenance Transactions

Simple maintenance was one of the first maintenance transactions available for OM data maintenance, and is still available in the latest release. The basic organizational plan framework is created from the simple maintenance transactions.

Components consist of organizational units, staff assignments, and task profiles. The initial screen of the simple maintenance transaction is accessed via Transaction Code PPOC_OLD, or from the menu path **Human Resources • Organizational Management • Expert Mode • Simple Maintenance • Create**. Whereas the menu path is contained in the expert mode transaction list, it is considered an organizational plan transaction, allowing you to maintain multiple object types in one transaction.

The initial screen is presented in Figure 8.9. Organizational units are used as the basis for entry in the transaction. When creating a new organizational plan structure in Transaction PPOC_OLD, you enter the starting object abbreviation and description. The validity period entered on the initial screen is used to maintain the record effective dates in the plan. Once you save the initial, or "root," organizational unit, the system switches from create mode to change mode. In the display (PPOS_OLD) or change (PPOM_OLD) transaction, the object manager can be used to search and select an initial organizational unit to edit, or you can simply enter the ID of the starting object. This organizational unit becomes the top organizational unit for the hierarchy display. Any objects related to the starting object are presented to the user for maintenance.

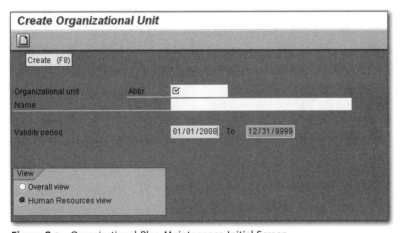

Figure 8.9 Organizational Plan Maintenance Initial Screen

Different views for simple maintenance are available because this transaction is designed for both HR users and SAP Business Workflow users. The overall view provides maintenance functions for the following objects in addition to the HR organization plan objects:

- ► Workflow tasks
- ► Workflow templates
- ► Rules

In change mode, additional views are provided for the reporting structure, account assignments, and further characteristics.

Creating the Organizational Plan

Figure 8.10 shows the HR view of simple maintenance. The simple maintenance mode provides a straightforward representation of the organizational plan. Objects are connected to one another via a line representing the relationship.

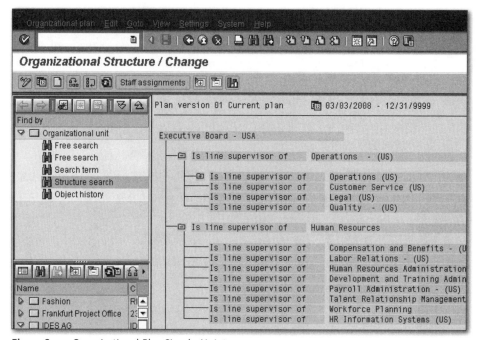

Figure 8.10 Organizational Plan Simple Maintenance

The function buttons provided along the screen header allow you to create objects and assign the objects to one another, thereby creating the necessary relationship records. Additional organizational units are created with the Create button, shown in Figure 8.11.

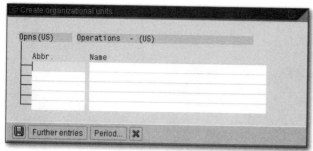

Figure 8.11 Creating New Organizational Units in Simple Maintenance

The object is created when you click on Save, and is displayed in the maintenance screen. In addition to Create, a variety of functions are available in simple maintenance, as described in Table 8.2. These options are also available through the Edit menu.

Function Option	Action Description
Create	Creates new objects
Change	Changes existing object properties
Delimit	Limits the validity period of the object
Delete	Deletes an object
Rearrange	Changes the sequence of the object
Prioritize	Changes the priority of the object
Move	Moves the object
Assign unrelated	Assigns an unrelated object to a selected object

Table 8.2 Simple Maintenance Function Options

Creating Staff Assignments

The Staff Assignments button can be used to add positions to the organizational plan and to create jobs. Similar to organizational units, you use the function buttons to create new position objects. When a position is created, you are prompted to specify the job with which the position will be associated. When a job is selected, the job abbreviation and description are automatically carried forward to the position's abbreviation and title. You can keep these text descriptions or overwrite them as necessary. Similarly, the validity starting period from the organizational unit is populated for the positions being created. You can also overwrite or change the starting effective date if needed. The position creation process lets you create one or multiple positions at once, as shown in Figure 8.12. The object and relationship infotypes are created automatically in the process when you click on Save.

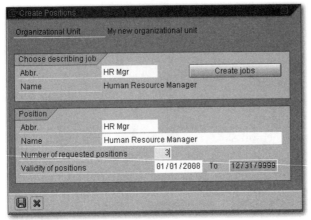

Figure 8.12 Creating New Positions in Simple Maintenance

Because the staffing assignments are built out in the organizational plan, the position objects are displayed in the hierarchy of the organizational units in which they were created, as shown in Figure 8.13.

Tasks can be assigned to positions in a similar fashion, using the Task profile button. Additional position characteristics, such as the Chief indicator, can be added to the positions once they are created.

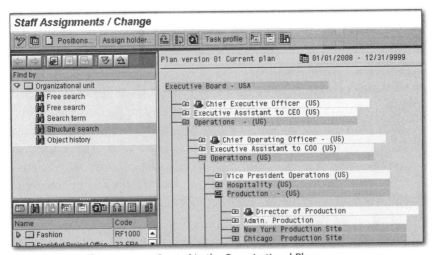

Figure 8.13 Staff Assignments Created in the Organizational Plan

Additional Information Functions

To keep the number of procedures a user has to follow to a minimum, some HR functions are not available in simple maintenance. You cannot create and maintain work centers, for example. All objects are created in active status as well.

The plan version used in simple maintenance always defaults to the active plan version set in configuration. To change the working plan version, you must exit the editing mode and change the plan version using the menu option **Settings • Plan version** on the initial transaction window.

Simple maintenance does allow you to maintain a reporting hierarchy among positions, cost center assignments, and certain infotype details. Note that the simple maintenance mode only utilizes the Overview screen in the work area. No infotype details for the objects are available for display in this view. To view object details, you can use the menu option **Goto • Object description**. From this option, you can select specific infotypes to maintain or display. Figure 8.14 displays all of the Goto options.

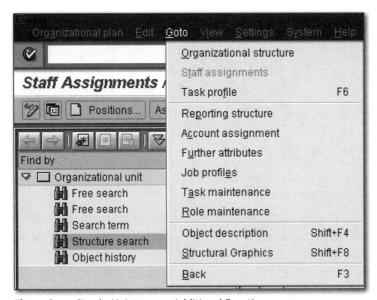

Figure 8.14 Simple Maintenance Additional Functions

From the Organizational Structure, Staff Assignment, or Task Profile screen, you can select various types of additional information by choosing the View menu. By default, only the short text description of the object is displayed, but additional options are available, as described in Table 8.3.

View Option	Item Displayed
Key on	The object type abbreviation and the object ID are displayed.
Relationship Text on	The relationship long text is inserted
Abbreviation on	The object abbreviations are displayed.
Object Period on	The validity period of the object is displayed.
Relationship Period on	The validity period of the relationships is displayed.
Percentage on	The system displays the staffing percentage.
Assignments • User on	The user assignment of employees in personnel management Infotype 0105 Communication appears.
Assignments • Substitute on	The substitute holder of the position is displayed.
Assignments • Chief on	The organizational unit chief position is indicated by a ▤ symbol.
Editing Period	A dialog box appears in which you can specify the start date of the editing period.
Color Legend	The colors assigned to infotypes are displayed on a color legend.
Switch Layout	The tree structure is compressed.

Table 8.3 Organizational Plan View Options

Pros and Cons of Simple Maintenance

One advantage of using simple maintenance mode is its ease of design. Because there's a simple graphical interface, users don't need a lot of training to understand what to do. Users can maintain objects in OM as well as those used exclusively in SAP Business Workflow. You can easily display additional data for the objects being maintained, such as infotype details or cost account assignments. You can also change the status of objects with the functions provided.

The primary disadvantage of the simple maintenance mode is that numerous screens are necessary to create all the plan data. Whereas a separate transaction function can ease segregation of duties, it can also be a heavy burden in a centralized maintenance function. The interface also requires that users be aware of the details that are required to be maintained for each object type, because these elements are not readily viewed or edited on the initial screen.

In summary, the interface can be used to quickly create, edit, and display plan objects. Getting to the object details for display or maintenance, however, is better left to more sophisticated transactions.

8.3.2 Organization and Staffing Maintenance Transactions

From the organization and staffing maintenance transactions, basic organizational plan components are created, as are infotype details for the objects. The organization and staffing plan is accessed via one of three transactions, depending on whether you want to create, change, or display the organizational plan. From the menu path **Human Resources • Organizational Management • Organizational Plan • Organization and Staffing**, you can select one of three transactions

- PPOCE: Create
- PPOME: Change
- PPOSE: Display

You are only required to use Create mode for the organization and staffing maintenance to create the initial organizational unit. Once the first organizational unit is created, you can create the remainder of the plan in either create or change mode, but you'll have better flexibility in maintaining the organizational plan if you switch to change mode.

Shown in Figure 8.15, the organization and staffing interface provides the most comprehensive functions possible in OM. Objects can be created and related to one another, and infotype records can be maintained for the objects. Additionally, with integration to personnel administration turned on, employee data for staff assignments is shown.

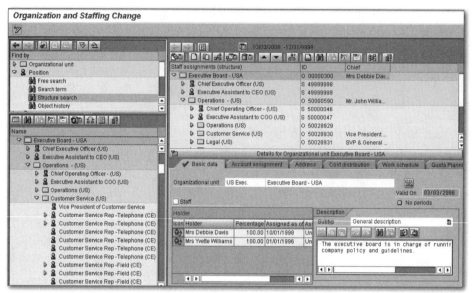

Figure 8.15 Organization and Staffing Interface – Change Mode

Creating the Root Organizational Unit

As the first step to building your organizational plan in OM, you need to create the root organizational unit. The root organizational unit represents the top-level organization in your enterprise structure. In most companies, this is generally equated with the department in which the company president resides. For enterprises with multiple companies, you can choose to represent the parent company as the root organization, with subsidiaries existing in the next-lowest level. In any case, the root organization is the basis from which all other organizational units can be created.

> **Tip**
>
> As a general guideline, your goal should be to have *one* root object in the organizational plan. Subsequent levels should have as few objects as is meaningful to the enterprise. This eases both the creation and ongoing maintenance process for the organizational plan.

The organization and staffing maintenance interface utilizes all four screen areas: search, selection, overview, and detail. When creating the initial organizational object, follow these steps:

1. Choose Transaction PPOCE Create. Enter the validity period as indicated in Figure 8.16. Click on the Enter ✔ button to continue.

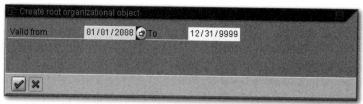

Figure 8.16 Initial Date Prompt in PPOCE

A new organizational object automatically appears in the overview area and in the detail area, as shown in Figure 8.17.

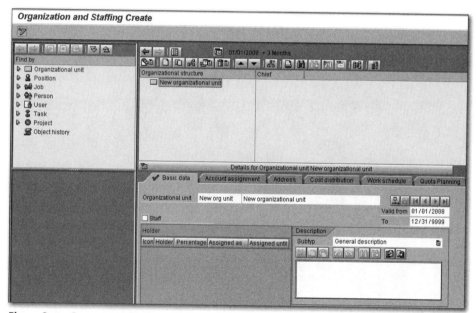

Figure 8.17 Creating a New Organizational Unit

2. Select the newly created organizational unit in the overview area by clicking on the object once.

When you select or place your cursor on the object New Organizational Unit in the overview area, your cursor is placed in the Basic Data object details entry window.

3. Enter the desired data in the Basic data tab. At minimum you should enter short and long names for your new organizational unit. You can also enter a description and select the Staff indicator if needed.

4. Click on Enter ✅ to transfer your entries back to the overview area.

5. You can navigate to the other tabs and add additional data.

6. Save 💾 your entries when done.

After the initial organizational unit object is created, change to the Organizational and Staffing Change interface, either through Transaction PPOME or from the main menu. In the overview area, the root organizational object that was created initially is presented, with the infotype information available in the detail area. To create new subordinate organizational units, follow and repeat these additional steps:

7. Click on the Create 🗋 button that appears just above the overview area.

   The new subordinate organizational unit is created in the structure, as depicted in Figure 8.18.

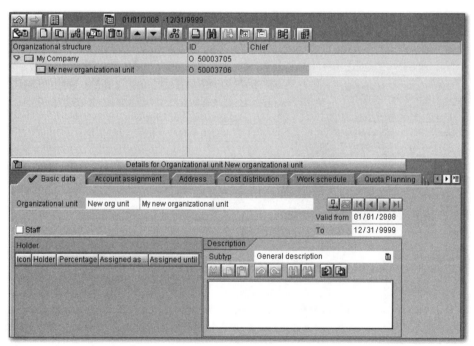

Figure 8.18 Newly Subordinate Organizational Unit Created

8. Enter the desired data in the Basic data tab. At minimum you should enter short and long names for your new organizational unit. You can also enter a description and select the Staff indicator if needed.

9. Click on the Enter ✅ button to transfer your entries back to the overview area.

10. You can navigate to the other tabs and add additional data.

11. Continue with steps 7 through 11 until your entire organizational structure is set up in the SAP system. Be sure to save 💾 your entries often, because data is not automatically saved for you.

Depending on how you want to use OM, you must decide which units you want to include in your organizational structure. For a rough depiction that can be used in testing the various functions within OM, you can restrict the structure. For example, you may only create a structure with the main departments. Alternatively, you may choose an organization that you know particularly well: Human Resources, for example.

Using Drag-and-Drop

As you determine the design of your organizational plan, you can create a more detailed depiction of the enterprise, including subsections and work groups, for example. As you refine your organizational hierarchy, you may find it useful to move organizational units around in the plan structure. This is easily done with drag-and-drop functionality. To move objects:

1. Select the object in the overview part of the work area.

2. Hold down the left mouse button and drag the object to the object to which you want to assign it. A relationship is created automatically.

3. Save 💾 your entry.

As alternatives to drag-and-drop functionality, you can also use the following function keys in the overview header area to change the information

Note that after you have made several changes to the organizational plan, you may be prompted to save the information. This helps prevent data loss. The number of steps that are carried out before the confirmation prompt appears is set in the IMG. Follow the menu path **Personnel Management • Organizational Management • Hierarchy Framework • Set Up Backup Prompt**. See the IMG documentation for more information.

Function	Result
	Assigns a selected object to another object in the hierarchy.
	Delimits an object or assignment. You are prompted to enter the date from which the object or assignment is to be ended.
	Deletes an object or assignment completely.
	Moves the organizational unit up or down within the hierarchy level.
	Moves up a level within a displayed structure. This affects the display only.
	Changes the data columns displayed in the overview. You are prompted to select the fields for display.
	Undoes or recreates the last change you made to data in the overview area but have not yet saved.

Table 8.4 Function Keys in the Organization and Staffing Overview Area

Creating Jobs

Jobs in the organizational plan can be created before, after, or concurrently with the organizational unit hierarchy. Because there is no direct dependency between jobs and organizational units, the order in which they are created isn't important. The only prerequisite to consider when creating the organizational plan design is that jobs should be created before positions are created.

When creating the jobs in the organizational plan, follow these steps:

1. Select Create jobs... in the Edit menu of the organizational and staffing maintenance interface, as shown in Figure 8.19.

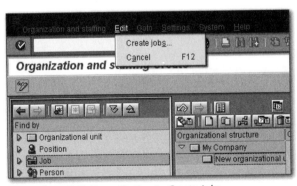

Figure 8.19 Edit Menu Option to Create Jobs

A Create Job window appears, shown in Figure 8.20. The job creation criteria are simplified in this interface. All that is required for entry is short and long text descriptions of the job to be created. You can scroll down the open text area to new rows to keep adding jobs to the list. Any jobs that have previously been created in OM are displayed in the lower portion of the dialog window.

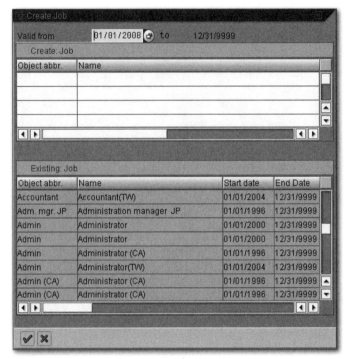

Figure 8.20　Create Jobs Entry Window

2. Enter the short and long text descriptions of the jobs you want to add.

3. When complete, click on the Enter ✔ button to transfer your entries to the overview area.

4. The text description for the job is transferred to the Basic data tab, as shown in Figure 8.21. You can add a detailed job description in the basic data tab, or navigate to the other tabs and add additional data.

   Keep in mind that characteristics of a job are inherited by the positions that are created using the job as a basis, so the more detail you provide, the more information can be inherited by the positions.

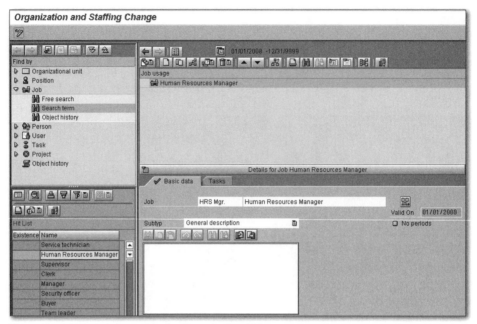

Figure 8.21 New Job Created in the Organizational Plan

5. Click on the Enter button to transfer your entries back to the overview area.

6. Continue with steps 4 and 5 until the details of all your jobs are set up in the SAP system. Be sure to save your entries often, because data is not automatically saved for you.

After jobs have been created, you can manage them in the overview and detail areas, similarly to organizational units. Functions to copy, delimit, delete, and assign jobs are available for use.

Creating Positions

The Staff Assignments function can be used to add positions to the organizational plan. To add positions and view their relationship to the organizational units to which they report, you first need to change the view of the organizational plan display.

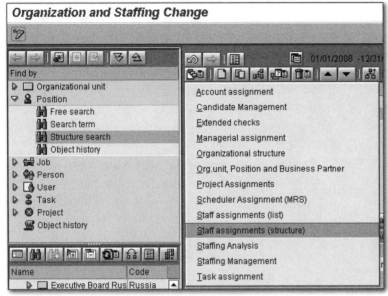

Figure 8.22 Overview Area Display Options Selection

Views are accessed from a drop-down window in the overview area, as shown in Figure 8.22. SAP provides multiple views in the maintenance interface. Views provide different display options for the various objects within OM.

Depending on the type of object you're working with, different views are available that provide different information displays. Figure 8.22 shows the view options for positions. Table 8.5 explains some of the various views that are available for the different organizational object types.

View	Information Available
Account Assignment	Structural display showing the assignment of a cost center to an object (organizational unit or position)
Managerial Assignment	Structural display showing the assignment of an organizational unit to a chief position and its holder (person or user)
Organizational structure	Structural display showing the assignment of an organizational unit to other organizational units

Table 8.5 Organizational and Staffing Maintenance Interface Views

View	Information Available
Staff Assignments (list)	List display showing the assignment of an organizational unit to the subordinate positions and their holders
Staff Assignments (structure)	Structural display showing an organizational structure and the assignment of each organizational unit to the subordinate positions and their holders
Task Assignment	Structural display showing the assignment of an object (position, job, person, or user) to tasks and activity groups
Reporting Structure	Structural display showing the higher- and lower-level assignments of positions to other positions
Job Usage	Structural display showing the assignment of a job to positions
Organizational Assignment	Structural display showing the assignment of a holder to position and higher-level organizational units
Task Hierarchy	Structural display showing the assignment of a task to other tasks and activity groups
Agent	Structural display showing the assignment of a task to other organizational objects

Table 8.5 Organizational and Staffing Maintenance Interface Views (cont.)

To switch between displays, select the required object and click on 🔄. The system shows you the various display types available. To create positions, the Staff assignments (structure) view provides the necessary information.

Creating Positions from Jobs

Positions can be created one of two ways in the organizational plan. The first way is to create positions generically from jobs, after which they can be assigned to the organizational units. To begin creating positions from jobs, follow these steps:

1. In the selection area, search for and double-click on the job from which you want to create positions. This will transfer the job to the overview area.

2. Click on the Create 🗋 button that appears just above the overview area. The new position is created in the interface, as depicted in Figure 8.23. The new position appears in both the overview and detail areas.

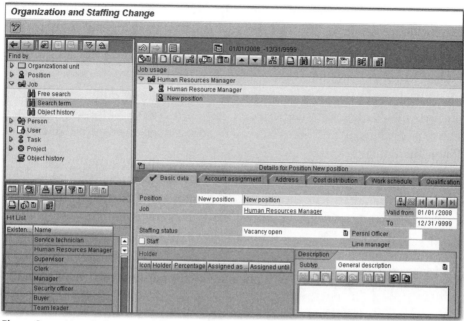

Figure 8.23 New Position Created From a Job

3. Select the newly created position in the overview area by clicking on the object once.

   When you select or place your cursor on the object New Position in the overview area, your cursor is placed in the Basic Data object details entry window.

4. Enter the preferred data in the Basic data tab. At minimum you should enter short and long names for your new position, and select the appropriate job to define the position. You can also enter a description and indicate whether the position is the chief or head of the organization.

> **Note**
>
> When you assign a job and press Enter, the job title is populated (inherited) into the position title. You can overwrite this as necessary.

5. Click on the Enter 🗸 button to transfer your entries back to the overview area.

6. You can navigate to the other tabs and add additional data.

7. Continue with steps 1 through 6 until all of your positions are set up in the SAP system. Be sure to save 💾 your entries often, because data is not automatically saved for you.

Creating Positions within Organizations

The second way positions can be created is directly in the organizational unit hierarchy. Using this method, the position is assigned directly to the organizational unit to which it reports. To begin creating positions in the organizational hierarchy, follow these steps:

1. Search for the organization in which you want to create positions. In the selection area, double-click on the organizational unit to transfer the organization to the overview area. Change to the Staff Assignment view.

2. Click on the Create 📄 button that appears just above the overview area.

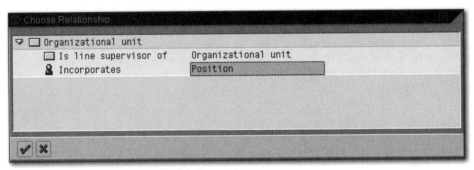

Figure 8.24   Creating a Position Staff Assignment

3. In the Choose Relationship window, select Incorporates Position as shown in Figure 8.24, and click on the Transfer ✔ button to proceed.

   The new position is created in the organizational structure, as depicted in Figure 8.25. The new position appears in the search results, in the overview area, and in the detail area.

4. Select the newly created position in the overview area by clicking on the object once.

   When you select or place your cursor on the object New Position in the overview area, your cursor is placed in the Basic Data object details entry window.

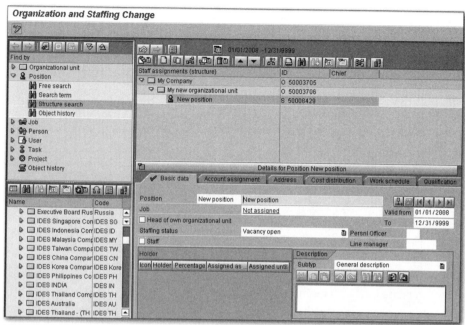

Figure 8.25   New Position in the Organization Hierarchy

5. Enter the preferred data in the Basic data tab. At minimum you should enter short and long names for your new position, and select the appropriate job to define the position. You can also enter a description and indicate whether the position is the chief or head of the organization.

Note

When you assign a job and press Enter, the job title is populated (inherited) into the position title. You can overwrite this as necessary.

---

6. Click on the Enter ✅ button to transfer your entries back to the overview area.

7. You can navigate to the other tabs and add additional data.

8. Continue with steps 1 through 7 until your entire organizational structure is set up in the SAP system. Be sure to save 💾 your entries often, because data is not automatically saved for you.

After the positions have been created, you can manage them in the overview and detail areas, similarly to organizational units and jobs. Functions to move, copy, delimit, delete, and assign positions are available for use.

Assigning Persons in the Organizational Plan

As previously described in Section 3.5.4, persons are typically assigned to the organizational plan via personnel administration Infotype 0001 Organizational Assignment. When persons are assigned to a position, a relationship between the position and person is created, allowing the person to be displayed in the organization and staffing interface. Each time you make changes to the organizational plan, the system checks whether any of these changes can have an affect on the personnel administration record.

> **Example**
>
> If you move a position to a different organizational unit, the person in that position should have a new organizational unit reflected on their Infotype 0001 Organizational Assignment as of the effective date of the move.

Once the system has successfully checked the consistency of the data changes, it saves the data in OM. The Infotype 0001 records of the persons affected by these changes are then read by the personnel administration database, changed to correspond with the OM data, and written back to the personnel administration database.

Note that whereas the OM data changes are written back to the personnel record for the employee, only the organizational assignment Infotype 0001 is maintained. The personnel actions Infotype 0000 is not created, and so must be maintained separately.

Additionally, there may be restrictions on personnel record changes that occur retroactively, or in the past. Personnel records are controlled by payroll control settings that dictate how far back in time personnel information can be changed. If a change in OM is made with an effective data earlier than the "earliest retroactive accounting period" for the employee, the change won't be allowed by the system. In this case, the system will reject the change, and you will need to change the effective date of your OM change to correspond with the retroactive accounting date.

Creating Additional Objects

The search area in the organization and staffing interface enables you to switch between various object types, allowing you to maintain the multiple aspects of the organizational plan. In addition to organizational units, jobs, positions, and persons, maintenance options delivered by SAP also exist for tasks and users. Through customizing options, you can also add any other objects that you may be using in your organizational plan. In all of these cases, the maintenance options that exist are essentially the same. You can create, change, delimit, and delete the objects and their infotype details. Because the functions themselves are very similar to those already described in this chapter, we won't go into full detail about how to maintain the information. Keep in mind the functions and processes for creating data described previously, because these instructions should generally apply to all the object types you may use.

Pros and Cons of the Organization and Staffing Maintenance Transaction

There are many advantages to using the organization and staffing maintenance transaction. First is the strong graphical interface. The interface provides a combination of simple and detailed infotype maintenance features, all housed together in one maintenance transaction. You can search, select, drag and drop, and maintain objects and their detailed characteristics. The graphical interface provides immediate feedback to the user on the effect of the change he has made. These transactions also store multiple object and infotype changes in memory, providing a means to preview changes visually before they have to be saved in the system. The screen layout is configurable, which is described in more detail in Chapter 9. This configurability provides great flexibility in designing a one-stop shop for your users to maintain all of the elements and details of the enterprise organizational plan.

The primary disadvantage of the organization and staffing maintenance transaction is that the interface itself is very complex. There are multiple aspects to learn, and those aspects change as users choose different object types to maintain in the organizational plan. For users outside of the Human Resources or Information Technology functions, the interface can be quite intimidating and require extensive training and support for the general or occasional user. Alternatively, significant configuration may be required to customize the interface to meet the needs of the various users of the transaction. These configuration activities are quite complex and can place a heavy burden on resources during implementation.

The organization and staffing transactions provide the most user-friendly graphical interfaces to display and maintain organizational plan information. Although some complex set up and training can be required up front to prepare users for task completion, this investment pays off in the long run. For more advanced users of the system, expert transactions may be necessary to maintain object characteristics. These expert transactions are described in the next section.

8.4 Expert OM Maintenance Transactions

In expert maintenance, you are restricted to editing one specific object type. Using these transactions, you can create and process individual objects and the relationships between them. You can also create, maintain, or display additional infotype attributes and characteristics for the objects. Table 8.6 lists some of the transactions available for expert maintenance.

Transaction	Expert Maintenance Transactions
PO01	Maintain Work Center
PO03	Maintain Job
PO10	Maintain Organizational Unit
PO13	Maintain Position
PFCT / PO14	Maintain Task
PP01	Maintain General Plan Data

Table 8.6 Expert Maintenance Transactions

The expert maintenance transactions are also referred to as detail mode or infotype maintenance in SAP help and reference documentation. With the various expert maintenance transactions, you create infotypes for the organizational objects individually. This infotype maintenance can be used to edit the organizational plan elements after the initial structure has been created in simple maintenance mode, or it can be used to create all of the elements of the plan.

Two options are available for editing data in expert maintenance. First, you can choose to edit a particular organizational object, such as a job or an organizational unit. For specific objects, there is a separate transaction, as listed in Table 8.6. Within these transactions, you can only edit the specific object type and the allowed infotypes for that object. For example, the maintenance interface for jobs is shown in Figure 8.26. As shown, the object type Job is preselected for maintenance. The user only needs to select the plan version and object ID number to maintain the data.

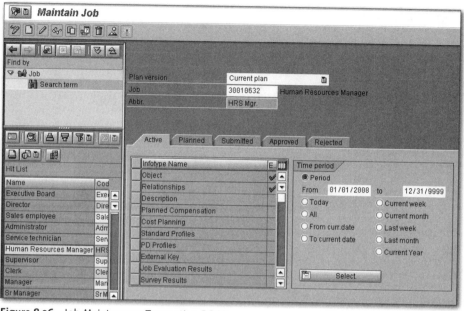

Figure 8.26 Job Maintenance Transaction PO03

Second, you can select and edit different objects using the general maintenance Transaction PP01. Here, you can select the object type to edit, and then maintain the infotypes allowed for that object. Because editing options are the same for the various transactions, let's focus on general maintenance navigation and functions.

The general maintenance interface provides multiple-object selection. Because you select the object type to maintain, you can work with objects that are used in the organizational plan as well as other objects. For example, you can call up the object type R – Resource type, which is used in the Training and Event Management component.

The general maintenance interface is similar to the simple maintenance interface in that the Object Manager consists of the usual search and selection areas from which you can choose objects to edit. Because the object type is selected from the available values list, the search criteria change dynamically to provide all search methods for that object type. Figure 8.27 provides a view of the general maintenance interface.

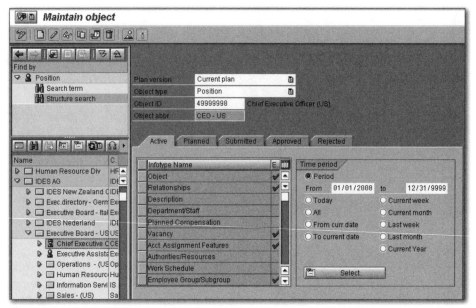

Figure 8.27 General Maintenance Interface

8.4.1 Using Expert Maintenance

The work area for expert maintenance is quite different from the simple maintenance interface. Rather than providing an overview and detail area, the interface
presents high-level information on the object selected in the overview portion of
the screen. From here, you can select or set the plan version to maintain, choose
the object type, and select an object ID to edit. The object abbreviation is displayed
automatically.

> **Tip**
>
> One condition must be met to maintain objects in the general maintenance interface.
> Infotype 1000 Object must be set in customizing to allow direct maintenance. This cus-
> tomizing setting was reviewed in Chapter 4, Section 4.2 Infotypes for OM. You cannot
> maintain infotypes for a particular object if Infotype 1000 Object has not been flagged
> as maintainable.

The lower portion of the work area provides a tabbed interface that presents the
user with the allowed infotypes for that object type, as well as a time period dur-

ing which to view, create, or edit infotype records. The time period start defaults to the current date, or you can reset this to another value to broaden or narrow the maintenance validity period. There is no detail area on the maintenance interface, because details on the infotypes are maintained in individual infotype screens. Infotypes are created, edited, and deleted manually by the user in this process.

8.4.2 Creating Object Records

Before you can create records for the various infotypes associated with the object, you must first create the object's "existence" in the system. This is done through the creation of a record in Infotype 1000 Object. When Infotype 1000 Object is present, the object itself exists in the system, and you can then associate additional infotype records with it. To create an object:

1. In the work area, set the plan version and object type you want to create. You should also select the appropriate tab to set the status of the object. Leave the object ID field blank.

2. Select the Object infotype as shown in Figure 8.28. Click on the Create ▯ button that appears just above the search area.

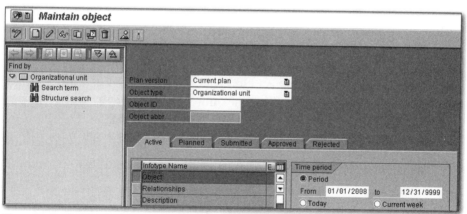

Figure 8.28 Creating a New Object in Infotype Maintenance

3. In the Create Object window, enter the short and long text names as shown in Figure 8.29. Click on the Enter ✅ button to validate your entry.

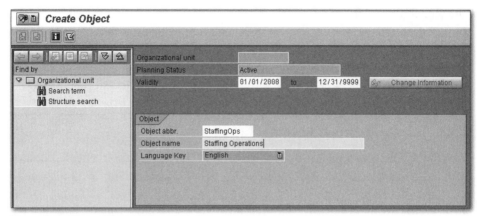

Figure 8.29 New Object Infotype Details

4. Save your entries.

After saving the Object infotype, you'll be returned to the general maintenance screen. An object ID will have been assigned to the new object, which appears in the work area field.

You can continue to create new objects in this manner, or maintain other infotype details for the new object as described in the next section.

8.4.3 Creating Additional Infotype Records

The procedure for creating additional infotype data varies slightly with each infotype, because the field-level details of the infotypes are different. The overall procedure remains the same, however, so it can be described broadly.

1. In the work area, set the plan version and object type you want to create. You should also select the appropriate tab to set the status of the object.

2. Using the search options, select the object for which you want to create infotype records. You can also enter the object ID directly.

3. Select the infotype you want to create or maintain. You may need to scroll up or down the list of infotypes to see all the infotypes available.

4. Click on the Create button that appears just above the search area.

5. In the infotype screen, enter the necessary details for your object. Save your entries when complete.

8.4.4 Changing the Status of Infotype Records

You can change the status of an infotype record when the status of that information changes in the organizational plan. Status changes can occur for a variety of reasons. For example, the status of an infotype may change from planned to active when it is approved. The general maintenance work area provides a tabbed interface that presents the user with the various status settings available. You can switch between tabs to check for the existence of infotype data in the various status values.

To change the status of an infotype is a simple process. Start on the tab that represents the current status of the object. Select the infotype. From the menu, choose **Edit • Status change**, and select the new status value.

Tip
If you have a large number of objects for which to change the status, use Report RHAKTI00 Change Status of Object. This report allows you to select multiple objects and infotypes whose status is to be changed.

8.4.5 Additional Infotype Functions

In expert maintenance mode, you can perform a variety of functions for the objects and infotypes in the organizational plan. Table 8.7 describes the function buttons that are available on the interface.

Function	Function Description
	Switches between display and edit mode in the maintenance transaction.
	Creates a new infotype record.
	Changes or edits an existing infotype record. Use this function to change information that was entered incorrectly.
	Displays an existing infotype record. You can navigate to the Next or Previous record if multiple infotype records exist.
	Copies an infotype to a new infotype record. All infotype information is copied so you can overwrite information as needed.

Table 8.7 Detail Maintenance Function Buttons

Function	Function Description
![icon]	Delimits an infotype record. You are prompted for the new validity ending period.
🗑	Deletes an existing infotype record. Only delete an infotype if it was created in error. If Infotype 1000 is deleted, this deletes all object infotype records.
![icon]	Displays all the infotype records in a list.
![icon]	Activates an infotype record. For example, a planned infotype can be approved or confirmed, and require activation.

Table 8.7 Detail Maintenance Function Buttons (cont.)

8.4.6 Country-Specific Infotype Records

Most OM infotypes are international, meaning they can be used for any country. Certain infotypes are not valid for all countries. These country-specific infotypes are not generally accessible in the detailed maintenance interface. To select and maintain data in these infotypes, the user must set the country code that corresponds to the infotypes.

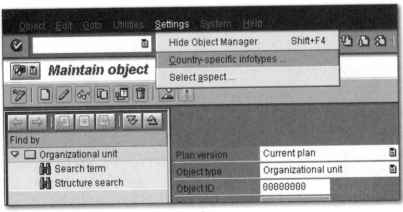

Figure 8.30 Choosing Country-Specific Infotypes

Figure 8.30 displays how you can access country-specific infotypes via the Settings menu. In the Country-Specific Infotypes pop-up window, the user can select to display no country-specific infotypes, all country-specific infotypes, or specific country infotypes. The country abbreviation is used to select the countries for display. Country values are available via a drop-down list or can be entered manually by the user, as in Figure 8.31. When selected, the country-specific infotypes then appear on the infotype list in addition to the international infotypes available.

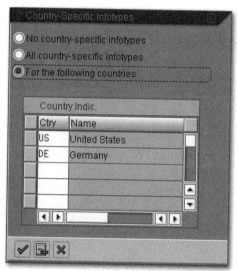

Figure 8.31 Selecting Country-Specific Infotypes for Display

Pros and Cons of Expert Maintenance

The primary advantage of expert maintenance is that the objects and their infotypes are directly accessed and maintained. There is no question about what data is being created or edited in this interface. The infotypes, their subtypes, and the details of the infotypes are presented to the user exactly as they are stored in the infotype. Users don't have to guess where the information is stored for later retrieval. This is particularly important when users perform ad hoc reporting on OM data. Often, the user has to know in which infotype the data is stored so that he can build the ad hoc query to retrieve the information. In addition, the multiple status values of object records are easily managed with the tabbed interface. A number of other transactions only allow you to work in one status value, restricting how freely you can edit the plan status.

The disadvantage of the expert maintenance transactions is in the interface itself. Drag-and-drop functionality is not available, and the user cannot view multiple objects at a time. Users are required to know which infotypes are mandatory when creating new objects. Additionally, because each infotype is maintained separately, multiple data entry screens require maintenance for a given object.

Given the specific knowledge required of the infotypes allowed and required for each object type in the organizational plan, the expert maintenance transactions are best left to advanced users of the system.

8.5 Action Maintenance

So far, we've discussed ways of creating and maintaining objects and infotypes that are heavily dependent on the user deciding which detailed information is necessary. Simple and detail maintenance transactions discussed until now require the user to create the Infotype 1000 Object, but other infotype records are at the discretion of the user to create and maintain. No additional infotype details are actually required of the user. Whereas this provides a lot of freedom in the organizational plan, allowing a user to pick and choose the details of the plan may not be in the best interests of the structure. It's quite easy for a user to forget critical details when creating a new job or a new organizational unit.

To ensure the completeness of the data maintained in the organizational plan, some customers use actions for organizational data maintenance. Actions are used in both the OM and PA components and simply refer to a chaining together of infotypes for a particular object type. In the case of OM, object types are those used in the organizational plan. The transactions for actions maintenance are listed in Table 8.8. You can use a general actions transaction (PP03) or specific transaction codes for certain object types.

Transaction	Detail Maintenance Transactions
PP03	Maintain Plan Data (action-guided)
PQ01	Actions for Work Center
PQ03	Actions for Job
PQ10	Actions for Organizational Unit
PQ13	Actions for Position
PQ14	Actions for Task

Table 8.8 OM Actions Transactions

In actions, the user is prompted to complete data entry for one infotype after another until all infotypes for the object are completed and saved. In this way, you can prompt the user to complete the infotypes that are necessary for the object type being maintained.

8.5.1 Using OM Actions

Actions for OM objects are defined by a series of infotype controls in the IMG. The initial screen of the general actions transaction prompts for an object type and object ID. When you create a new object, leave the object ID blank. If you're performing a subsequent action on an existing object, you can use the search and select areas to choose an object ID, or enter it directly in the ID field. In the task selection area, you can set the planning status, validity period, and an action type to use.

When the user clicks the Execute ⊕ button to begin the action, the series of infotypes that are chained together in the action appear one at a time. The user completes the infotype information, and when the infotype is saved, the next infotype in the action appears. This process continues until all infotypes in the action are complete and saved, at which point the user is returned to the actions transaction. Figure 8.32 shows the general actions transaction and action options for an organizational unit object.

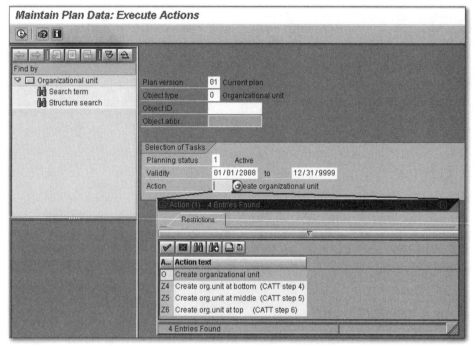

Figure 8.32 Actions for Organizational Unit

Figure 8.33 provides an illustration of what an action may include for an organizational unit. In this case, the infotypes maintained in sequence include:

- Infotype 1000 Object
- Infotype 1001 Relationship
- Infotype 1002 Description

Actions can be used for a variety of maintenance purposes. In addition to creating new objects, you can use actions to change object characteristics. For example, you may want to create an action such that when a job title changes to include an update to the job description on Infotype 1002, the user is prompted to update any task assignments (via the relationships Infotype 1001) for the job.

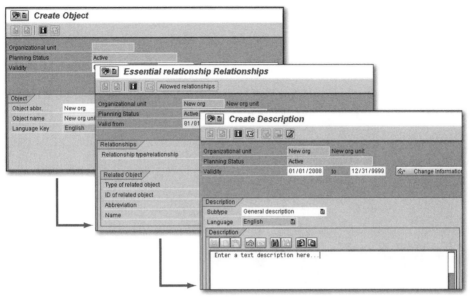

Figure 8.33 Infotypes Chained Together to Form an Action

Pros and Cons of Actions Maintenance

The clear advantage of actions-based maintenance is that you can control and prescribe which infotypes (and subtypes) the user should complete when creating or maintaining an object. This takes the guesswork out of the task, eliminating situations where a user forgets to create critical information. All objects and infotypes can be maintained in this fashion.

The downside of the action-based transaction is in the presentation and requirements on the user. Because the actions are infotype driven, the user has to know what each infotype function is and how the information should be stored. The screens and views of the infotypes are not configurable, so users need to be trained on how the system works as delivered. Lastly, there is no graphical interface, so the user is not given direct visual clues that the object is being created in the hierarchy in the correct placement. Users can switch to one of the more graphical interfaces to check their data entry visually, but that process is not inherent in the action transaction.

8.5.2 Modifying or Creating Your Own OM Actions

SAP delivers a number of actions for the main objects in the organizational plan: organizational unit, job, position, task, and work center. You can use these transactions and create actions of your own. Actions for OM objects are defined by a series of infotype controls in the IMG. Follow the IMG menu path **Personnel Management • Organization Management • Maintain Personnel Actions**.

Action	Info	Action text
A		Create work center
B		Create training program
C		Create job
D		Create course type classroom
DECC		Create curriculum type
DETE		Create course type Static WBT
DETR		Create course type Web-Based Training
DETX		Create course type for external LMS
DEVC		Create course type Virtual Classroom

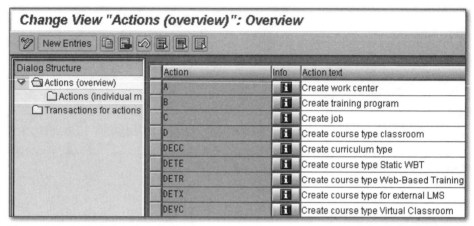

Figure 8.34 IMG: OM Actions Defined

Act.	Action text	SNo	Plan v...	Obj. ty...	Infoty.	Subtyp	Plan stat	Vari...	Func...	FCode s
O	Create organizatio...	1	**	O	1000				INSE	MASS
O	Create organizatio...	20	**	O	1002	0001			INSE	MASS
O	Create organizatio...	30	**	O	1003				INSE	MASS
O	Create organizatio...	40	**	O	1001	A011		K	INSE	

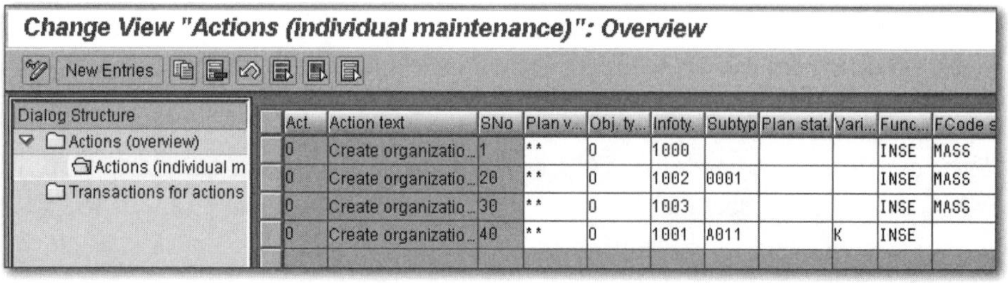

Figure 8.35 IMG: OM Actions Detail

The action is first defined by a four-character (nnnn) action name, shown in Figure 8.34. In the subsequent IMG view, the details of the action are defined, as shown in Figure 8.35. The action is directed by the sequential number in each row of configuration. The system performs each row in sequence, from lowest to highest. The sequence field is a three-character number from 001 to 999, so you can theoretically have 999 steps in the action. With the configuration settings you can control:

- The plan version to set for the infotype. Value ** provides a default to use the active plan version set in customizing.
- The object type to maintain. Only one object type can be maintained in an action.
- The infotype and subtype to maintain.
- The plan status (blank = active).
- For relationships, the target object type for the relationship.
- The function for the infotype (e.g., Insert, Copy, Delimit, Delete).
- The function code to use in the action. This is only used in conjunction with the INSE (insert) function. Valid options are DUTY = mandatory infotypes and MASS = prevents fast entry.

When creating OM actions, you should ensure that Infotype 1000 Object is created first. In delivered actions, this infotype always has sequence number 001. All other infotypes can be created in the order of your choosing, although it is best practice to separate the sequential numbers by some value (for example, multiples of 5 or 10), so that if you need to insert an infotype in between two others at some later point, you do not have to resequence the entire configuration set.

In the subsequent IMG view Transactions for actions, you can set the default action to use for the PQ** transaction codes delivered by SAP (Table 8.8), or you can define your own transaction codes and associate them with actions here as well.

8.6   Supplemental Maintenance Functions

Two additional interfaces are available to assist in the maintenance of the organizational plan. These functions are meant to supplement the organizational plan transactions that have already been described.

8.6.1   Structural Graphics

Structural graphics is an interface tool that enables you to display and maintain your organizational objects graphically. Using the structural graphics tool, you can, for example, move individual objects or whole substructures around the organizational plan. Structural graphics can be accessed from within the simple maintenance transaction interface, or you can access it directly from Transaction PGOM or the menu path **Personnel Management • Organization Management • Info System • General • PD Graphics Interface**. Figure 8.36 shows the structural graphics interface.

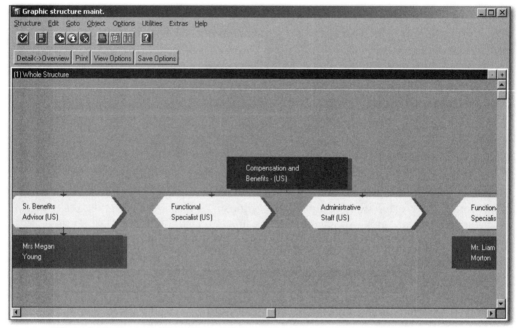

Figure 8.36 Structural Graphics Interface

Procedures for working with objects are simplified in structural graphics. The interface is first accessed from a report selection screen, in which you can specify the portion of the organizational plan structure with which to work. Once inside the interface, the organization is represented graphically in the upper portion of the window. A toolbox provides the various functions available. In the Utilities section are functions to create, move, change, delimit, and delete objects. The Extras menu has further functions that allow you to display or maintain additional attributes or characteristics of the objects. Both toolbox options are shown in Figure 8.37.

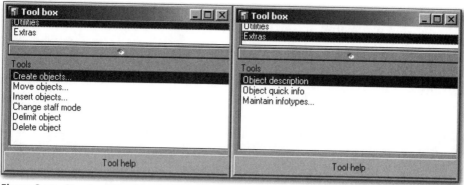

Figure 8.37 Structural Graphics Toolbox Windows

Selecting objects in structural graphics is easy. Users can simply select an object, press the Shift key to select multiple objects, or use the mouse to drag across and select a large group of objects at once. Structural graphics also lets you change the shape and colors of the objects displayed. However, not all of the functions available in the detail or simple maintenance transactions are available in structural graphics. For most functions and object details, the user has to open many additional windows in which to display information or perform data maintenance.

8.6.2 Matrix Organizations

As mentioned during the discussion of relationships, in addition to one-to-one object reporting relationships, you can have one-to-many relationships in the organizational plan. For certain object types such as positions and organizational units, it's useful to have multiple views of the objects and their reporting relationships. A matrix organization is an example of this alternate view, in which relationships between both functions and disciplines are represented. In this scenario, multiple hierarchies of the organizational units exist in the SAP system, providing different viewpoints of the organizational plan.

Matrix organizations are particularly useful for organizations that do project-based reporting, where persons and positions work in organizations that are different from their direct manager. Projects can be defined as organizational units and reported on separately from the usual hierarchical structure. Alternatively, manufacturing organizations can choose to represent resources that work along product lines. Resources can report to a central resource management organization but be assigned to various products for manufacturing and distribution purposes. Whatever the purpose, matrix organizations can be used to facilitate this multidimensional reporting view.

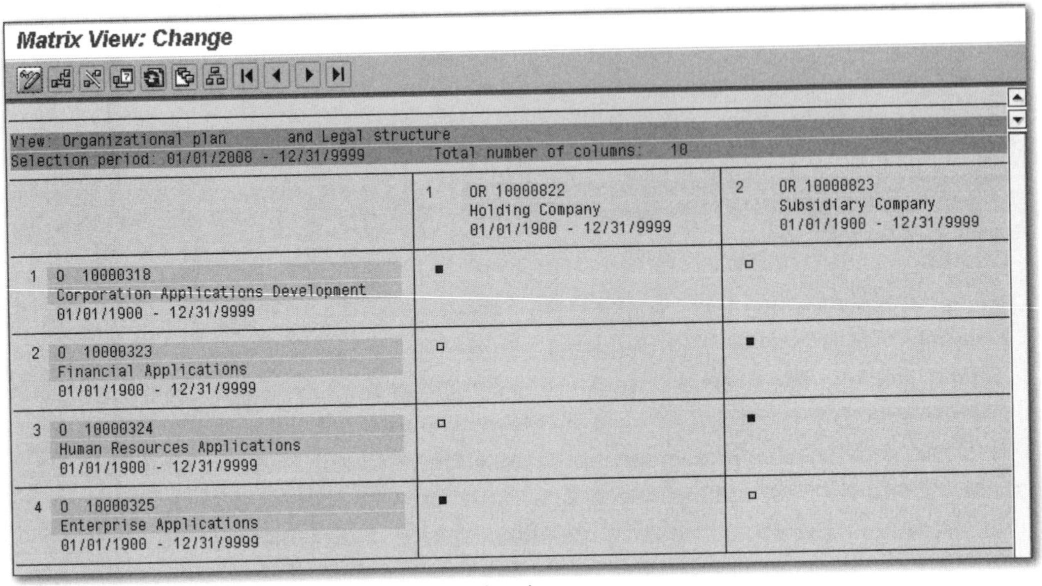

Figure 8.38 Matrix Organization Displayed

A sample matrix organization is displayed in Figure 8.38, in which a combination of objects, O organizational units and OR legal entities, are utilized to demonstrate the bi-directional reporting hierarchy. The organizational units are represented in the usual organizational plan hierarchy, and also report to these legal entities in the matrix view. You can access matrix organization functions via the menu path **Personnel Management • Organizational Management • Organizational Plan • Matrix • Display** or **Change**, or via Transaction Codes:

▶ PPMS Display Matrix Organization

▶ PPME Change Matrix Organization

In matrix organization planning, you define a matrix type that is used to represent the structure. SAP provides some standard matrix types to use, or you can create your own. The matrix type defines the object types, objects, and relationships to use and display in the structure.

8.7   Which Interface Is the Right One To Use?

Now that you have an understanding of the organizational plan maintenance options, the question of which one to use must be asked. The answer is, "It depends." There are many different types of users with different informational needs and different responsibilities when it comes to keeping the organization structure current.

Some users will want to access the data occasionally to simply look up a cost center or a person in the organization. Other users will have complex reporting and analysis needs. More advanced users will be required to keep the organizational plan details up to date. Maintenance users can also vary greatly, from distributed field managers and HR representatives who may manage their own organizational structures, to centralized HR operations functions that manage the entire enterprise organizational plan.

The wide variety of potential users of the plan data generally means you will need to use a combination of transactions in OM. Keeping in mind the five basic methods of maintenance, the following table provides some guidelines about the targeted users of the application and which transaction or interface is best suited to their use.

Maintenance Mode	Targeted User
Simple maintenance	▸ Users requiring an introduction to OM ▸ Novice users processing specific responsibilities: separate transactions for organizational unit, job, and position allow for clear segregation of duties in data maintenance ▸ Infrequent users who want a visual display of the organization
Organization and staffing maintenance	▸ Advanced users of OM who maintain the overall organizational plan: multiple objects can be maintained in conjunction with each other ▸ Novice or infrequent users who want a visual display of all the organizational plan elements
Expert mode or infotype maintenance	▸ Advanced users of OM who maintain specific infotype details or change object status values or determine solutions to specific problems

Table 8.9 Maintenance Modes for Targeted Users

Maintenance Mode	Targeted User
Actions maintenance	▶ Novice users becoming familiar with the specific steps required to maintain OM objects
Structural graphics	▶ Advanced users of OM performing planning or prototype activities

Table 8.9 Maintenance Modes for Targeted Users (cont.)

Because most enterprises have multiple types of users of the organizational plan, it's likely that you will use more than one interface in the SAP system to view and manage data. Some customers use all the transactions available, ensuring that the needs of the user population are best served by the appropriate transaction. Whatever the needs of your users may be, there is a transaction to suit their OM needs.

8.8 Conclusion

In this chapter we've reviewed the wide variety of maintenance interfaces available to manage the organizational plan. Given the different types of users who may exist in your organization, you can choose to utilize one or many of the options. Simple maintenance, organization and staffing, expert mode, actions, and structural graphics each provide many options for maintaining the many organizational objects you'll use. Now you have an understanding of how data may be maintained. The next chapter will discuss some of the technical tools and utilities available to help prepare your system for data maintenance.

Most maintenance users want one place to go to perform their work. The organization and staffing interface is just that place for OM. It is a one-stop shop that provides everything you need to effectively maintain your organizational structure. Getting the user interface to have everything needed is the challenge that will be met by customizing the hierarchy framework interface.

9   Customizing the Hierarchy Framework

In Chapter 8, we discussed the various transactions available to create and maintain the organizational plan. The organization and staffing maintenance transactions are the most flexible user interfaces in OM. The transactions allow you to create, change, or display the organizational plan components in one user interface. In the organization and staffing interface (Figure 9.1), objects can be created and related to one another, and all infotype records can be maintained. Because there are so many elements to work with, you'll want to customize the hierarchy framework interface to meet your needs.

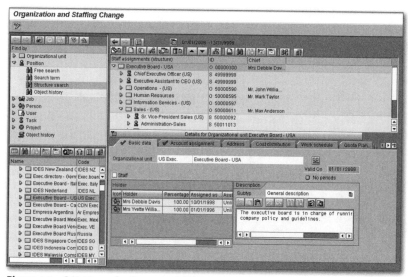

Figure 9.1   OM Hierarchy Framework View

9.1   The SAP Hierarchy Framework

As we just discussed in Chapter 8, the hierarchy framework is broken into four main areas:

▶ Search area: To find organizational objects

▶ Selection area: To select objects to display and maintain

▶ Overview area: To display key object characteristics

▶ Detail area: To create or edit object infotype details

Although the standard hierarchy framework provides a comprehensive user interface, you may sometimes want to alter the interface. For example, there may be too much information or too many options for your users, and you're looking to simplify the interface. Alternatively, you may want to add objects or infotypes that you want users to maintain.

Whatever the reason may be, the hierarchy framework is flexible, and the IMG provides the necessary activities for altering both the function and appearance of the interface. Each of the interface areas has varying configuration options, so let's take a look at them all.

9.1.1   Setting User Parameters for Customizing

Before you begin the customizing activities for the hierarchy framework, it's important to set some user parameters. To set user parameters, select the menu option **System • User Profile • Own Data**. Go to the **Parameters** tab as shown in Figure 9.2.

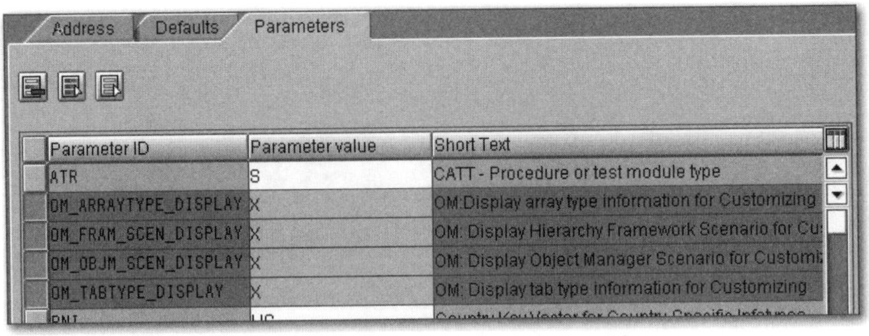

Parameter ID	Parameter value	Short Text
ATR	S	CATT - Procedure or test module type
OM_ARRAYTYPE_DISPLAY	X	OM:Display array type information for Customizing
OM_FRAM_SCEN_DISPLAY	X	OM: Display Hierarchy Framework Scenario for Cu
OM_OBJM_SCEN_DISPLAY	X	OM: Display Object Manager Scenario for Customi
OM_TABTYPE_DISPLAY	X	OM: Display tab type information for Customizing
PNL	US	Country Key Vector for Country Specific Infotune

Figure 9.2 Setting User Parameters for the Hierarchy Framework

Enter the following user parameter IDs with parameter value "X":

▶ OM_OBJM_SCEN_DISPLAY: Object Manager Scenario

▶ OM_ARRAYTYPE_DISPLAY: Column Framework

▶ OM_TABTYPE_DISPLAY: Tab Page Key

▶ OM_FRAM_SCEN_DISPLAY: Framework Scenario

These user parameters help identify the technical names of the components you'll be adjusting in the IMG activities. Some of the user parameter settings have an immediate effect on the transaction display. Compared with Figure 9.1 you can see in Figure 9.3 that there are three identified changes in the interface. At the top of the screen, the scenario OME0 is identified; at the top of the search area, the scenario OMEO00 is identified; and to the right of each detail tab heading, a technical name is now visible. Additional technical information is available as a result of the column framework setting, which we'll review later.

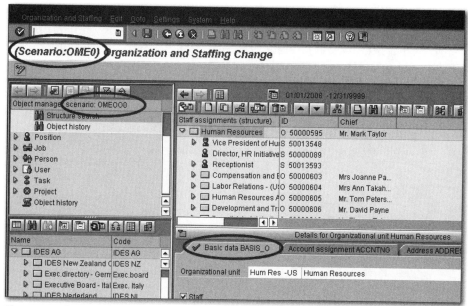

Figure 9.3 OM Interface with User Parameter Settings On

In this chapter, we'll review how to customize each of the organization and staffing interface areas. Let's begin by examining how to customize the search area.

9.2   Adjusting the Search Area

With the standard delivered search area, also called the Object Manager, you can search for and select organizational units, positions, jobs, users, persons, and tasks. Each object contains its own search methods, or ways to search for data. One or more methods of search may available for each object. In some cases, the search methods are the same for multiple objects.

> **Example**
>
> In your own implementation, you may want to remove objects that you do not use, or add new objects that you have created yourself. Alternatively, you may want to remove search criteria that you do not find useful, or add additional search methods that are more helpful to your users. Any of these options is possible via the IMG customizing activities.

9.2.1   Finding the Object Scenario

Before you can begin customizing, you need to know the technical name of the Object Manager scenario. The Object Manager scenario defines which objects can be searched for and selected, as well as how you can search for the objects. The standard scenario used in the OM transactions for organization and staffing is OMEO00.

User parameter OM_OBJM_SCEN_DISPLAY displays the Object Manager scenario that is actively being used in the search area, as shown in Figure 9.4.

Figure 9.4 Object Manager Scenario OMEO00

Now that you know the scenario name, you can access the customizing activities via the IMG path **Personnel Management • Organizational Management • Hierarchy Framework • Object Manager**, or directly via Transaction Code OOOBJ-MANCUST. In the IMG menu, multiple activities are listed, but all can be accessed via the first activity, so we'll describe navigation from within that view.

> **Note**
>
> The object manager customizing activities are client independent. Any changes you make will affect all SAP clients in your system, so take care when adjusting these entries, because you won't be able to recover the table entries from another client.

9.2.2   Defining Search Objects

The objects that are listed in the search area are defined as a search node, which is the top activity in the customizing table. In the search area, the node is represented by an icon and name, and functions like a folder. When you expand the folder, the search methods are listed.

In the customizing table, the search node key can be up to 10 characters. Usually, the node definition is similar to the name of the object type, as in the case of the organizational unit (O) or person (P) as shown in Figure 9.5. The node is assigned an object type and an icon to display in the search area. You can provide a name for the search node, but if a name is not provided, the node will adopt the name of the associated object type.

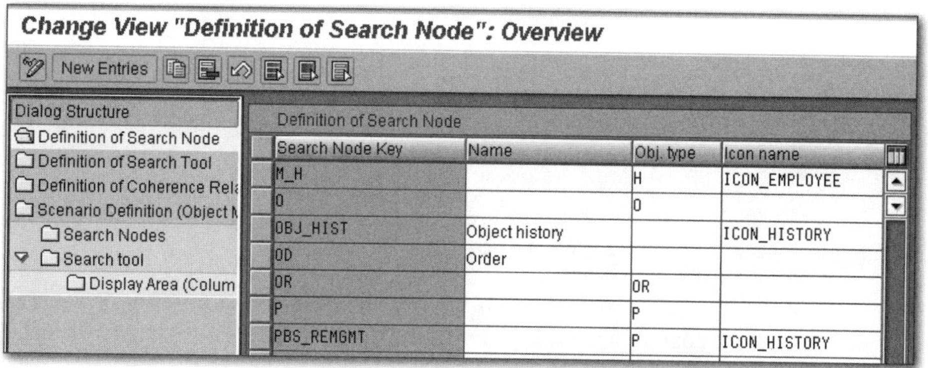

Figure 9.5   IMG: Definition of a Search Node

Sometimes, nodes may not be associated with a specific object. These types of search nodes use a program to determine what objects to utilize. This program name is defined in a following section.

9.2.3 Specifying the Search Methods

Once the search node is defined, you must determine what search methods or tools to use for that object. The search tools are defined generically in the IMG (Figure 9.6) and then assigned to the objects. Search tools are program routines that determine how a particular object is found in the system. There are many search tools that you can use with various objects. Search tools are technically defined as an ABAP object class. To understand more about how a specific search tool works, you can enlist the help of a technical ABAP resource, which can view the source code via the Class Builder (Transaction Code SE24).

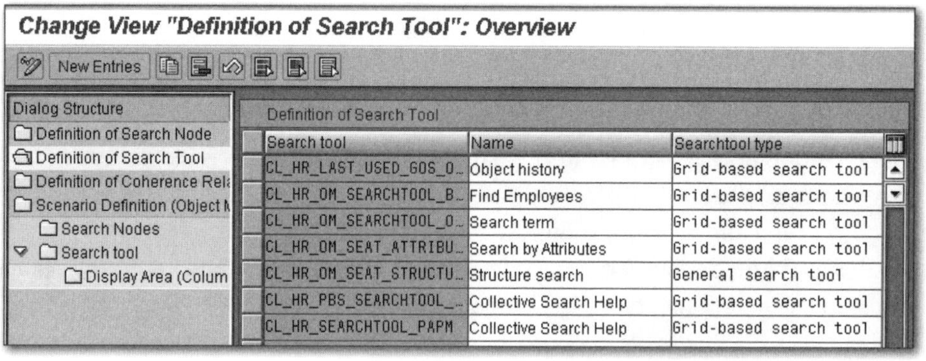

Figure 9.6 IMG: Definition of a Search Tool

Search tools can either be grid based, which provides results of the search in a table format, or they can be general, in which case the program determines the output format.

9.2.4 Associating Search Methods and Objects

Assignment of the search criteria to the object search nodes is a two-step process within the Object Manager scenario definition (Figure 9.7). The scenario can be set up to allow selection of a single object or multiple objects. As was previously identified, Scenario OMEO00 is the standard in OM.

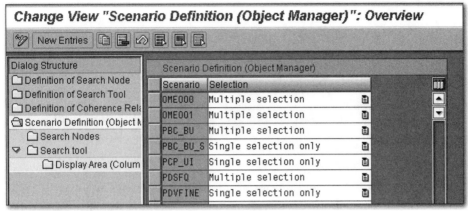

Figure 9.7 IMG: Scenario Definition (Object Manager)

Selecting the scenario, you navigate to the Search Nodes activity, which is shown in Figure 9.8. Here, the scenario and search node key are combined, which defines the node and related object as a search option in the transaction. In this customizing view, you can also specify an alternate name for the search node. This allows you to refer to the search node with one name in one scenario and another name in another scenario. The search nodes assignment view also gives you the ability to change the order of the search nodes using the position setting. You can order the nodes from 1 to 99, with 1 being the top node displayed in the user interface.

Change View "Search Nodes": Overview

Dialog Structure
- Definition of Search Node
- Definition of Search Tool
- Definition of Coherence Rel
- Scenario Definition (Object M
  - Search Nodes
  - Search tool
    - Display Area (Colum

Search Nodes

Scenario	Search Node Key	Name	Position	Column group	Header type
OME000	C		3		
OME000	O		1		
OME000	OBJ_HIST		99	OBJ_HIST	
OME000	P		4		
OME000	S		2		
OME000	T		6		
OME000	US		5		

Figure 9.8 IMG: Search Nodes Assigned to Scenario

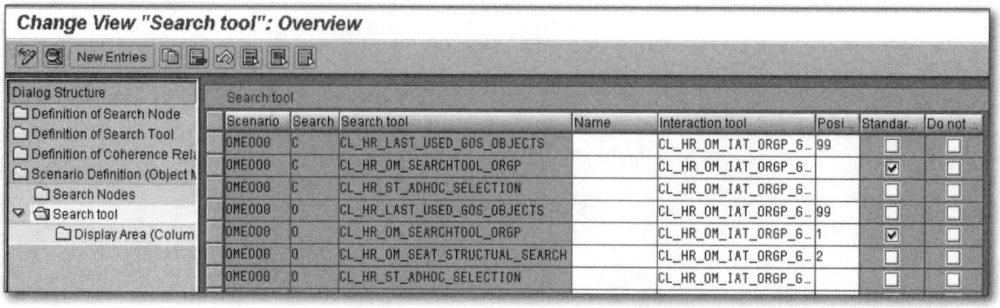

Figure 9.9 IMG: Search Tool Assigned to Scenario

The final activity is to assign the search tools to the scenario and node. In this customizing activity, shown in Figure 9.9, the scenario, the search node, and the search tool serve as the table key. Again, in this view you have the option of defining a custom name for the search tool used in the scenario for the specific node. You must specify at least one search tool per search node.

The interaction tool setting in this view defines which actions a user can carry out on search results shown in the display area and what the system does in response to the user action. Examples of actions include double-click, and drag-and-drop. Tool CL_HR_OM_IAT_ORGP_GOS_CD is *the* interaction tool used for all OM search tools.

The position field is used to sort the search tool entries for a node. Similar to the sort setting for the nodes, you can number searches from 1 to 99. Two final options exist for customizing the searches. You can specify that one search tool per node is considered the standard search; this is the default search that is used when you click on the node rather than a search tool in the user transaction. The final option is a checkbox that hides the default or standard search tool from the list of displayed search tools for that node.

9.2.5 Objects and Search Tools Summary

Whether you are adding or changing objects or search methods, the activities can be summarized in three steps:

1. Determine the Object Manager scenario used in the transaction you are using. The scenario defines the objects and searches to be used.

2. Define the search node, which identifies the objects to include and in what order to present them to the user.

3. Specify the search tools that you want to use for each node in the scenario. Search tools provide the various means to search for objects.

> **Tip**
>
> When removing elements that you don't want to use from the search area, the customizing activity is performed in reverse. You simply remove the customizing entries that assign the search tool to the search node and scenario, and remove the search node from the scenario as well. You do not have to (and should not) delete the customizing entries that define the node or the search tools.

Now that you know how to customize a search node to find objects in your organizational plan, let's examine how those objects are displayed in the selection and overview screen areas.

9.3 Changing the Column Layouts

When you have used the Object Manager to search for data in the organizational plan, the resulting data can be displayed in two areas.

9.3.1 Locating the Selection and Overview Column Groups

The selection area displays the direct results of the search. The overview area displays the results from the selection area for which you have performed an action (e.g., double-clicking on the data). Both the selection and overview areas of the user interface use a column layout configuration to display data. Each data element for a specific object is displayed in a separate column. Figure 9.10 provides a sample of the selection area column layout, which includes the object name and code. In the selection area, you can use the columns ⊞ icon in the header area to see all columns that are available to view. Selecting the Technical information button shows the technical names of the fields used and the column group.

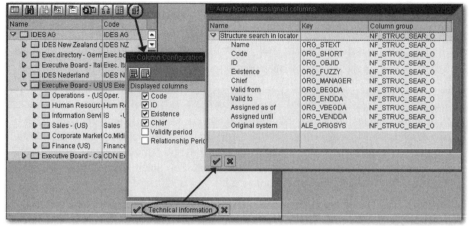

Figure 9.10 Column Layout Technical Information

The column group name is displayed when the user parameter OM_ARRAYTYPE_ DISPLAY is turned on. Similar technical information is also available in the overview area. The column group defines the fields that can be displayed in each column, whether the fields are fixed or can be turned on and off by the user, and the order in which they appear.

With the column group name identified, you can access the customizing activities via the IMG path **Personnel Management** • **Organizational Management** • **Hierarchy Framework** • **Column Framework** or directly via Transaction Code OOCOLFRAMCUST. In the IMG menu, multiple activities are listed, but all access the same customizing table, so you can simply choose the activity Define Your Own Column.

> **Note**
>
> The column group customizing activities are client independent. Any changes you make will affect all SAP clients in your system, so take care when adjusting these entries.

9.3.2 Adjusting the Columns Displayed

Columns are first defined individually, before being assigned to a group. SAP provides several hundred predefined columns that you can use to display object information in either the selection or overview areas. The customizing view for the column definition is shown in Figure 9.11. The entry defines the column heading, the alignment of the data (left, center, right, or justified) in the column, whether an icon is displayed in the column along with the data, the field length, and any data conversion needed to display the data properly.

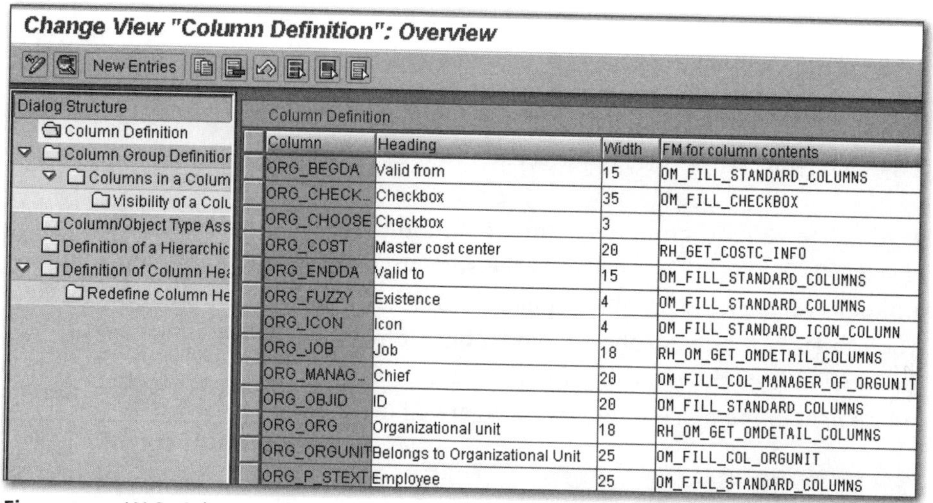

Change View "Column Definition": Overview

Column	Heading	Width	FM for column contents
ORG_BEGDA	Valid from	15	OM_FILL_STANDARD_COLUMNS
ORG_CHECK...	Checkbox	35	OM_FILL_CHECKBOX
ORG_CHOOSE	Checkbox	3	
ORG_COST	Master cost center	20	RH_GET_COSTC_INFO
ORG_ENDDA	Valid to	15	OM_FILL_STANDARD_COLUMNS
ORG_FUZZY	Existence	4	OM_FILL_STANDARD_COLUMNS
ORG_ICON	Icon	4	OM_FILL_STANDARD_ICON_COLUMN
ORG_JOB	Job	18	RH_OM_GET_OMDETAIL_COLUMNS
ORG_MANAG...	Chief	20	OM_FILL_COL_MANAGER_OF_ORGUNIT
ORG_OBJID	ID	20	OM_FILL_STANDARD_COLUMNS
ORG_ORG	Organizational unit	18	RH_OM_GET_OMDETAIL_COLUMNS
ORG_ORGUNIT	Belongs to Organizational Unit	25	OM_FILL_COL_ORGUNIT
ORG_P_STEXT	Employee	25	OM_FILL_STANDARD_COLUMNS

Dialog Structure:
- Column Definition
- Column Group Definition
  - Columns in a Colu
    - Visibility of a Colu
  - Column/Object Type Ass
- Definition of a Hierarchic
- Definition of Column Hea
  - Redefine Column He

Figure 9.11 IMG: Column Definition

Column content is determined not by the direct selection of infotypes and fields, but rather by the use of a function module. Meant to be reused throughout the SAP system, function modules are procedures that are defined in special ABAP programs. Function modules in this context define the technical infotype fields that can be displayed throughout the OM interfaces and transactions. To understand more about how the delivered function modules work, you can enlist the help of a technical ABAP resource that can view the source code via the Function Builder (Transaction Code SE37). Programmers can also create new code or copy code from existing function modules to create your own column display definitions.

Once columns are defined individually, they must be grouped together to be assigned to a transaction. The column group is defined by a 15-character code and description, as shown in Figure 9.12.

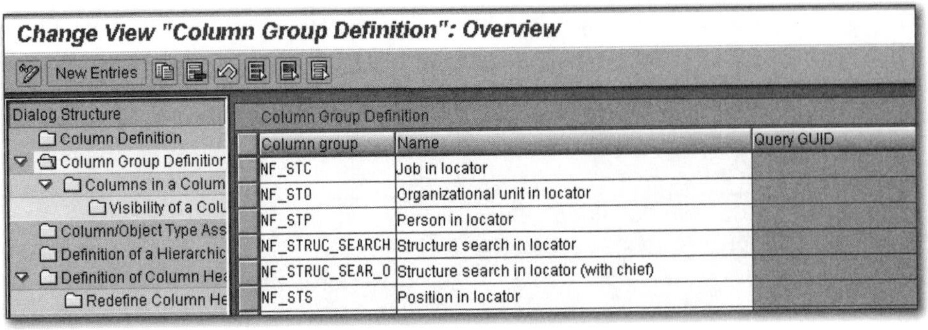

Figure 9.12 IMG: Column Group Definition

Within the column group, you then define the individual columns that can be displayed (Figure 9.13), as well as the sort order (left to right) for the columns. Columns can be fixed, meaning the user cannot remove the field from the display. You can also identify a coherence relationship between fields, which means you can only hide or show those columns as a unified block. In the case of coherence, if one field in the block is displayed, so are all other fields in the block.

Example

Object effective starting and ending dates are typically grouped, because users generally prefer to see both the beginning and ending effective dates of an object versus just one date.

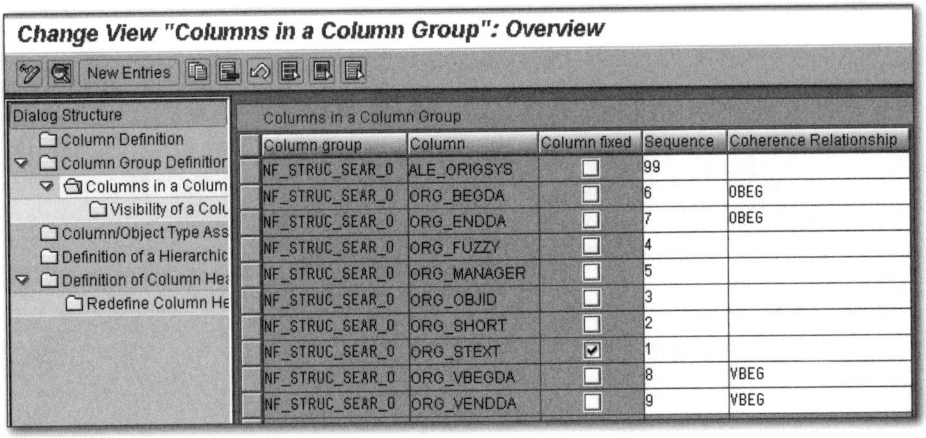

Figure 9.13 IMG: Columns in the Column Group

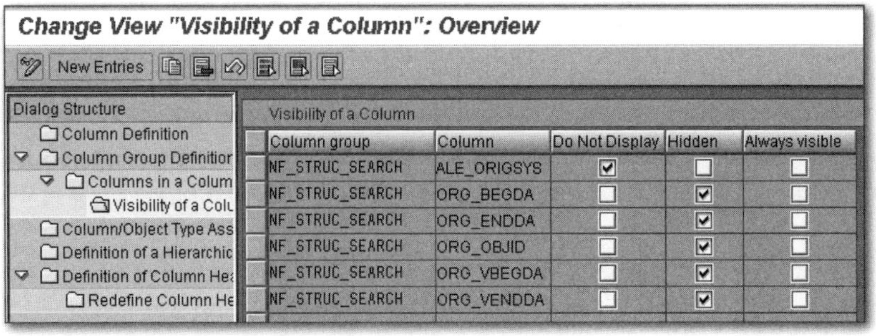

Figure 9.14 IMG: Visibility of a Column

You can also specify additional behavior for the columns in the Visibility of a Column view (Figure 9.14). You can choose to include the contents of a column in a group but not allow the user to display the field contents at all. Selecting the option Hidden hides the column when the user initially displays the column group, but allows the user to select the column for display manually using the column configuration icon. Alternatively, you can set a field to always be visible, in which case the user cannot remove the column from view.

9.3.3 Object Assignment to Columns

Typically, the function module that determines the contents of a particular column is designed to use a particular object type. Some function modules can be used with multiple object types, however. For these functions, you must associate the column with a specific object type.

The object-to-column configuration is shown in Figure 9.15. For example, the columns ORG_JOB and ORG_ORG use the same function module to call the column contents: RH_OM_GET_OMDETAIL_COLUMNS. The program is generic, so specifying the object type here fills the column with the right object type details.

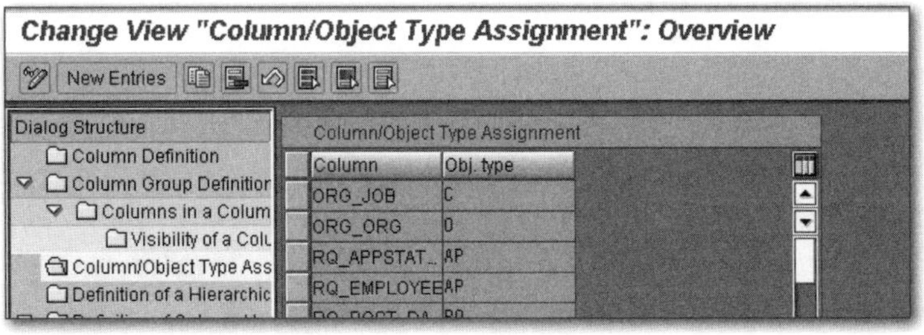

Figure 9.15 IMG: Column/Object Type Assignment

9.3.4 Creating Hierarchical Column Groups

With a typical column group definition, you list the individual columns that can be displayed. In some cases, you may want or need to create a column group that is a combination of the multiple column groups. Hierarchical column groups allow you to perform this combination. An example of this use is the hierarchical view for organizational units.

In a hierarchical column group definition, the system performs a recursive check of each column group and uses them sequentially. The column group that is the key field in the table is read first, and all columns belonging to that column group are displayed. The next assigned column group is then read, and any additional columns are displayed. This process is repeated for the final column group. The hierarchical column configuration is shown in Figure 9.16 for column group NF_GEN_OV_ORG.

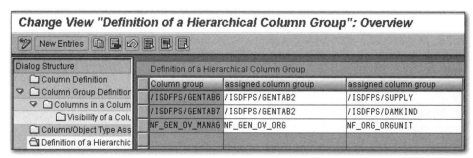

Figure 9.16 IMG: Define Hierarchical Column Group

This recursive behavior allows you to build additional columns when hierarchical data is displayed, so you can show some data that may be related among the levels of the hierarchy.

9.3.5 Assigning Columns in the Scenario

For the selection area, a specific table entry is used to determine which column group will be used to display the results of the search. The IMG activity is the last in the selection scenario configuration tables, shown in Figure 9.17. For each scenario, search node, and search tool, you specify the column group to use. For grid-based search tools, you can also specify whether to display icons in the column group and whether the user has a free choice of which columns to display in the results list.

Change View "Display Area (Column Group...)": Overview

New Entries

Dialog Structure
- Definition of Search Nod
- Definition of Search Tool
- Definition of Coherence I
- ▽ Scenario Definition (Obje
  - Search Nodes
- ▽ Search tool
  - Display Area (Col

Display Area (Column Group...)

Scenario	Search Node Key	Search tool	Column group	Head
OME000	0	CL_HR_LAST_USED_GOS...	OBJ_HIST	
OME000	0	CL_HR_OM_SEARCHTOOL...	NF_STO	
OME000	0	CL_HR_OM_SEAT_STRUC...	NF_STRUC_SEAR_0	
OME000	0	CL_HR_ST_ADHOC_SELE...	NF_STO	
OME000	OBJ_HIST	CL_HR_LAST_USED_GOS...		
OME000	0	CL_HR_LAST_USED_GOS	OBJ_HIST	

Figure 9.17 IMG: Assignment of Column Groups to Scenario

For the overview area, the use of column groups is more complicated. You do not directly assign the column groups to be used with specific object types in customizing. In the organization and staffing transactions, the use of views dictates that there may be a variety of column groups for a particular object type. Views were explained in Chapter 8, Section 8.3.2 (see Figure 8.22 for reference).

The IMG activities for view service definition are accessible via Transaction Code OOFRAMEWORKCUST. In the configuration activities for the view service attributes for a specific object type, you can specify the column group to be used in that view. This customizing table is shown in Figure 9.18.

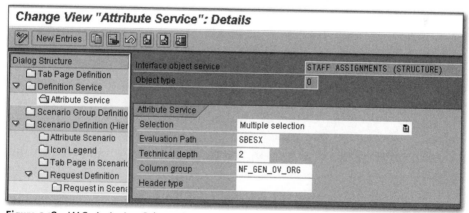

Change View "Attribute Service": Details

New Entries

Dialog Structure
- Tab Page Definition
- ▽ Definition Service
  - Attribute Service
- Scenario Group Definitio
- ▽ Scenario Definition (Hier
  - Attribute Scenario
  - Icon Legend
  - Tab Page in Scenari
- ▽ Request Definition
  - Request in Scen

Interface object service   STAFF ASSIGNMENTS (STRUCTURE)

Object type   0

Attribute Service

Selection	Multiple selection
Evaluation Path	SBESX
Technical depth	2
Column group	NF_GEN_OV_ORG
Header type	

Figure 9.18 IMG: Assigning Column Groups to View Services

9.3.6 Column Groups Summary

When configuring column groups to meet your needs, you have two choices in customizing approach. The first is to understand which column groups are being used in the transactions and views that you're using and to simply modify them. You can change the field attributes, reorder the field sort, and add or remove fields from the column groups. The second option is to create your own column groups and assign them to the search node or view configuration. In either case, the activities can be summarized in four steps:

1. Determine the column group used in the area of the transaction you are using. The column group determines the fields to be displayed.

2. Define the column, or select columns that are predelivered. Remember that function modules determine the contents of the column.

3. Assign the columns to the appropriate column group. Set the visibility controls to determine which fields are always visible and which may be controlled by the user.

4. Assign the column group to either the search node or the overview view. Keep in mind that these assignment activities are not in the same IMG folder as the column configuration activities.

> **Tip**
>
> When removing fields from the column groups that you don't want to use, the customizing activity is performed in reverse. Remove the customizing entries in the visibility tables before removing fields from the column group. Take care not to leave orphaned table entries. You do not have to (and should not) delete the customizing entries that define the column itself.

We've reviewed how to configure the search area and column layouts for the selection and overview areas. There is one final component of the hierarchy framework that can be customized. In the next section we'll examine how to adjust the detail area.

9.4 Infotype Tab Pages

When you have selected organizational plan data in the selection area, the data is displayed in both the overview and detail work areas. The detail area displays any infotype information that either currently exists for the object selected or provides data entry fields in which to input new information. The detail area presents infotype information to the user in the form of a tabbed interface. The tabs can represent a single infotype or can be a combination of infotypes.

In your use of the organization and staffing interface, you may want to remove infotype tabs that you don't use or add tabs for existing infotypes or new infotypes that you have created. Customizing these options is possible via the IMG customizing activities.

9.4.1 Determining Which Tab Pages Are in Use

Similar to the search scenario and column group definitions, there are user parameters that can help you determine which tab pages are being used in your transactions. In the case of tab pages, two user parameters are required. User parameter OM_TABTYPE_DISPLAY is used to display the technical name of the tab page. This technical name is displayed in all caps next to the tab page description. User parameter OM_FRAM_SCEN_DISPLAY is used to display an overall scenario that is defined for the entire transaction. Figure 9.19 highlights both these elements, which together control the tabs that are available to the user.

With the scenario and tab page names identified, you can access the customizing activities via the IMG path **Personnel Management · Organizational Management · Hierarchy Framework · Integrate New Infotype** or directly via Transaction Code OOFRAMEWORKCUST. In the IMG menu, multiple activities are listed, but you can access all customizing tables via the activity Add Infotype as Tab Page in Detail Area.

> **Note**
>
> The tab page and scenario customizing activities are client independent. Any changes you make will affect all SAP clients in your system, so take care when adjusting these entries.

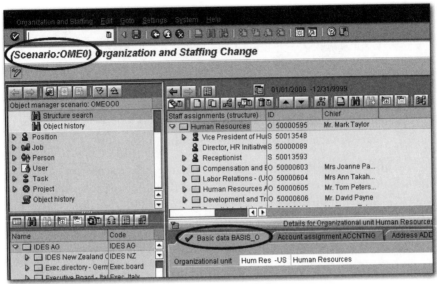

Figure 9.19 Overall Scenario and Tab Page ID Identified

9.4.2 Defining Tab Pages

Tab pages are defined by an up–to-eight-character code (Figure 9.20). Tab pages can represent a single infotype, in which case the tab page definition specifies the infotype number and is marked as infotype specific. Tab pages can also be made up of multiple infotype views, such as the Basic Data tab page. Tab pages that are not infotype specific are defined further with additional customizing.

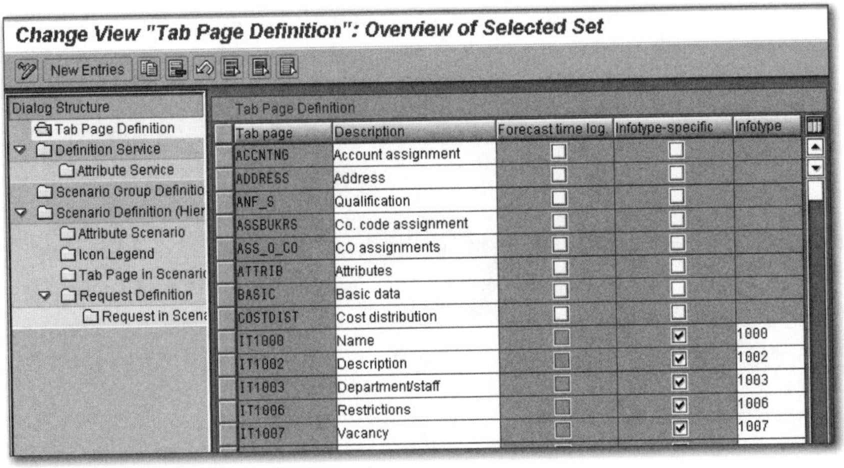

Figure 9.20 IMG: Tab Page Defnition View

9.4.3 Assigning Tab Pages

To control tabs, we need to know the hierarchy framework scenario used in the overall user interface. The scenario is used to set a variety of attributes. The scenario includes the Object Manager scenario, as reviewed in Section 9.2.1, and the overview area views that are available for each object type. In addition, the scenario configuration includes assignment of the tab pages to the various object types.

In the customizing view shown in Figure 9.21, the scenario used is the OM standard OME0. The scenario and object type are combined with the tab page definition to form the table key. For all tab pages assigned to the object in the scenario, you can indicate the left-to-right order in which the tab pages are presented by sequencing the entries from 1 to 99. For tab pages that are not infotype specific, the customizing entry must contain a report name. The report name is the ABAP program that defines what the tab page will contain in both content and layout.

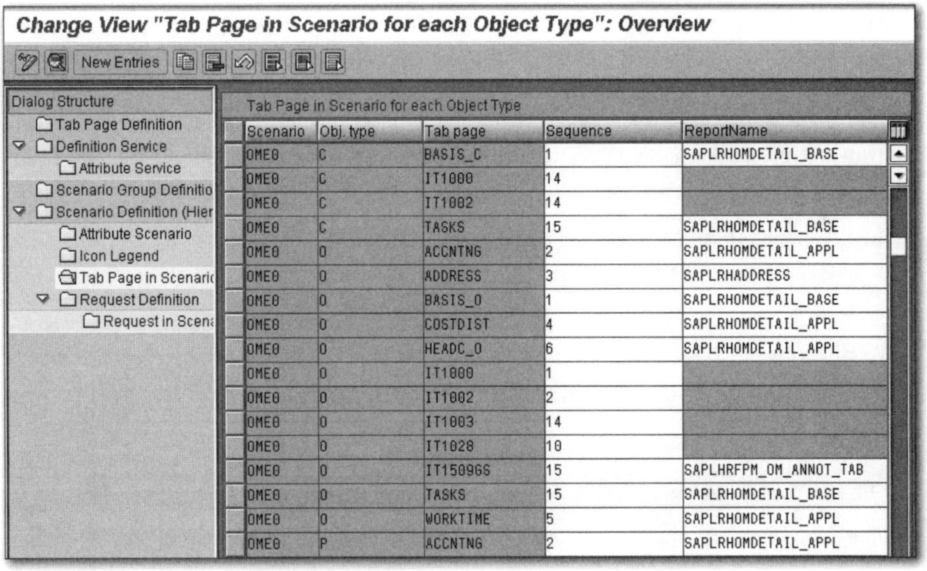

Change View "Tab Page in Scenario for each Object Type": Overview

New Entries

Dialog Structure
- Tab Page Definition
- ▽ Definition Service
  - Attribute Service
  - Scenario Group Definitio
- ▽ Scenario Definition (Hier
  - Attribute Scenario
  - Icon Legend
  - Tab Page in Scenari
- ▽ Request Definition
  - Request in Scen

Tab Page in Scenario for each Object Type

Scenario	Obj. type	Tab page	Sequence	ReportName
OME0	C	BASIS_C	1	SAPLRHOMDETAIL_BASE
OME0	C	IT1000	14	
OME0	C	IT1002	14	
OME0	C	TASKS	15	SAPLRHOMDETAIL_BASE
OME0	O	ACCNTNG	2	SAPLRHOMDETAIL_APPL
OME0	O	ADDRESS	3	SAPLRHADDRESS
OME0	O	BASIS_O	1	SAPLRHOMDETAIL_BASE
OME0	O	COSTDIST	4	SAPLRHOMDETAIL_APPL
OME0	O	HEADC_O	6	SAPLRHOMDETAIL_APPL
OME0	O	IT1000	1	
OME0	O	IT1002	2	
OME0	O	IT1003	14	
OME0	O	IT1028	10	
OME0	O	IT1509GS	15	SAPLHRFPM_OM_ANNOT_TAB
OME0	O	TASKS	15	SAPLRHOMDETAIL_BASE
OME0	O	WORKTIME	5	SAPLRHOMDETAIL_APPL
OME0	P	ACCNTNG	2	SAPLRHOMDETAIL_APPL

Figure 9.21 IMG: Tab Page in Scenario Definition

For custom infotypes, you can either create your own program or examine the delivered programs to determine if one is able to read, display, and process your new infotype data. The programs SAPLRHOMDETAIL_APPL and SAPLRHOMDETAIL_BASE are used in multiple tab pages, because the program routines are general enough to apply to multiple infotype structures. You can examine the program code via Transaction SE38.

With the tab page in scenario configuration, you can control a variety of options for the tabs that are presented for each object in the organization and staffing interface. You can change the order of the tabs by simply changing the sequence of the tab page order. You can remove tabs altogether by removing the tab page entry for the object type or for all object types. If you create your own infotypes, you can insert them easily into the tab order by creating an entry in the customizing table.

9.4.4   Tab Pages Summary

When configuring the choice and layout of standard or custom tab pages, there are few customizing activities. By understanding which tab pages are used in the transaction scenario, you can modify the customizing entries to rearrange or remove tab pages that you may not be using, or add pages that you want to have maintained for the objects in your organizational plan. The customizing activities can be summarized in three steps:

1. Determine the tab page name and scenario used in the organization and staffing transaction you are using. The scenario and tab page work together to determine the infotypes to use.

2. Define the tab page, or select tab pages that are predefined. Remember that ABAP programs determine the contents of tab pages that are not specific to one infotype.

3. Assign the tab pages to the appropriate scenario and object type. Set the order in which tabs are displayed left-to-right by sequencing the entries from 1 to 99.

> **Tip**
>
> When removing tab pages that you don't want to use from the scenario, the only customizing activity necessary is to remove the customizing entries in the tab page in the scenario table. You do not have to (and should not) delete the customizing entries that define the tab page, nor do you need to change any other customizing setting for the scenario.

So far, we have discussed how to customize the various parts of the organization and staffing transaction: the search area, selection area, overview area, and detail area. Before concluding this chapter, it will be useful to provide a bit more context around the general interface scenario definition, which was touched upon in the tab page definition.

9.5 Transaction Scenarios

The interface scenario, also called the hierarchy framework scenario, defines and brings together all of the customizing elements: the object manager scenario, column layouts, and tab page definitions. The SAP system provides multiple hierarchy framework scenarios (Figure 9.22), which are used in different transactions throughout the system.

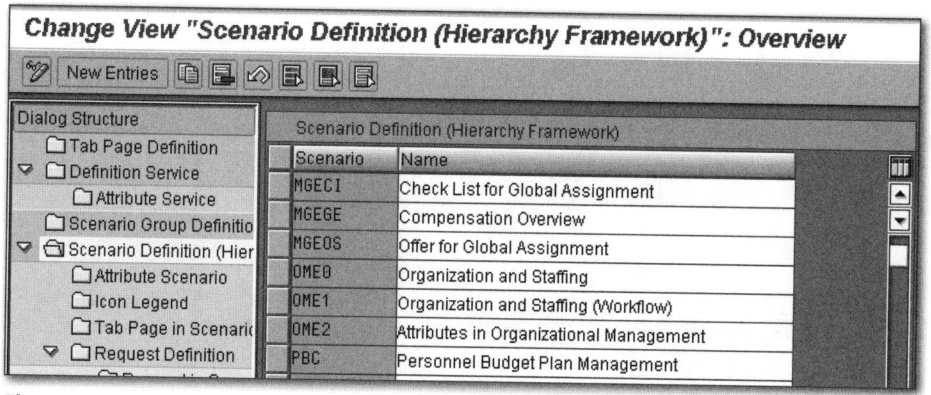

Change View "Scenario Definition (Hierarchy Framework)": Overview

Dialog Structure	Scenario Definition (Hierarchy Framework)

Scenario	Name
MGECI	Check List for Global Assignment
MGEGE	Compensation Overview
MGEOS	Offer for Global Assignment
OME0	Organization and Staffing
OME1	Organization and Staffing (Workflow)
OME2	Attributes in Organizational Management
PBC	Personnel Budget Plan Management

Dialog Structure:
- Tab Page Definition
- Definition Service
  - Attribute Service
  - Scenario Group Definitio
- Scenario Definition (Hier
  - Attribute Scenario
  - Icon Legend
  - Tab Page in Scenari
- Request Definition

Figure 9.22 IMG: Scenario Definition (Hierarchy Framework)

Scenario OME0 is the standard scenario used in the organization and staffing interface. The scenario is defined by an up–to-eight-character code and description, as shown in Figure 9.23. The scenario attributes are shown in Figure 9.23. Although we won't explain what all the attributes are, four are of particular interest, and are important to understand. In the attribute configuration, you specify which Object Manager scenario will be used to form the search area. Transaction codes are also specified that will use the scenario to display, change, or create data. These settings are particularly important if you want to utilize a different user interface for the various users of your organizational plan data. Rather than creating transactions that will use different scenarios, you create this assignment in the reverse. One scenario definition contains multiple transaction codes. Therefore, to provide different interface layouts, you must create different hierarchy framework scenarios.

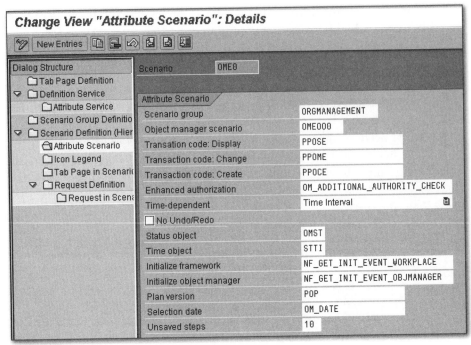

Figure 9.23 IMG: Scenario Definition Attributes

Tip

Creating multiple hierarchy framework scenarios is the one mechanism by which you can create a custom user interface without developing your own ABAP code for the interface itself.

You can copy and create different object manager scenarios to limit the objects a user can search for and display, including limiting how they can search for data. You can utilize different column groups and layouts to determine what data a user is presented in both the search and overview areas. You can reassign and reorder the tab pages that present and maintain data in the detail area. Lastly, you can combine all these custom elements in a scenario that is then tied to a specific transaction code.

Providing users with separate transaction codes for each hierarchy framework scenario in essence provides them with a custom transaction that you have controlled entirely thorough configuration.

9.6   Conclusion

In this chapter we've reviewed the customizing options that are available to alter the organization and staffing maintenance interface. Changing the search options, the display of search results and overview data, and the options and order of the tab pages are all possible through customizing. These options can enable you to give your users a customized user interface without having to create custom programs, which can help increase user adoption and ease maintenance of the organizational plan data. Now you have an understanding of how the organizational and staffing interface can be customized. The next chapter discusses some of the technical tools and utilities available to help prepare your system for data maintenance.

A variety of technical utilities and tools in OM are helpful to master. Whether you're a member of the SAP technical team or a business process owner, these programs cannot only ease the implementation process for you, but are very helpful in ongoing maintenance and enhancement of the OM system.

10 Technical Tips and Tools

In addition to the user interface procedures such as simple maintenance and organizational reporting, users of the OM system will find it helpful to understand and use a number of technical tools and utilities available to help set up, maintain, and manage the organizational plan. SAP ERP HCM users can apply these tools throughout the lifespan of their SAP systems.

The tools are appropriate for use in initial implementation, where the organizational plan may need to go through several iterations of design and development before the final structure is decided upon. On an ongoing basis, the functions are useful in creating and managing organizational plan data for testing enhancements or adjustments to the system. The tools can speed the process by which data is created in one or more HR systems, allowing you to rapidly prototype and test functional and technical design and data changes.

Let's look first at tools that prepare your SAP system when you're beginning to create the organizational plan in OM.

10.1 Setting the Stage for Data Maintenance

The organizational plan data is maintained on a client-dependent basis. There can be multiple clients in one SAP system, each with its own set of master records and tables. When you log in to the SAP system, you choose a client instance in which to log in. The client is defined by a three-character code (i.e., 100) that you specify when you log in.

When you first install your SAP system, SAP predelivers some data in the various OM functions. This data is referred to as the "model company," and can be used for testing and training purposes. SAP also provides an international demo system called IDES that can be installed in a separate system. The IDES system contains even more data for process demonstration and testing out of the box. In some functions, it would be quite tedious to set up every aspect of the application master data to see how the functionality works. Having this out-of-the-box data is handy for getting things working fast.

When preparing to create your own organizational plan, this data may not be particularly useful to keep around. Although having sample jobs is interesting, the data may not represent the job functions that your company uses. To start with a clean slate when setting up your own organizational plan, you should delete the initial data. Similarly, as you are creating your own organizational plan, you can go through several iterations of designing the hierarchy format. In between iterations, you may want to clean out any test organizational plan data and start from scratch. To make this process easy, SAP provides some useful utilities to remove data from the OM functions.

10.1.1 Cleaning Out the SAP Datasets

Before defining the company organization structure, you should delete the organizational model examples delivered by SAP from the system. This process can be completed for each object individually: job, organizational unit, position, and so on. You can also delete multiple objects at the same time by using an evaluation path to select related objects to delete.

SAP delivers the program Delete Data Records from Personnel Planning Database. This program's technical name is RHRHDL00, and can be used to delete OM data from the system. This program can be used to clean out organizational management, personnel development, training and events, and any other OM data that may exist in your system.

Selection criteria are quite flexible in this program, allowing for selection of specific objects, infotypes, and subtypes in varying statuses. With the various selection parameters, you can select and delete data according to the following criteria:

▶ Plan version
▶ Object type

► Object ID (single or multiple values can be entered)

► Search term (all matching entries can be deleted)

► Object status

► Effective date (multiple reporting period methods are available)

► Structure parameters as found via the use of an evaluation path

► Infotype and subtype

The program is accessed via Transaction RE_RHRHDL00 or via the menu path **Organizational Management • Tools • Database**. The program selection screen is shown in Figure 10.1.

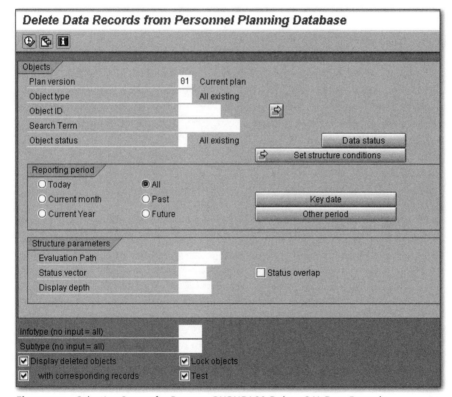

Figure 10.1 Selection Screen for Program RHRHDL00 Delete OM Data Records

Additionally, the program selection allows you to display all the objects and their corresponding records. You can choose to lock the records for maintenance while the program is running to avoid people trying to maintain the records you are trying to delete. Lastly, a test run parameter shows you what records would be deleted if you ran the program, but it does not actually delete the information.

When run, the system confirms your deletions as shown in Figure 10.2. This process can be run for individual objects, for all objects of a particular object type, or for all objects in the organizational plan. If you specify an evaluation path as part of the structure selection criteria, the process will select all objects along the evaluation path for deletion.

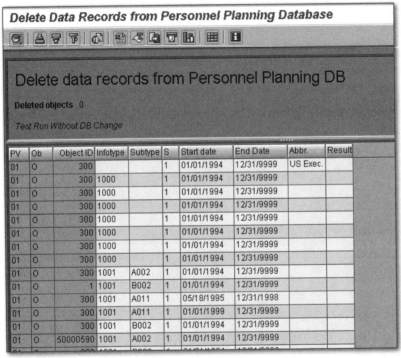

Figure 10.2 Program RHRHDL00 Results in Test Mode

When deleting master data in the organizational plan, you may need to run the deletion program multiple times using different evaluation paths and selecting certain object types. For example, you can delete organizational units and positions only via evaluation path O-O-S, leaving jobs intact in the initial run. Jobs can then be deleted in a separate program run if needed.

> **Tip**
>
> If you delete all organizational plan objects, it may also be useful to reset the number range settings associated with the plan. Refer to Section 3.9 for information on number ranges.

The RHRHDL00 program deletes all infotype records associated with an object. If you require more specific deletion processing, you can also use program RHRHDC00 Delete Individual Personnel Planning Records. This program can be used to delete specific infotype records for objects, but cannot be used to delete the object itself. Selection criteria for this program are slightly limited: You can specify the object type, status, reporting period, and evaluation path. The specific infotype and subtype can then be selected for deletion. Unlike the first program, however, this program does not provide a test option. Once it is run, the records are immediately deleted from the system, so care should be taken when using this program.

As a cautionary word regarding deletion, it's important to make a distinction between deletion of master data and deletion of configuration settings.

Deleting Datasets versus Configuration

As mentioned in the outset of this chapter, SAP provides much sample data that youwon't find useful in your implementation. Deletion of this master data is expected, which is why the PD dataset deletion tools are provided. Similarly, many configuration settings are provided that you will also not use in your implementation. Object types, infotypes, subtypes, and relationship configuration are just a few of the areas where delivered configuration may not meet your business needs.

> **Tip**
>
> Although the temptation to delete this delivered configuration is hard to resist, it is extremely important that you remember and heed this one message regarding deletions: **do not** under any circumstances delete this configuration information from your SAP system.

Many a customer implementation has been sabotaged by meaningful yet misguided deletion of such configuration elements. Once you have deleted the primary configuration of object types or relationships, you can find yourself in customizing tables where this information is a dependent entry. The lack of the dependent object or infotype definition will cause system errors that will render the table virtually uncustomizable until you restore the dependent information. Similarly, if you have removed the defining ABAP programs and screens for infotypes, and find that you want to use them at a later time, they will be unavailable. It's a painstaking process to either recreate this information yourself or to try to copy it from some reference system where it still exists.

Do yourself a huge favor and simply do not delete any of these core configurations in the system. It's far easier to restrict user access to the information via authorizations and other customizing, such as allowed relationships per object type, than to try to remove it from the system completely. More information on authorizations is provided later in this chapter. Let's now discuss some other tools that can further help you set up the OM system.

10.2   OM Configuration Setup Consistency Check

When implementing OM, there are dozens of configuration tables that can be maintained. Creating or adjusting objects, relationships, infotype subtypes, actions, time constraints, and other field values can all be part of the configuration tasks performed. Because there's a high degree of dependency among OM tables, the system provides a configuration consistency check program, RHCHECK0. The program is accessible one of two ways: via Transaction Code OOCH or in the IMG path **Personnel Management** • **Organizational Management** • **Basic Settings** • **Data Model Enhancement** • **Check consistency of installation**.

When run, the installation check performs some basic table checks and reports back on configuration inconsistencies it finds regarding infotypes, subtypes, relationships, time constraints, or integration settings. The system checks that data is present in all tables where appropriate. If data is not found where the system expects an entry, the information is flagged and presented to the user in a summary report, as shown in Figure 10.3. From the report summary, the user can select an error category and see the details of the errors in the lower portion of the report display. The installation check results may or may not require correction, depending on your interpretation of the results.

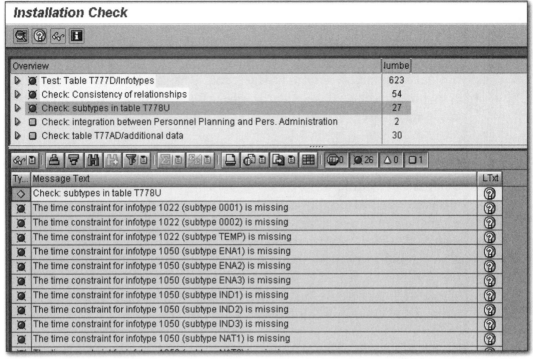

Figure 10.3 Program RHCHECK0 Installation Check Results

Example

Let's say you have created a new object type and after saving the entry, determined that it's no longer required. The program identifies this as inconsistent data. You are not mandated to remove the partial configuration from the system. The report output is simply an indication of where problems may exist should you require the use of the configuration elements outlined in the report summary. In general, it's good practice to know where partial configuration exists in the system so that you can either prevent its use in production, or remove or complete the partial configuration settings.

This tool is primarily concerned with the consistency of the organizational plan configuration on its own, and not with anything related to how you may actually use the data. SAP also provides tools that look at the organizational plan data used in the PA integration scenario. These tools are explained next.

10.3 OM–PA Integration Tools

When you think about crafting the organizational plan and setting up your employee master, multiple strategies are available for creating this data. You can create the organizational plan manually, and simply assign employees to the relevant positions one by one. Alternatively, you can create the organizational plan and load employees together through a data conversion process.

10.3.1 Creating OM Master Data from PA

One strategy that can be used for creating master data is to use the personnel master data as the basis for creating some or all of the organizational plan. In this scenario the employee master does not necessarily rely on the organizational plan for data. Personnel records are loaded into the PA component with the various OM data objects directly attached to the personnel record. Organizational units, jobs, and positions can be loaded into PA without a relationship to any OM object, and that data can then be used to either create the OM data entirely, or to create the relationships among existing OM data.

SAP provides program RHINTE00 Transfer Data from Personnel Administration to copy the objects and relationships that have been set up in PA to OM. The program can be found via Transaction Code RE_RHINTE00 and in the IMG path **Personnel Management · Organizational Management · Integration · Integration with Personnel Administration · Transfer Data from Personnel Administration**.

> **Example**
>
> In the most extreme case, you can create all OM data from PA. With OM-PA integration turned off, you create an employee master in PA, including Infotype 0001 Organizational Assignment. In the Organizational Assignment infotype, you have loaded an employee with value 389012 in the cost center, 30277190 in the position, 21200534 in the job, and 10000300 in the organizational unit.
>
> You then turn OM-PA integration on. When program RHINTE00 is run, the system creates an object for each of the organizational plan elements: organizational unit, job, and position. The program also creates the relationship A 011 (cost center assignment) between organizational unit 10000300 and cost center 389012, relationship A/B 002 (reports to / belongs to) between organizational unit 10000300 and position 30277190, relationship A/B 003 (defines / is defined by) between job 21200534 and position 30277190, and relationship A/B 008 (holder) between position 30277190 and the employee.

The selection parameters associated with the program are quite diverse and provide many options for creating data. As with many SAP ERP HCM reports, the program includes some general selection criteria that allow you to select certain PA records for processing; only those records are read to determine which OM data to create. The selection parameters determine how much data is created and how data is created by the program. The lower portion of the selection screen is shown in Figure 10.4.

You can use the program to create the entire organizational plan, but the plan objects require updating to provide other infotype information. In practice, many customers use the program to create only the relationships between the employees in the enterprise. The organizational plan objects are created in OM, and integration is turned off so that the employees' records can be loaded with the position, job, and organizational unit. Following the employee data load, the program is run in test mode to identify any employees who are assigned a position that does not exist in OM or employees who are assigned no position. The employee data is corrected, integration between OM and PA is turned on, and the program is run again to create the holder relationship only. The result is a batch input session that will create the relevant position-to-holder assignment and a complete organizational structure.

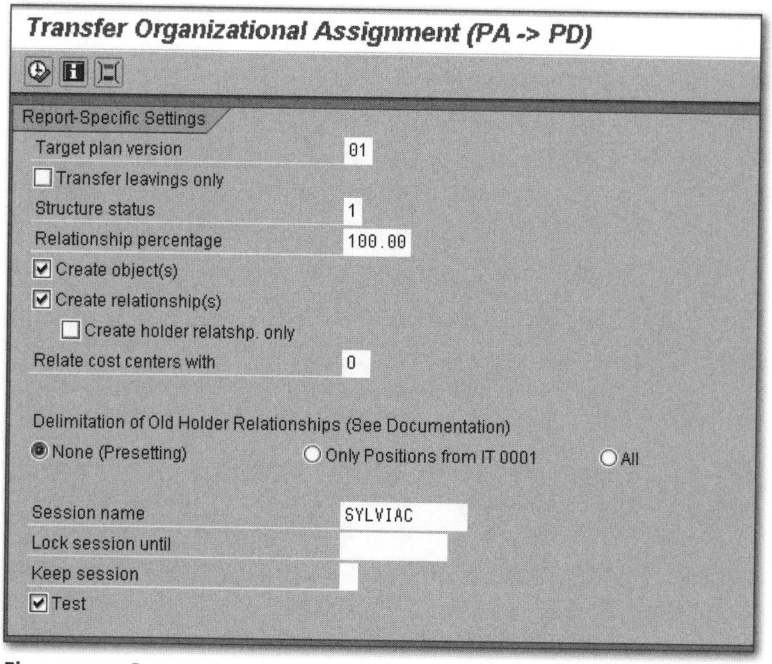

Figure 10.4 Program RHINTE00 Transfer OM Data From PA Selection Screen

Table 10.1 provides a detailed explanation of each of the selection parameter functions. You can use all or some of the functions depending on your requirements for creating data in OM.

Parameter	Use Explanation
Target plan version	Sets the plan version for objects being created. You can set any plan version, but only one at a time for each program run.
Transfer leavings only	Used when you want to process personnel separations only (e.g., terminations). The system determines the position holder and creates a vacancy record for the vacated position.
Structure status	Sets the object status in OM. The default status is Active.
Relationship percentage	Provides the default percentage for person-to-position holder relationships.
Create object	Check when you want the system to create OM object records for the objects included. Objects that can be created are organizational unit, job, position, and work center.
Create relationship	Check when you want the system to create OM relationship records between the objects included. Possible relationships include: ▸ C to S: job describes position (A 007) ▸ O to S: organizational unit includes position (B 003) ▸ O to K: cost center assignment (A 011) ▸ S to K: cost center assignment (A 011) ▸ S to P: person is holder of position (B 008) ▸ A to P: person is holder of work center (B 008)
Create holder relationship only	Check when the only relationship you want created is S to P: person is holder of position (B 008) or A to P: person is holder of work center (B 008)
Relate cost centers with	Indicates the object type to which you want to relate the cost center. You can only choose one object type for a single program run. The organizational unit (O) is the default object type.

Table 10.1 Program RHINTE00 Selection Parameters

Parameter	Use Explanation
Delimitation of old holder relationship	Controls the system reaction when a position is already held by a person and another record is due to be created. There are three options: ▶ **None:** Do not delimit any existing holder relationships. If multiple holders are identified, all records will be created at the percentage identified, which could result in positions being occupied at more than 100%. ▶ **Only positions from Infotype 0001:** Only delimit positions from which the holder originates in PA Infotype 0001 Organizational Assignment. ▶ **All:** Delimit any position holder records in conflict. This includes any position assignment that may originate from Infotype 0001 or from anywhere else, such as workflow users assigned to positions.
Session name	Name of the batch input session to create. This session holds the data to be created in OM for later processing.
Lock session until	Date up to which the batch input session will be kept for processing.
Keep session	Set to "X" to keep the batch input session after it is processed; you have to delete it manually. If not set, the session is deleted immediately after it is processed.
Test	Test flag. When checked, the system only simulates the program output, but does not create data or a batch input session. This provides a "what if" view on the data to be created.

Table 10.1 Program RHINTE00 Selection Parameters (cont.)

When the program is run, the system can either create OM data records directly, or you can use batch input to process the resulting data at a later time. If you enter the batch input session parameter, a session is created that must subsequently be processed. A batch input session is a system-generated recording that enters data noninteractively in the system. Batch input basically simulates user input for transactional screens via an ABAP program. If you don't specify a batch input session, the program will process the data in real time.

> **Tip**
>
> Whether or not you have a large volume of data, always use batch input. Online processing can utilize system resources heavily. Batch input allows you the option of processing the data after regular business hours, when system use is at its lowest and more system resources are available.

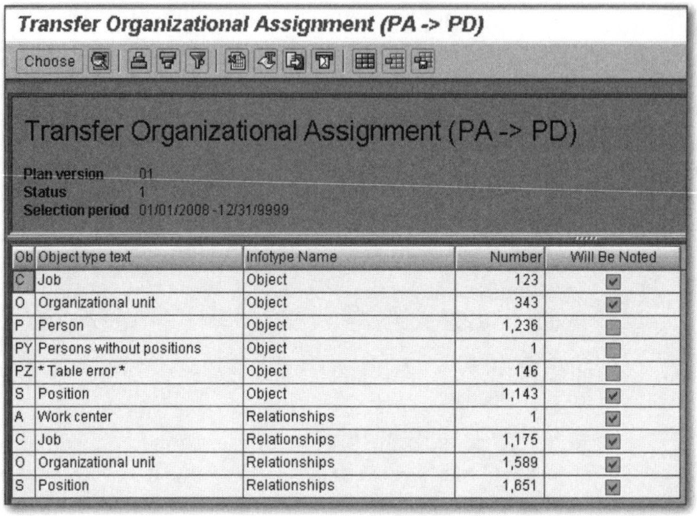

Transfer Organizational Assignment (PA -> PD)

Choose

Transfer Organizational Assignment (PA -> PD)

Plan version   01
Status   1
Selection period   01/01/2008 - 12/31/9999

Ob	Object type text	Infotype Name	Number	Will Be Noted
C	Job	Object	123	☑
O	Organizational unit	Object	343	☑
P	Person	Object	1,236	☐
PY	Persons without positions	Object	1	☐
PZ	* Table error *	Object	146	☐
S	Position	Object	1,143	☑
A	Work center	Relationships	1	☑
C	Job	Relationships	1,175	☑
O	Organizational unit	Relationships	1,589	☑
S	Position	Relationships	1,651	☑

Figure 10.5   Program RHINTE00 Transfer Organizational Assignment Output

Figure 10.5 shows a sample output screen from the program run in test mode. In this output, you can see that both objects and relationships can be created in the process. Persons without positions (PY) and table errors (PZ) are also identified. Using the program test mode is an excellent mechanism for locating and correcting errors in the organizational assignment infotype as you're planning and testing employee data conversions. In addition to the summary information, you can drill-down on any item from the summary to see the object details. Figure 10.6 provides an example of the job detail from the sample run provided in Figure 10.5. Here, 123 jobs have been defined in PA that are not present in OM, so objects can be created. Similar information is presented for all object and relationship data.

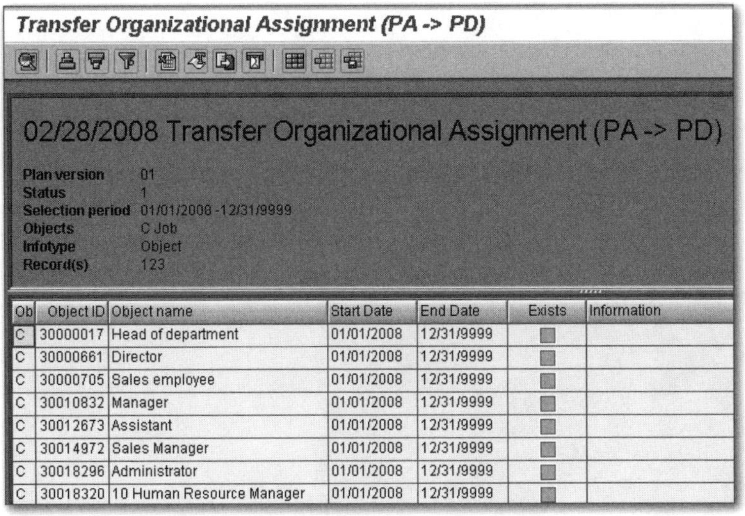

Figure 10.6 Program RHINTE00 Object Type Detail View

In addition to program RHINTE00 to create data from PA, there are programs that will allow you to ensure that OM and PA data are consistent with one another. Used in conjunction with program RHINTE00 or on their own, the programs can help ensure that your organizational plan data is reflected properly in personnel administration. These programs are described in the next section.

10.3.2 Preparing PA Check Tables

When using OM with active integration to PA, specific SAP ERP HCM tables are maintained when organizational units, jobs, and positions are created in OM. The table names vary by object type:

- **Jobs:** Tables T513 and T513S

- **Organizational units:** Table T527X

- **Positions:** Tables T528B and T528T

- **Work centers:** Tables T528B and T528T

Jobs, positions, and work centers have separate tables for the object ID and the text descriptions of the tables; organizational units have only one table. Usually, each time one of these object types is created in OM, the corresponding entry is created in the above-mentioned PA table. Sometimes, however, the tables can become out of sync.

Example

If you have implemented PA before implementing OM, you can create the PA table entries directly using either the PA IMG activities or the general table maintenance interface (Transaction Code SM30), in which case the corresponding OM object is not present. Similarly, if OM data is converted into SAP by a custom program, the PA tables may not have been updated in the process. In either case, the tables become out of sync.

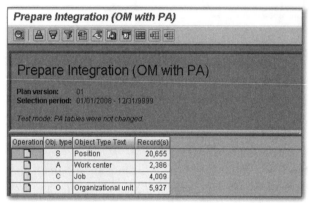

Figure 10.7 Program RHINTE10 Prepare Integration Sample Output

Whatever the reason for the tables being out of sync, SAP provides a utility to check the consistency of these tables and remedy the inconsistency. The program RHINTE10 Prepare Integration with Personnel Administration (Figure 10.7) is provided to transfer any objects and relationships that have been set up in OM to the relevant PA tables. The program can be found via Transaction Code OOHP and in the IMG path **Personnel Management • Organizational Management • Integration • Integration with Personnel Administration • Prepare Integration with Personnel Administration**.

An example of the program run in test mode is shown in Figure 10.7. Selection criteria for the program are very similar to most other OM reports. You can select object data by object type, object ID, or validity period. You can specify an evaluation path to select multiple object types, or you can leave all of these parameters blank to select any relevant data that may be out of sync. An object status parameter is also provided, but only objects in active status are written to the PA tables. The program also includes a test parameter so that you can simulate the program run and simply list the data out of sync.

In addition to the RHINTE10 program, SAP also provides a utility to examine data from the employee master to determine whether tables are inconsistent, which is explained next.

10.3.3 OM-PA Data Consistency Check

The program RHINTE20 Check Integration Consistency is provided to determine whether data for the OM objects relevant to integration with PA are available in both components. Sample program output is shown in Figure 10.8. The program can be found via Transaction Code OOPP and in the IMG path **Personnel Management • Organizational Management • Integration • Integration with Personnel Administration • Check Integration Consistency**.

The program output lists objects that are either present in the PA tables yet don't have a matching OM object, or are present in OM yet don't have a corresponding entry in the relevant PA tables. Unlike the program RHINTE10 report output, the missing entries can be created directly from the program RHINTE20 output display. A checkbox is present next to each entry so that objects can be selected and created using the Create object icon on the screen. This allows for a great deal of control when processing data, because you can choose the objects to create, or leave as-is those objects you don't want to create.

Keeping the PA and OM tables in sync ensures that the OM organizational plan data is reflected properly in PA. There are other processes that may allow data between OM and PA to become out of sync, for which additional utilities are provided.

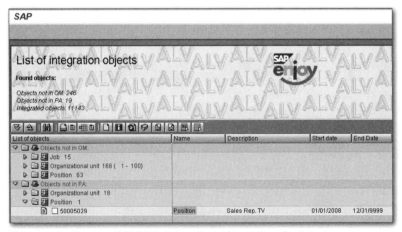

Figure 10.8 Program RHINTE20 Integration Objects Sample Output

10.3.4 Keeping PA Organizational Assignments in Check

The organizational plan transactions in OM allow you to edit and maintain not only the organizational plan object but also the persons in the organizational plan. As described back in Section 5.3.7, persons can be holders of positions and assigned from either the Organizational Assignment Infotype 0001 from PA, or can be assigned directly from the organizational plan maintenance views. There are three ways you can update PA master data when OM changes affecting persons are carried out. You can change master data directly, by batch input, or either directly or by batch input depending on the number of persons affected.

When changes are made online within OM, you can have the system compile a list of the personnel numbers affected by the changes, rather than allowing corresponding changes to be made immediately within PA. The system automatically checks whether the OM changes have any affect on PA master data. You can then use program RHINTE30 to create a batch input session to make the required PA changes for these persons.

You can also perform several OM changes and then run program RHINTE30 to create a common batch input session for all of the persons affected. This is helpful when you are reorganizing large sections of the organizational plan and must update the organizational assignment for multiple employees.

Batch input sessions that are processed in the OM system do not change PA master data. To change the data resulting from OM batch input updates, you must start program RHINTE30 for the persons concerned, and process the resulting batch input session to update the affected employees' organizational assignment records.

Example

Batch input loads can be used to create the organizational plan relationships. If a relationship between a position and person is created in a batch, often the assignment of the job and organizational unit may not be passed to the employees' organizational assignment record. Program RHINTE30 finds the position-holder relationship and updates the organizational assignment of the employee to inherit the job and organizational unit data.

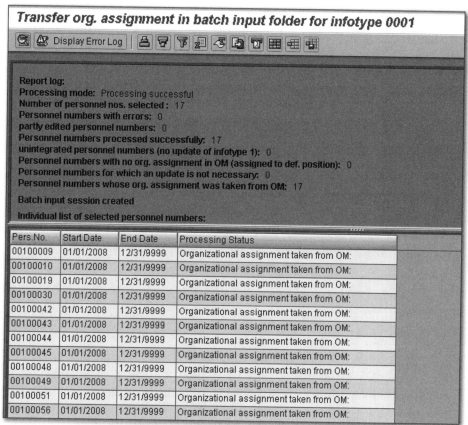

Figure 10.9 Program RHINTE30 Transfer OM in Batch to PA Infotype 0001

The program RHINTE30 Transfer Organizational Assignment in Batch Input Folder for Infotype 0001 is provided to update any organizational assignments that have been carried out in OM and need to be transferred to PA. Sample program output is shown in Figure 10.9. The program can be found via Transaction Code OOHQ and in the IMG path **Personnel Management • Organizational Management • Integration • Integration with Personnel Administration • Transfer Data to Personnel Administration**.

The selection criteria for the program consist of means to select the relevant personnel. You can choose personnel master records by personnel number, company code, personnel or employee structure data (personnel area, subarea, etc.), and validity date. You can run the program in test mode, in which case no batch input session is created. The selection criteria also allow you to process all persons regardless of their need for Infotype 0001 change; all persons are selected, and information is displayed regarding their disposition to change Infotype 0001.

The RHINTE30 program is particularly useful for customers who have just turned on integration between OM and PA. Program RHINTE30 essentially re-creates Infotype 0001 in PA, which takes into account and inherits any information related to the position assigned to the employee in the infotype.

With data shared between OM and PA, multiple utilities are present to help keep the information consistent. So far, we have been discussing keeping information consistent within one SAP system. Similar issues can occur when data is shared and transferred among multiple systems. For multisystem data sharing, programs are available to help keep data in sync.

10.3.5 Moving OM Data between SAP Systems

When implementing an SAP system, it is usual to have multiple systems in which to perform configuration activities and testing. Typical customer system scenarios have development, test, and production systems. Because the organizational plan can ultimately have thousands of objects and infotype records, it is not uncommon for implementation teams to build the entire structure in the development system and transfer the approved and final design of the organizational structure to the test and production systems.

Similarly, an SAP ERP HCM organizational plan can also be used in other SAP components such as SAP Business Workflow or Enterprise Buyer Procurement. If the SAP ERP HCM components reside in the same physical SAP system as the other functions, it is very easy to share this information. In some customer implementations, however, the HR system may be in a separate SAP system, requiring the OM data to be transferred to another SAP system.

These types of system setups may require that the HR organizational plan data be transferred to an SAP system other than the one in which the data is created or maintained. If you have set up an organizational plan in a different client or a separate SAP HR system, you can move the data from one system to another using the SAP transport system. Transports are a mechanism used throughout SAP components to move data and configuration settings from one SAP client or system to another.

OM Data Transport

Set up activities for the transport of OM data are accomplished via a customizing setting in the IMG, shown in Figure 10.10. The activity can be found via Transaction Code OOCR and in the IMG path **Personnel Management • Organizational Management • Transport • Set Up Transport Connection**. Three settings are possible in transporting OM data:

▶ **Blank:** Automatic transport connection

▶ **"X":** No automatic transport (i.e., manual transport)

▶ **"T":** Manual transport using object lock

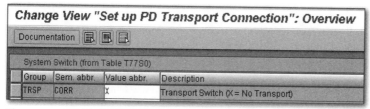

Figure 10.10 IMG: OM Transport Connection Setting

For automatic transport, OM object and infotype records are written to a transport as they are maintained. The OM user is prompted for a transport request each time he saves organizational plan information. With manual transport, the objects are not automatically written to a transport. Objects can be added to a specified transport request through a delivered program. Two options exist in this case:

▶ **Program RHMOVE30 Manual Transport Link**
This program adds OM and PD objects (no external objects) to a specified transport task and, if necessary, deletes the objects in the source and target systems. This is used with TRSP CORR setting X. The program is accessed via Transaction Code RE_RHMOVE30 or via the SAP menu path **Organizational Management • Tools • Data Transfer • Manual Transport**. The program is also accessible in the IMG menu immediately following the configuration activity.

▶ **Program RHMOVE50 Transport of Objects Using Object Lock**
This program also adds OM and PD objects (no external objects) to a specified transport task. This is used with TRSP CORR setting T. When objects are maintained, they are flagged (the so-called object lock) so the program knows which

objects to include in the transport. Once the object is added to the transport, the lock flag is removed. This program is not associated with a transaction code, so it can be run from Transaction Code SA38 ABAP Reporting or SE38 ABAP Editor.

The selection screen of either program allows you to identify which objects you want to manually transport. You can select any combination of plan version, object type, object, status, and reporting period. Additionally, you can utilize an evaluation path to select objects that are related to one another to ensure that the full reporting structure is included.

Tip

Additional settings in the program selection criteria provide the option of deleting the object in the source and target systems. This ensures that the object is completely replaced in case it already exists.

A sample of the data selected for transport with program RHMOVE30 is shown in Figure 10.11. In this example, the program is run in test mode, so a transport is not created. The program selection parameters include a test setting so that you can list and verify the objects to be transported before the transport request is actually created and populated.

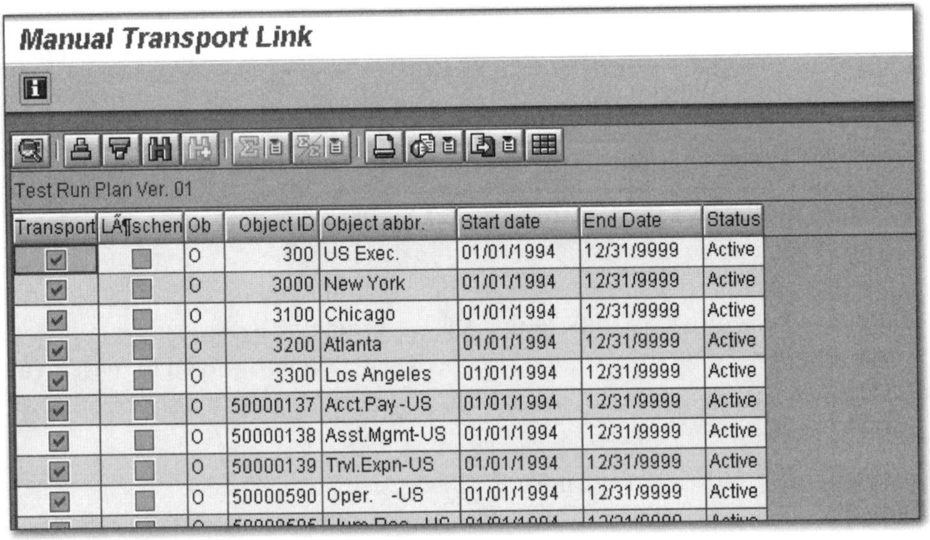

Transport	LÃ¶schen	Ob	Object ID	Object abbr.	Start date	End Date	Status
☑	☐	O	300	US Exec.	01/01/1994	12/31/9999	Active
☑	☐	O	3000	New York	01/01/1994	12/31/9999	Active
☑	☐	O	3100	Chicago	01/01/1994	12/31/9999	Active
☑	☐	O	3200	Atlanta	01/01/1994	12/31/9999	Active
☑	☐	O	3300	Los Angeles	01/01/1994	12/31/9999	Active
☑	☐	O	50000137	Acct.Pay-US	01/01/1994	12/31/9999	Active
☑	☐	O	50000138	Asst.Mgmt-US	01/01/1994	12/31/9999	Active
☑	☐	O	50000139	Trvl.Expn-US	01/01/1994	12/31/9999	Active
☑	☐	O	50000590	Oper. -US	01/01/1994	12/31/9999	Active

Figure 10.11 Manual Transport Program RHMOVE30

> **Note**
>
> With either program RHMOVE30 or RHMOVE50, external objects such as persons or cost centers are not transported in the process. If the external object already exists in the target system, only a relationship is created to that object. If the object doesn't exist in the target system, the transport data will fail and produce an error, and no data will be imported.

Once you have moved OM data to the production system client, you can choose to create and maintain any further organizational plan data in this system only. In this case, it's important to set the TRSP CORR setting in the production SAP client to "X" so that users are not prompted for transport requests as production data is created or maintained.

The transport system is only one way to move data into an SAP system. It's particularly useful for moving data between SAP systems. For data exchange between SAP and non-SAP systems, or when you want to manipulate data before import, you may find other tools useful. These tools are described next.

OM Data Import and Export

SAP also provides tools to export and import the organizational plan from system to system without using the transport system. Three programs are available to support this process:

▶ **Program RHMOVE00 Create PD Sequential File**
This program generates a sequential data file of your organizational plan data. This is run from the source SAP client and creates a data file in the SAP system directory structure. This program can be accessed via Transaction Code OOMV or via the SAP menu path **Organizational Management • Tools • Data Transfer • Create Sequential File.**

▶ **Program RHMOVE40 Display PD Sequential File**
This program displays the data file generated by Program RHMOVE00, and allows users to edit the data in the file. This program is a subprogram within RHMOVE00, accessible via an icon in the RHMOVE00 report display. It can also be run independently from Transaction Code SA38 ABAP Reporting or SE38 ABAP Editor.

▶ **Program RHALTD00: Legacy Data Transfer**
This program imports the data from the sequential file into the target SAP system. This program can be accessed via Transaction Code OODT or via the SAP menu path **Organizational Management • Tools • Data Transfer • Legacy Data Transfer.**

When the RHMOVE00 program is run, a list of the data to be transferred can be displayed as shown in Figure 10.12.

Transport Personnel Planning Data Records to Sequential File

&° Display File · 🖉 Change File · 🚚 Legacy Data Transfer

List of transported records

Number of Objects: 8
Number of Records: 140

TESTRUN

PV	Ob	Object ID	Infotype	Subtype	S	Pr	Start date	End Date	Var.field	RNo
01	C	50029026	1000		1		01/01/1994	12/31/9999	R	
01	C	50029026	1000		1		01/01/1994	12/31/9999	S	
01	C	50029026	1000		1		01/01/1994	12/31/9999	Z	
01	O	300	1000		1		01/01/1994	12/31/9999	D	
01	O	300	1000		1		01/01/1994	12/31/9999	E	
01	O	300	1000		1		01/01/1994	12/31/9999	F	
01	O	300	1000		1		01/01/1994	12/31/9999	J	
01	O	300	1000		1		01/01/1994	12/31/9999	P	
01	O	300	1000		1		01/01/1994	12/31/9999	S	
01	O	300	1000		1		01/01/1994	12/31/9999	Z	
01	S	49999998	1000		1		01/01/1994	12/31/9999	D	
01	S	49999998	1000		1		01/01/1994	12/31/9999	E	
01	S	49999998	1000		1		01/01/1994	12/31/9999	F	
01	S	49999998	1000		1		01/01/1994	12/31/9999	P	
01	S	49999998	1000		1		01/01/1994	12/31/9999	S	

Figure 10.12 Program RHMOVE00 Sequential File Data Output

From the program RHMOVE00 list output, you can also perform functions on the data. At the right end of the icon bar across the top of the output are three functions: Display File, Change File, and Legacy Data Transfer. The Display File icon calls program RHMOVE40, which provides a list display of the data in the sequential file that has been created. The next icon, Edit File, allows you to both display and edit or change the data file contents. This is useful if you want to alter some data for testing purposes. The final icon, Legacy Data Transfer, takes you to the import program RHALTD00.

These sequential file tools are useful in transferring data between SAP systems. In addition, you can use the tools to transfer data from a previous HR information system that may be replaced with SAP. By formatting legacy system data to the file layout used in the data file produced by program RHMOVE00, you can import the organizational plan from your legacy system to SAP.

Now that we've reviewed some of the tools that will help prepare your system for creation of the organizational plan, let's take a look at a few utilities that are useful for ongoing maintenance activities.

10.4 Object and Infotype Utilities

As discussed in Chapter 3, OM uses a status setting for objects and infotype data records to assist in managing the organizational plan data. In this section we'll look at changing the object status and copying plan versions.

10.4.1 Changing the Object Status

Objects and infotypes can be one of five status values:

- Active (1)
- Planned (2)
- Submitted (3)
- Approved (4)
- Rejected (5)

The status identifies the current state of the object or data record in the organizational plan. If your enterprise uses a decentralized method of maintaining the organizational plan objects and records, you may find the status values helpful in managing the request and approval process for the organizational plan data. Typically, users are restricted to maintaining records in a particular status based on their user authorizations (see Section 10.5). An organizational unit manager will usually not be able to submit a change, approve it, and activate it.

The approval process requires multiple parties to be involved along the process chain so they can complete their activity. There may, however, be situations where you want to bypass the multistep approval process and alter the status of proposed object and infotype changes in mass. Program RHAKTI00 Change Object Status is provided to allow you to change multiple objects and infotypes at once. You can access the program via the menu path **Organizational Management • Tools • Object • Change Status**.

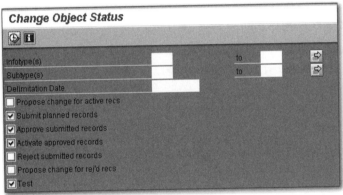

Figure 10.13 Program RHAKTI00 Change Object Status Selection Screen

A portion of the selection screen for the program is shown in Figure 10.13. In addition to the usual criteria that allow you to select the object type, object IDs, reporting period, and evaluation path, there are also status-related selection criteria. With these options, you select the object and infotypes (and/or subtypes) for which you want to change the status. The options allow you to change statuses in step or in combination. You can move objects from one status value to another, such as changing approved records to active. If you choose multiple options, the objects can be moved through multiple statuses.

If you select the three options, Submit planned records, Approve submitted records, and Activate approved records, you will effectively *activate* records in planned status. Records are moved from planned to submit, submit to approved, and approved to active sequentially and in one program run.

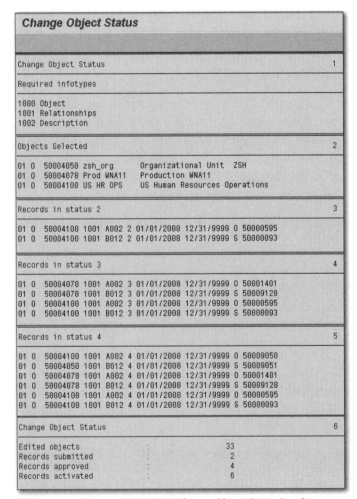

```
Change Object Status

Change Object Status                                               1

Required infotypes

1000 Object
1001 Relationships
1002 Description

Objects Selected                                                  2

01 0  50004050 zsh_org       Organizational Unit  ZSH
01 0  50004078 Prod WNA11    Production WNA11
01 0  50004100 US HR OPS     US Human Resources Operations

Records in status 2                                               3

01 0  50004100 1001 A002 2 01/01/2008 12/31/9999 0 50000595
01 0  50004100 1001 B012 2 01/01/2008 12/31/9999 S 50000093

Records in status 3                                               4

01 0  50004078 1001 A002 3 01/01/2008 12/31/9999 0 50001401
01 0  50004078 1001 B012 3 01/01/2008 12/31/9999 S 50009128
01 0  50004100 1001 A002 3 01/01/2008 12/31/9999 0 50000595
01 0  50004100 1001 B012 3 01/01/2008 12/31/9999 S 50000093

Records in status 4                                               5

01 0  50004100 1001 A002 4 01/01/2008 12/31/9999 0 50009050
01 0  50004050 1001 B012 4 01/01/2008 12/31/9999 S 50009051
01 0  50004078 1001 A002 4 01/01/2008 12/31/9999 0 50001401
01 0  50004078 1001 B012 4 01/01/2008 12/31/9999 S 50009128
01 0  50004100 1001 A002 4 01/01/2008 12/31/9999 0 50000595
01 0  50004100 1001 B012 4 01/01/2008 12/31/9999 S 50000093

Change Object Status                                              6

Edited objects          :           33
Records submitted       :            2
Records approved        :            4
Records activated       :            6
```

Figure 10.14 Program RHAKTI00 Change Object Status Results

When the program run is complete, the system will display a multipage output of the changes performed. In the example in Figure 10.14, the program has searched through Infotypes 1000, 1001, and 1002 for objects that are in need of status change. Three objects are selected among the 33 processed for status changes. One object had two relationship records changed from planned (2) status through to active, another pair was changed from submitted (3) to active, and yet another pair was changed from approved to active.

This tool is particularly useful when you have large numbers of records that you want to change and activate. Let's look now at another way of changing large numbers of records, this time through the use of the plan version.

10.4.2 Copying Plan Versions

As mentioned in Chapter 3, Section 3.7, the organizational plan can exist in one or more plan versions. One plan version is active at any given time and is the plan version that is used actively in the SAP system and in the various day-to-day business processes throughout SAP ERP HCM. In other plan versions, you can model and plan additional organizational scenarios. These are very useful, for example, if you have large parts of the organization that may be reorganized.

Example

A large department or functional reorganization can involve hundreds of organizational units, positions, and persons undergoing change. Rather than making these changes in the active plan version in a planned status, you can make an alternative plan version that is completely separate from your active plan. This enables you to model the new organization in isolation.

With the program Copy Plan Version (RHCOPL00), you can copy objects and infotypes from one plan version to another. You can access the program via the menu path **Organizational Management • Tools • Plan Version • Copy**. Objects are selected from one plan version, typically the active plan, and copied into the specified plan version.

Note

Objects and infotypes have to be copied in such a manner that they do not conflict with existing plan data. A particular object ID or infotype record cannot already exist in the destination plan version. The target plan version either needs to be completely empty, or you have to copy portions of the organizational plan that don't already exist in the plan version.

You can select objects by object type and object ID, and specify an evaluation path along which related objects can also be copied. The validity period selection parameters allow you to select records that exist on or over a particular time period. In addition to specifying the target plan version, you can select the specific infotypes, with subtype if necessary, that should be copied. This is useful to restrict the copy process to only those elements you need to model. For example, you may only need the Object and Relationship infotype, and no information about planned compensation or work schedules. When the program is run, a summary of the objects and infotype records can be displayed, as shown in Figure 10.15.

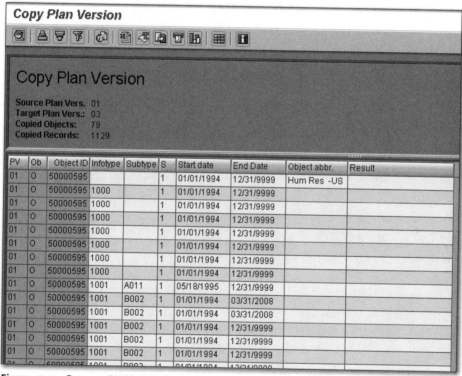

Figure 10.15 Program RHCOPL00 Copy Plan Version Results

You can further compare the current organizational plan with the planning scenarios and transfer data from the simulated structures into the current organizational plan, as described in the next section.

10.4.3 Comparing and Reconciling Plan Versions

The Reconcile Plan Versions comparison program (RHCOPLPT) gives you the ability to identify and analyze the impact of the different organizational plan version on any or all of its components and to copy the different plan elements to the active plan. You can access the program via the menu path **Organizational Management • Tools • Plan Version • Compare**.

The program processes data in two steps. In the first step, the objects and infotypes in the alternate plan version are selected and compared to the other plan version you specify. The results of the comparison are displayed in a tree structure format (Figure 10.16) that outlines the differences in the plan versions.

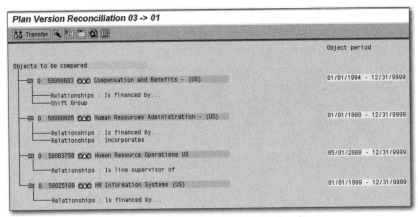

Figure 10.16 Program RHCOPLPT Compare Plan Version Results

In the second step, individual infotype records, all records for an object, or all objects and their records can be selected using the Select ⬛ icon. A colored stoplight status icon indicates the extent to which the objects are comparable in both plan versions. The options are:

▶ Green: The objects and infotypes are the same in both plan versions.

▶ Yellow: The object exists in both plan versions, and infotype records are partially similar in both plan versions.

▶ Red: The object only exists in the source plan version.

The Transfer button ⬛ Transfer reconciles the objects and selected infotypes, meaning the selected information is copied to the target plan version and saved.

Now that we've reviewed many of the technical tools and utilities available in OM, let's turn our attention to securing the data. Authorization management is typically a broad area of responsibility that is managed centrally by customer SAP support teams. OM data incorporates two authorization concepts that are important to understand broadly, because the concepts may influence the structure of your organizational plan and the object or infotype details that you maintain for the plan.

10.5 Authorizations and the Role Concept

Authorizations protect unauthorized access to transactions and programs in the SAP system. Authorizations are grouped by broad authorization classes; Human Resources is one authorization class that is further broken down into over 30 authorization objects. These authorization objects are the bottom-line level of detail in the authorization concept. Each object contains up to 10 fields to which you can assign a value, which represents either data or action permissions. Authorizations are then specific configurations of an authorization object.

> **Example**
>
> "Write access for Infotype 1002" is an authorization. "Reading access for Infotype 0001" is an authorization. "Read and Write access to object type S Position" is an authorization.

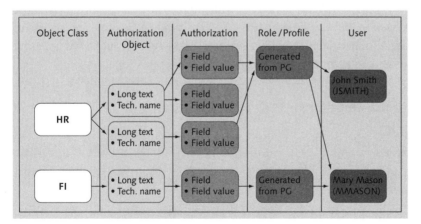

Figure 10.17 Overview of the SAP Authorization Concept

The actual value entries that you can use are directly limited and defined by the authorization object being used. Authorizations are not assigned to users directly. Rather, authorizations are grouped and assigned to profiles, which can then be assigned to users. Profiles can be single, containing only one authorization, or they can be composite, containing multiple single profiles. Profiles can be assigned to users directly or compiled in a role, which is then assigned to the user. Figure 10.17 provides an overview graphic that explains the entire authorization concept.

When a user logs on to the SAP system to perform his job duties, certain responsibilities and processes must be executed. The role assigned to the user presents the user with the relevant processes collected in the role. Combined with the authorizations, the role controls what the user can see and do. Depending on the individual, one or more roles may be assigned.

Example

A purchasing manager in the procurement organization can be assigned three roles: employee, manager, and purchase approver. The employee role can be assigned to every employee in the enterprise, enabling all employee users to use self-service functions such as benefits enrollment. The manager role can be assigned to supervisors of personnel, enabling them to conduct performance reviews and salary adjustments. The purchase approver role is specific to the job in procurement, so can only apply to select persons.

The roles and profiles used in authorization management can contain authorization objects from one or many SAP components, depending on which components are used in your enterprise. General or cross-functional authorization objects allow access to transaction codes, reporting tools, and customizing activities regardless of component. In the next sections we'll review the OM-specific authorizations that you should take into account when planning your organizational structure.

10.5.1 Authorizations for OM

Two basic authorization objects control access to organizational plan data. With these authorization objects, you can create authorizations that allow or restrict access to the organizational plan by object type, plan version status, and infotype. The authorization objects are:

- PLOG: Personnel Planning
- PLOG_CON: Personnel Planning with Context

These authorization objects control access related to personnel planning and organizational management objects and infotypes. When any function in OM is performed, the system conducts a check against the PLOG and PLOG_CON authorization objects to determine what a user can see and do.

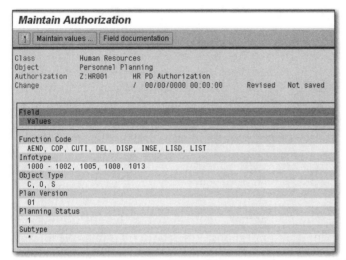

Figure 10.18　Human Resources Personnel Planning Authorization PLOG

The PLOG authorization object (Figure 10.18) is the most basic OM authorization. With this authorization object, you control access to the various parts of the organizational plan. Authorization fields include the following:

▸ **Function code**
Defines the system action that is allowed. There are over 30 different functions for OM data (see Appendix D). Examples include display (DIS), LIS (list), create (INSE), change (AEND). and delete (DEL).

▸ **Infotype and subtype**
Listed as separate fields, the infotype and subtype work together. The four-character infotype number is entered in the authorization field.

▸ **Object type**
The object type ID is used.

▸ **Plan version**
The two-character plan version is used.

▸ **Status**
The one-character code for the status is used.

289

An example of a PLOG authorization is provided in Figure 10.18. In this example, a broad range of functions are allowed for Infotypes 1000 Object, 1001 Relationships, 1002 Description, 1005 Planned Compensation, 1008 Account Assignment, and 1013 Employee Group/Subgroup for jobs, organizational units, and positions. Only active data in plan version 01 is allowed. Every relationship is allowed by the specification * in the subtype field.

> **Tip**
>
> When creating PLOG authorizations, you should keep authorizations for infotype with subtypes separate from other infotypes so you can specify the subtypes more clearly. When multiple infotypes with subtypes are included in the same authorization, you may inadvertently provide authorizations that you don't mean to. For example, Infotypes 1002 Description and 1028 Address can both use a custom subtype Z001. You may want a use to display the description Z001 and edit the address Z001. Including both functions, both infotypes, and the subtype Z001 in the same relationship will give read and edit access in both infotypes, which is not what you want.

Similar to access conflicts within an authorization, there may be situations where conflicts exist when combining authorizations. When a user has multiple roles in an organization, the authorizations assigned to him may provide broader access than is intended.

> **Example**
>
> A user is a manager of employees in the HR operations organization. In his role as manager, the user can propose position changes such as promotions or reclassifications for his employees. This role requires write access to Infotype 1000 to request new positions and Infotype 1001 Relationships to propose new staff assignments.
>
> In the role as HR operations manager, the user can display the entire organizational structure to support reporting or inquiry support requests from the enterprise. This requires read access to all objects and infotypes in the organizational plan.
>
> With both of these authorizations assigned to one userid, the authorizations are combined. The user would end up having write access to Infotypes 1000 and 1001 for all objects in the plan.

To assist in resolving the application of the PLOG authorization, you can use the PLOG_CON authorization, which provides a context link for authorizations to the profile in which it is used. This context solution enables you to make a technical connection between the individual authorization object and the profile for which the authorizations are designed.

Taking the example above, the resulting authorization setup would require association of the different authorizations to two separate profiles. The authorization providing write access to Infotypes 1000 and 1001 would be assigned to the manager profile, while the authorization providing read access to all objects would be assigned to the HR operations profile. Both profiles would be assigned to the user, and each would work independently to determine the user's overall access controls.

Figure 10.19 shows the configuration of the PLOG_CON authorization. As opposed to the general PLOG authorization shown in Figure 10.18, the addition of the Authorization Profile field in the object provides the connection to the context in which this access is used.

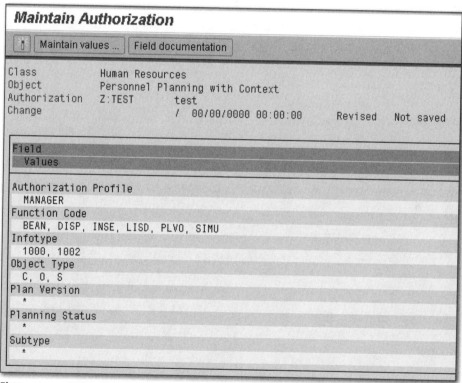

Figure 10.19 PLOG_CON Context Authorization

With context-driven authorizations, you have the added flexibility to manage multiple authorizations more easily. Because enterprise users have multiple roles in the organization, problems may arise when the authorizations required for different tasks overlap. You can avoid these conflicts by providing the profile context, which will resolve conflicts automatically.

The OM authorization objects provide access controls for plan data rather broadly. Access to an object type is general, meaning all objects of that particular type are assumed to be accessible in the authorization. If an authorization includes read access to object type S, all positions are available to read. You may want to restrict the authorizations to a particular subsection of the organizational plan rather than allow such broad access. In this case, you'll also need to implement the structural authorization checks.

10.5.2 Organizational Plan-Based Authorizations

Authorizations can be based on the organizational plan structure to limit the objects that a user can process. These structural authorizations utilize a combination of the traditional object-based authorizations and the organizational plan structure to determine a user's access.

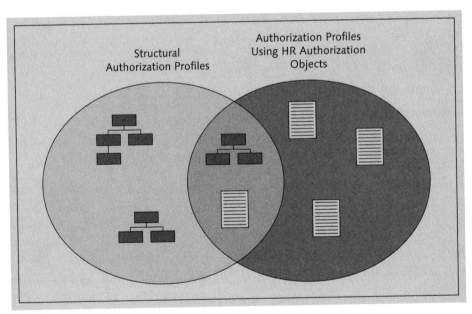

Figure 10.20 Structural Authorization Concept

Depicted in Figure 10.20, the traditional authorizations exist in the system utilizing the PLOG and PLOG_CON authorization objects. Structural authorization profiles are then created that identify portions of the organizational plan for which access is to be limited. When combined in the user profile and role, the authorizations provide access controls around objects and infotypes in a particular part of the organization. The PLOG and PLOG_CON authorizations determine the object and infotype access, and the structural authorization determines the appropriate organization.

Tip

Structural authorizations are particularly useful when distributing HR-related tasks throughout the enterprise. Manager Self-Service functions use the structural authorization concept to determine the organizations and personnel to which that a manager may have access.

Structural authorizations must be activated in the system in order to work. They are accessible via Transaction Code OOAC or IMG path **Personnel Management • Personnel Administration • Tools • Authorization Management • Maintain Authorization Main Switches**. A subset of the customizing table entries is shown in Figure 10.21.

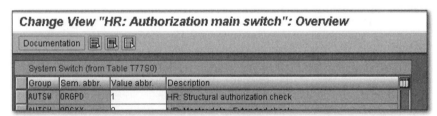

Figure 10.21 IMG: Edit Authorization Main Switches

In the customizing table, the entry AUTSW ORGPD provides the activation switch for structural authorizations. For all the authorization switches in this table, value "0" deactivates the switch and value "1" activates the check.

Three additional customizing activities are necessary to set up structural authorizations. All activities are available via the IMG path **Organizational Management • Basic Settings • Structural Authorization**. In the first customizing activity, also accessible via Transaction Code OOSP, the structural authorization profile is defined by name and long text description. In the detail customizing view, shown in Figure 10.21, the profile is assigned organizational plan elements. A sequential number from 01 to 99 allows for up to 99 different plan object assignments.

When determining which objects are restricted, you have two options that can be implemented independently or together. The first option is to enter plan information directly. In the structural authorization definition you can specify the plan version, object type, specific object IDs, and evaluation path to restrict objects. The technical depth identifies how many levels deep along the organizational structure the authorization check should search for and authorize objects. The period determines how the profile evaluates the validity period of the structure: value "D" for current day is a common setting.

The second method for determining objects uses the function module parameter. You can specify a function module that dynamically determines a root object when the authorization check occurs. You must at minimum specify a plan version and object type. SAP provides two function modules for structural authorizations to achieve common restriction requirements:

▶ **RH_GET_MANAGER_ASSIGNMENT**
This determines as the root object the organizational unit to which the user is assigned as manager via relationship A012 (is manager of). This function module works within the key date parameter used in the transaction or report that is being run in the system. It only finds organizational units of which the user is manager on the key date or during the period specified.

▶ **RH_GET_ORG_ASSIGNMENT**
This determines as the root object the organizational unit to which the user is assigned organizationally.

Change View "Authorization profile maintenance": Overview												
New Entries												
Dialog Structure	Auth.profile	No.	Plan...	Obj...	Obje...	Maint.	Eval.path	Status vec	Depth	Sign	Period	Function module
▽ ☐ Authorization	MANAGER	0	01	O		☑	PERSON	12			D	RH_GET_MANAGER_ASSIGNMENT
☐ Authoriza	MANAGER	1	01	Q		☑	QALL	12				
	MANAGER	3	01	QK		☑	QUALCATA	12				
	MANAGER	4	01	BA		☑						
	MANAGER	5	01	BS		☑						
	MANAGER	6	01	BG		☑						
	MANAGER	7	01	RQ		☑						
	MANAGER	8	01	R		☑						
	MANAGER	9	01	SO		☑						

Figure 10.22 IMG: Maintain Structural Profiles (Detail)

The structural authorization profile configuration is shown in Figure 10.22. In this example, the MANAGER profile is accorded access first (row 0) to organizational units in plan version 01 along the evaluation path PERSON. The function module RH_GET_MANAGER_ASSIGNMENT dynamically determines the organizational unit to which the user is the assigned manager. The PERSON evaluation path specifies to find the related persons reporting to the resulting organizational unit. This combination of factors provides managers of an organization access to their employees.

In this customizing view, the MANAGER profile goes on via additional line items to provide the user access to additional objects, some via evaluation paths, in the organizational plan.

Once the structural authorizations are defined, they must be assigned to the relevant user IDs. This is accomplished via the second IMG activity, shown in Figure 10.23, which is also accessible via Transaction Code OOSB. In this view, the user name and profile are assigned a validity effective period. When the user logs in to the system, the authorization checks read this table to determine if a structural authorization applies to the user name, and processes the organizational plan data accordingly.

Figure 10.23 IMG: Assign Structural Authorization

Because there can be hundreds of thousands of users and authorization profiles to maintain, it is neither expected nor recommended that the structural authorization table be maintained manually. Rather, the assignment of the profiles to users is accomplished via the assignment of the relevant profiles to Infotypes 1016 Standard Profiles and 1017 PD Profiles for the jobs, positions, work centers, or organizational units in the plan.

When authorizations are assigned to the organizational plan objects via Infotypes 1016 and 1017, you can use program RHPROFL0 Generate User Authorizations to automatically fill the structural authorization table. The program RHPROFL0 uses evaluation path PROFL0 to locate and temporarily save all users in the organizational structure. The system then reads all valid related objects for which Infotypes 1016 or 1017 are maintained, up to the next-highest organizational unit. The program checks the users assigned to holders of positions in the plan and creates user IDs if they are not found in the system. Finally, the system enters authorization profiles for all users found in the organizational plan in the customizing table.

By running the RHPROFL0 program on a regular basis, you can automatically maintain the structural authorization assignments for users in the system so that they are up to date. Many customers schedule this program to run nightly so that user authorizations are refreshed each morning.

The final IMG activity required for structural authorizations is to save user data in memory. Structural authorization performance is known to be slow for higher-level managers who have access to a large organizational structure. To avoid performance problems for users with extensive authorization profiles, you can enter the user names in the structural authorization memory table, shown in Figure 10.24.

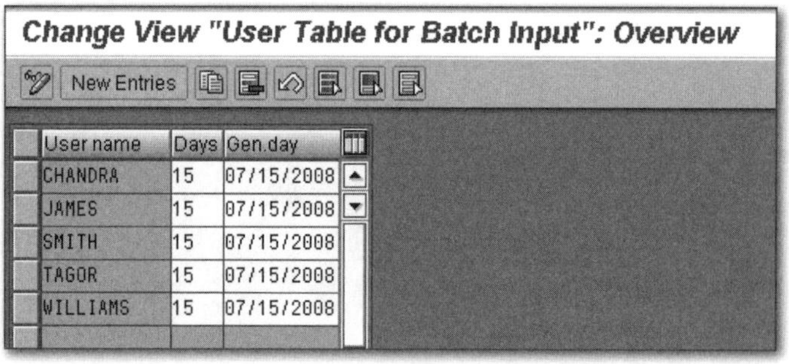

Figure 10.24 IMG: Save User Data in SAP Memory

You can fill the memory table manually or use two programs that SAP provides to fill the tables automatically. The first, program RHBAUS02 Check and Compare T77UU, reads the structural authorization assignment to user tables and checks if the users have authorization to more objects than a threshold value specified when the program is run. The default threshold is 1000, but you can decrease or increase the value as needed. Any users who have authorization to more objects than the threshold are added to the memory table. If users who already exist in the memory table fall below the threshold, they are removed from the memory table.

Once program RHBAUS02 is run, you must then run program RHBAUS00 Regeneration of INDX for Structural Authorization. Program RHBAUS00 regenerates indexes for the structural authorization users who are in the memory table. Indexes for quick access to organizational structures are only available for these users. Both programs RHBAUS02 and RHBAUS00 must be run from Transaction Code SA38 ABAP Reporting or SE38 ABAP Editor, as neither are present in the SAP or IMG menu paths.

When the structural authorization memory table and indices are completely maintained, users will be able to view and maintain the organizational plan or employee data appropriately. Users who are high in the organization hierarchy should experience fast system response to their inquiries along the organizational plan, resulting in effective use of the authorizations you have set up in OM.

10.6   Conclusion

In this chapter we've covered a wide variety of technical tools, processes, and utilities to help you make the most of your organizational plan structure. These tools are not only helpful when you are first implementing organizational management, but will help keep your system running smoothly for its lifespan. The next and final chapter discusses integration of OM to other components in SAP. Whether integrating to SAP ERP HCM components or other SAP functions, organizational management is a powerful tool that can help you make the most of you SAP solution.

*OM is a core component that has integration ties to just about every SAP ERP HCM component that exists. As such, it is one of the areas where you should focus your attention early in any implementation. **This focus will** ensure that your OM design will deliver the benefits available throughout SAP ERP HCM.*

11 Integration of OM with other SAP Components

This chapter involves integration of OM to the various functions within SAP ERP HCM and to other SAP ERP components. With the object types, infotypes, and relationships that are created in the organizational plan, these various components can use information about the enterprise to run and plan the business processes that rely on organization-based information. Let's first take a look at integration within SAP ERP HCM.

11.1 OM and SAP ERP HCM Function Integration

SAP ERP HCM allows you to transform your traditional human resource functions into a comprehensive human capital program. Whether you implement all components or parts, certain functions are central in design and focus throughout SAP ERP HCM. OM is one such component. OM has many integration ties to other SAP ERP HCM components that enables the components to share common master and transactional data.

Sharing data helps ensure that processes have the most up-to-date information possible. As such, it's one of the areas where you should focus your attention early on in any implementation of SAP ERP HCM. When you first begin implementing SAP ERP HCM, you should take a step back and have a high-level look at all the components you'll be using. When you have a view of all components, you can determine what data elements are shared, which will help you choose how the data will be designed and maintained on a regular basis.

11.1.1 Personnel Administration Integration

Core to OM integration is its ties to Personnel Administration (PA). Positions provide the key to integration with personnel administration, because they are the organizational object that is directly assigned to people in the SAP system. In PA, only the position is selected as the integration point to OM. By assigning the employee to a position, you implement integration between OM and PA.

Position assignments to employees are stored on the Organizational Assignment Infotype 0001. Employees are assigned to a position through the use of a personnel action, which first begins with maintenance of Infotype 0000 Actions. In the Actions infotype, shown partially in Figure 11.1, the position can be entered in the Organizational Assignment section of the screen. When saved, this data is transferred to Infotype 0001 Organizational Assignment, creating a record of the same effective starting and ending period. If you leave the position blank on the Actions infotype, you can enter it in the Organizational Assignment infotype.

Create Actions

Organizational assignment		
Position	10000666	Human Resources Manager
Personnel area	1010	Headquarters
Employee group	1	Company Employee
Employee subgroup	U2	Salary

Figure 11.1 Use PA Infotype 0000 Actions to Assign Positions

Tip

Although you can wait to assign a position on Infotype 0001 Organizational Assignment, you may realize the additional benefit of having the Personnel Area, Employee Group, and Employee Subgroup fields auto-populated when you assign the position on Infotype 0000 Actions. When the Infotypes 1008 Account Assignment and 1013 Employee Group/Subgroup are maintained in OM, this data can be used to default values in PA upon assignment of the position, which can save you entry steps.

The position is ultimately stored in the PA Infotype 0001 Organizational Assignment, shown in Figure 11.2. When the position is transferred to the organizational assignment, other relevant data is also carried forward. The job key, Exempt (FLSA status) indicator, organizational unit, and cost center are inherited from the position assignment. So, as the position changes over the lifecycle of the employee, so does this data by relationship.

The relationship data is the primary vehicle for integration between OM components and other SAP ERP HCM components in SAP. By relating persons and positions, you carry out integration between PA and OM. By relating organizational objects within OM, you enable those objects to be related to the assigned person in PA. You must carefully determine which relationships are required in your organizational structure to properly reflect information in PA.

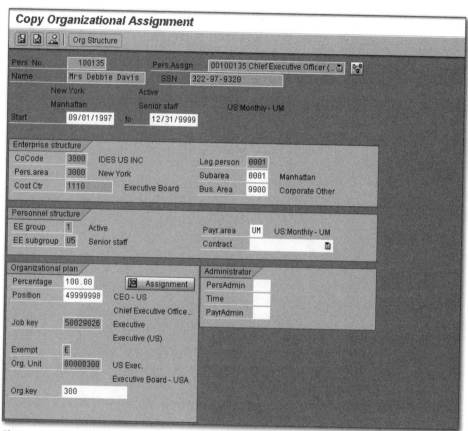

Figure 11.2 PA Infotype 0001 Organizational Assignment

In addition, two key features are important to understand in the organizational assignment: the Percentage field and the Assignment button. The staffing percentage indicates which percentage of an employee's time is to be spent in the position entered in the Position field. Typically, employees hold one position at 100%. However, there may be cases where an employee holds multiple positions concurrently. When this is the case, the staffing percentage field is used to represent the percentage of time that the employee is allocated to the position displayed.

> **Example**
>
> In the case of concurrent employment, a person can hold multiple positions concurrently at varying percentages. When the percentage allocation is totaled, it equals one full-time equivalent employee. In another case, an employee may temporarily be responsible for another position that is vacant. In this case, the person holds two positions at varying percentages until the interim position is permanently filled, and the staffing percentage remains at less than 100% for both positions.

The staffing percentage works in conjunction with the Assignment button. When selected, the Assignment button calls up another window where you can add the multiple assignments as shown in Figure 11.3.

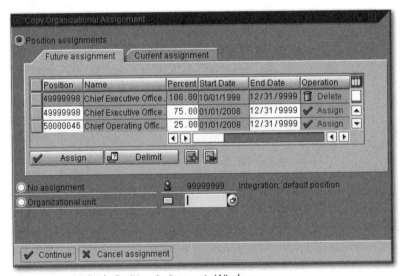

Figure 11.3 Multiple Position Assignments Window

Of course, when an employee only holds one position, there is only one position assignment present. When multiple positions are assigned, however, each position is listed separately with its relevant percentage allocation. The number of position assignments is only restricted by your ability to assign and allocate them to the employee. The percentage allocation should generally not exceed 100%; however, you can control this in customizing to some extent.

In the Assignments window, you also have additional options for OM integration. When you want to store personnel information on persons in the enterprise who are not specifically assigned a position, you can choose the options for No Assignment or Organizational Unit instead. Let's discuss these in reverse order.

The assignment to an organizational unit alone is useful when you don't want to assign a person to a position, but you still need the ability to determine the organizational unit to which the person reports. This is useful in cases where you store information on contingent or contract workers in the SAP system as persons. You likely don't have a regular position to assign them to, but you want to know on what department or project they are working.

By contrast, the option to associate No Assignment to a person is useful when you don't have any organizational assignment connection to the person. In this case, the system assigns a default position, 99999999, to the person as a placeholder in the position field. The value 99999999 doesn't represent an actual position in the organizational plan but is just a filler value that can be used by multiple persons. The use of the default position essentially eliminates the integration of OM and PA for the person to whom it is assigned.

> **Tip**
>
> Keep in mind that the integration of positions and persons is one of the more compelling integration points throughout SAP ERP HCM and will enable you to take full advantage of all SAP ERP HCM functions for your workforce. However, the use of the default position in SAP for regular employees should be kept to a minimum to ensure best use of the SAP ERP HCM functions for employees.

Integration is carried out from both OM and PA perspectives in the SAP system. In addition to the PA Infotype 0001 Organizational Assignment record being maintained, an infotype is also maintained in OM simultaneously. Person assignments to positions are maintained as a relationship record in OM. The relationship A/B 008 (holder) is maintained whenever a person and position are associated. This information is stored in OM Infotype 1002 Relationships for the position assigned.

In addition to the person-to-position assignment processes, two other factors affect integration between OM and PA, so let's look at these now.

Locating Objects for Integration

Not all positions or organizational units can be assigned to persons in PA. Depending on your implementation of SAP ERP HCM, two data characteristics may be useful in determining which position or organizational unit objects can be assigned to your employees.

First, use of the Department flag in Infotype 1003 Department/Staff can limit the ability to assign some organizational units to persons in PA. Some organizational units can be created that don't have assigned positions because you may not want employees to be assigned to these organizations. Flagging an organizational unit as a department allows only those data records marked from OM to be written to PA. If you use the department flag, the assignment of organizational units in PA will be limited accordingly.

Second, in addition to marking departments assignable, you can also choose to identify positions as vacant for PA integration. The maintenance of OM Infotype 1007 Vacancy defines a position as available to be assigned in PA. By assigning positions as vacant, you can maintain a history of when a position was open and able to be filled, as well as when the position is occupied. When a position vacancy is filled by assigning the person to the position, a historical record of the vacancy is created. This vacancy management helps ensure that positions are not assigned inadvertently to multiple persons in the enterprise.

Let's take a look now at how OM integration with PA is set up in the system.

Setting up Integration with Personnel Administration

A baseline assumption for the discussions in this book is that integration between OM and PA is active. So for OM and PA to be integrated, you must activate integration. Activating integration between OM and HR master data in PA ensures that data is consistent between both applications. Two customizing settings are necessary to activate OM-PA integration. The integration settings are accessible via the IMG path **Organizational Management • Integration • Integration with Personnel Administration • Set Up Integration with Personnel Administration**. In this case, two customizing activities are present.

In the first customizing activity, also accessible via Transaction Code OOPT, you access a control feature in SAP ERP HCM that determines whether a person participates in integration. The feature PLOGI utilizes a decision tree to determine whether the person participates in integration. The possible return values for the feature are "X" for participation or blank for no participation. The default value for the feature is "X" for active participation by all persons, as shown in Figure 11.4.

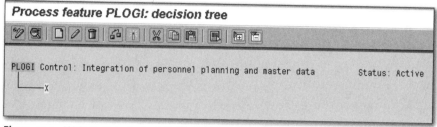

Figure 11.4 IMG: Participate in OM-PA Integration

The second IMG activity (Figure 11.5), also accessible via Transaction Code OOPS, provides the system control Table T77S0, in which one master setting is required for integration and several other optional settings are provided. The entry PLOGI ORGA must contain value "X" to activate integration.

Change View "HR Master Data Integration": Overview

Documentation

System Switch (from Table T77S0)

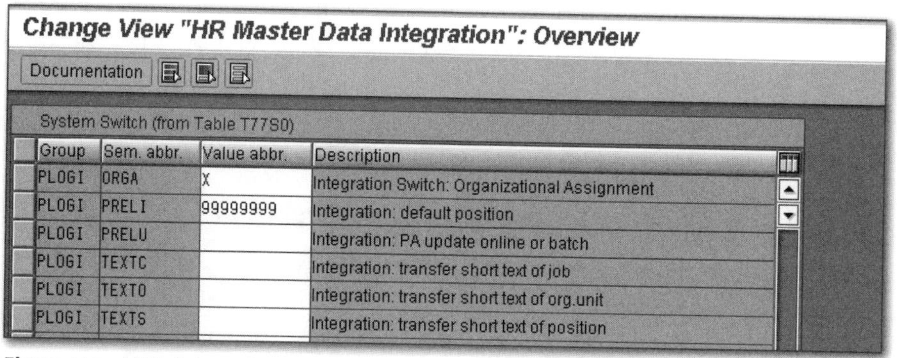

Group	Sem. abbr.	Value abbr.	Description
PLOGI	ORGA	X	Integration Switch: Organizational Assignment
PLOGI	PRELI	99999999	Integration: default position
PLOGI	PRELU		Integration: PA update online or batch
PLOGI	TEXTC		Integration: transfer short text of job
PLOGI	TEXTO		Integration: transfer short text of org.unit
PLOGI	TEXTS		Integration: transfer short text of position

Figure 11.5 IMG: Integration Basic Settings

This setting works in conjunction with the PLOGI feature value and the customizing setting for the active plan version to determine the plan version to reference for integration. In addition to the PLOGI ORGA switch to turn on integration, you can use the following integration settings:

- **PLOGI PRELI**
  Provides the default position number to use when a person is not assigned a position in the organizational assignment.

▶ **PLOGI PRELU**

Determines whether changes made in OM that affect personnel records in PA are made online or in batch. If the value is blank or 0, all changes are made online. Any other numeric value serves as a threshold: if the number of persons affected exceeds the value, the changes are written to a batch input session. Value BTCI forces all changes made from OM to a batch input session.

▶ **PLOGI TEXTC/TEXTO/TEXTS**

Determines whether the short or long text description of the relevant object type (C-job, O-org unit, S-position) will be displayed in PA in the organizational assignment infotype. Value X transfers the short text, and blank transfers the long text.

> **Tip**
>
> In general, the customizing settings are delivered by SAP such that integration is active. If you've been using SAP for some time without using SAP ERP HCM functions, you may need to check that integration is active. Many customers turn integration off to use OM for non-HCM purposes, such as SAP Business Workflow or Enterprise Buyer Procurement.

Keep in mind, though, that PA integration to OM goes beyond the infotype records. So in addition to linking persons in the organizational plan, you can use OM information in PA reporting, as we'll see in the next section.

11.1.2 Personnel Administration Reporting Integration

Reporting plays an important role in PA. Many standard reports are provided that allow personnel administrators to evaluate the large volumes of data entered into the system. Reports also enable you to define search criteria and create reports of employees and employee data, and to perform statistical evaluations.

SAP standard reports are started from the main information system in the SAP menu. When a specific report is accessed, a selection screen containing a series of selection options is presented that lets you specify the criteria used to execute the report. Most SAP ERP HCM reports share common selection criteria, such as selecting the validity period for infotype data and the personnel number. With integration to OM active, some reports can also utilize selection based on the organizational plan. The selection screen for one such report, the Employee List (technical report name RPLMIT00), is shown in Figure 11.6.

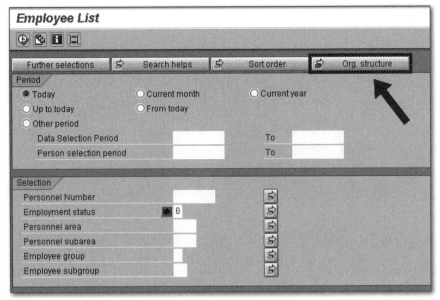

Figure 11.6 Report RPLMIT00 Employee List Selection Screen

The selection option for the organizational structure is highlighted at the top of the selection criteria. When selected, the user is presented with the organizational hierarchy. In this case, you can choose one or many organizational units from the organizational plan to include as selection criteria. This is an easy way to conduct reporting by organizational structure when multiple versions of reports are required for different parts of the enterprise.

In addition to running reports from the PA information system, there is the option of using the Human Resources Information System (HIS), which was described in Chapter 6.

PA is probably the first component in SAP ERP HCM where the benefits of OM integration are achieved for most customers, but let's look at the other application areas where OM data and processes are integrated.

11.1.3 Compensation Management Integration

The Enterprise Compensation Management component controls and manages the remuneration policy in your enterprise. It provides processes and control mechanisms for implementing the policy, facilitating compensation planning and budgeting, and decentralized administration.

Compensation Management also lets you perform job pricing, with which you can save and evaluate the results of external job evaluation systems and salary surveys. Using these results, you can prepare and propose salary structures that can be assigned to jobs and positions in the form of planned compensation. By using this process, you can ensure that the internal values of jobs and positions in your enterprise are competitive with the market.

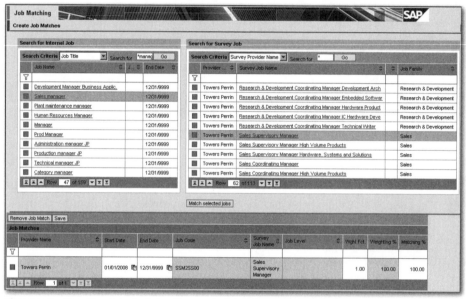

Figure 11.7 Matching Jobs to Salary Surveys in Job Pricing

Figure 11.7 shows an example of job pricing. The job codes created in the organizational plan are used as the basis for identifying a match to the survey job codes. Then the evaluation or survey match information is stored in Infotype 1050 Job Evaluation Results, or 1051 Salary Survey Results.

Subsequent functions in Compensation Management allow you to get analysis and summarizations of the survey results from the matched jobs. You can use the resulting information as input for creating salary structures, which you can then associate back to the job and specific positions in Infotype 1005 Planned Compensation. (We reviewed this infotype in Chapter 7.

In addition to job pricing, Compensation Management includes functions for budgeting that are integrated with the organizational plan. The budgeting function enables you to plan and control expenses for compensation adjustments given to employees, such as merit awards and promotional salary increases. You can assign budgets to organizational units and roll up budgets to higher-level organizational units in the plan. When creating budgets, keep in mind that the organizational structure and job or position data from OM are basic inputs.

Audit Report for Budgets

Monitoring of Compensation Budgets

Budget Type   49 Bonus Budget
Budget Period 01/01/2009 to 12/31/2009
Currency   USD

Budget Unit	Object ID	Total Budget	Total Spent	Total Rest	Distributable ...	Spent Budge...
▽ ① Human Resources	50036151	2,800,000.00	0.00	2,800,000.00	49,000.00	0.00
☐ Human Resources	50000595					0.00
▽ ① Compensation and Benefits - (US)	50036152	73,450.00	0.00	73,450.00	73,450.00	0.00
☐ Compensation and Benefits - (US	50000603					0.00
▽ ① Labor Relations - (US)	50036153	1,225,400.00	0.00	1,225,400.00	1,225,400.00	0.00
☐ Labor Relations - (US)	50000604					0.00
▽ ① Human Resources Administration - (	50036154	145,200.00	0.00	145,200.00	145,200.00	0.00
☐ Human Resources Administratio	50000605					0.00
▽ ① Development and Training Admin - (U	50036155	128,250.00	0.00	128,250.00	128,250.00	0.00
☐ Development and Training Admin	50000606					0.00
▷ ① Payroll Administration - (US)	50036156	355,000.00	0.00	355,000.00	355,000.00	0.00
▷ ① Human Resources Operations (US)	50036157	243,200.00	0.00	243,200.00	243,200.00	0.00
▷ ① Talent Relationship Management(US	50036158	345,500.00	0.00	345,500.00	345,500.00	0.00
▷ ① Workforce Planning	50036159	120,000.00	0.00	120,000.00	120,000.00	0.00
▷ ① HR Information Systems (US)	50036160	115,000.00	0.00	115,000.00	115,000.00	0.00

Figure 11.8 Budget Allocation to Organizational Units

Compensation budgets can be created and managed at the individual organizational unit, or at a higher level. Figure 11.8 shows how the budgets of multiple organizational units can roll up to a higher-level organization. The budget structure is a hierarchy, similar to the organizational plan hierarchy.

Budgets can also be created and related to the organizational units as an independent process, or they can be created using data from cost planning processes. Compensation Management includes processes that let you upload planned budget information to the budget structure, so let's see how this works.

11.1.4 Cost Planning Integration

With Personnel Cost Planning you can project costs related to personnel for a future time period, and you can gather information from multiple SAP ERP HCM components to generate planned costs for employees and positions. Data from the organizational plan is a critical element in cost planning, because jobs, positions, and organizational units can have information relevant to cost planning. Jobs and positions can also store planned compensation information to be used to plan for vacant or unoccupied positions. Also, organizational units can have information regarding planning headcount increases or decreases in the Quota Planning infotype.

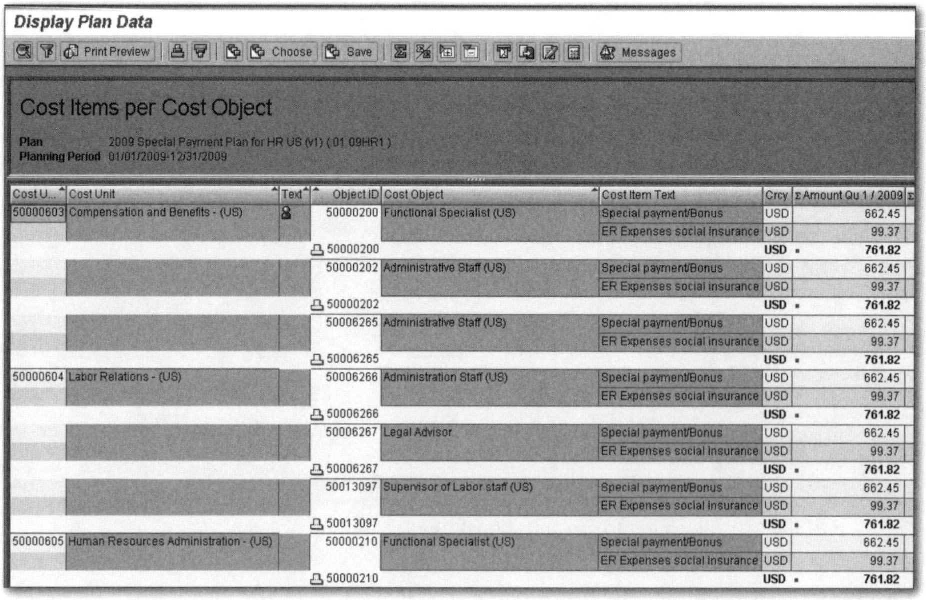

Figure 11.9 Display of Planned Costs for Bonus Payments by Organizational Unit

When the cost planning run is complete, as shown in Figure 11.9, you can store the projected cost planning data in the organizational object in Infotype 5010 Cost Planning. You can store information in the organizational unit, job, or position, depending on how you want to store planned costs elements. One or more cost planning runs can be conducted, which allows you to either separate or aggregate different cost elements, such as salaries, benefits, social insurance and taxes, special payments, and long-term incentives. The cost planning processes are fairly flexible, so you can design scenarios to capture any costs that can be related to the objects in the organizational plan.

In addition to planning costs and compensation, implementing OM also enables you to plan for employee development and career progression.

11.1.5 Personnel Development Integration

The functions in Personnel Development (PD) help you maximize the value of your employees by letting you plan and implement specific personnel and training measures to promote their professional development. You can also increase employee satisfaction and engagement by giving consideration to their personal and career aspirations. PD achieves these objectives through the use of qualification and skills profiles.

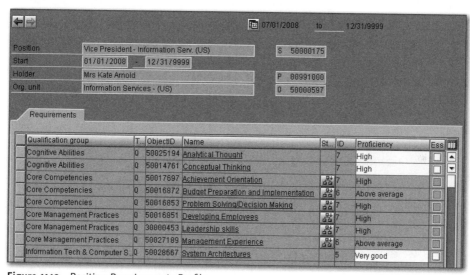

Figure 11.10 Position Requirements Profile

Through the integration of PD and OM, you can access objects within the enterprise structure and assign qualifications to positions and jobs by creating a requirements profile, as shown in Figure 11.10. All qualifications (object type Q) are stored centrally in a catalog that you can access and assign to multiple object types. The inheritance principle works in the requirements profile definition for organizational objects, and requirements can be defined broadly for jobs. Then positions can inherit the job requirements, and you can further refine the requirements of the specific position.

> **Example**
>
> As you can see in Figure 11.10, core competencies and core management practices are inherited from the job, as indicated by the ⊞ icon. These requirements are defined generally for all positions defined by this job, so they are not editable. However, additional competencies specific to the position can be added and tailored to the position, and these proficiencies are editable.

When job and position requirement profiles are created, you can compare the requirements to the qualifications of the position holder. Similar to the requirements profile, a person has a qualification profile that identifies his skills, competencies, and training. This comparison allows you to determine where additional development or training is required so that the person can fulfill his position expectations. This can further integrate to both Career and Succession Planning to Training and Event Management, which we'll discuss next.

11.1.6 Career and Succession Planning Integration

Career and Succession Planning lets you fulfill two goals:

▶ Encourage the professional development of your employees

▶ Ensure that critical positions are filled with appropriate headcount

With Career Planning, you can identify possible career paths and goals for employees, and then integrate that with the organizational plan in OM to determine the jobs and positions that will be included in their career paths (careers).

Careers are the specific paths within an organizational structure that are not specific to any person. So you can use careers to show employees the potential career opportunities open to them as they progress within your company. Because careers can contain jobs and positions in any combination, you can represent both vertical and horizontal movement within a career.

The system arranges organizational objects in careers so that the lowest in the hierarchy appears at the bottom of the career, and objects higher up in the hierarchy appear toward the top of the career. Objects that are equivalent or within the same hierarchy level appear beside one another in the career. Figure 11.11 shows a sample career using both jobs and positions.

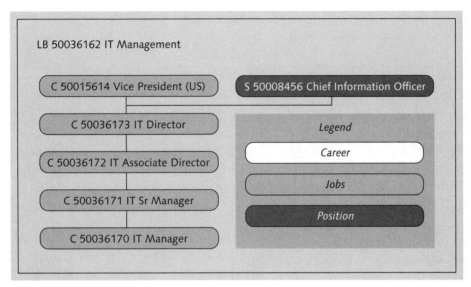

Figure 11.11 Jobs and Positions in a Career

Using the careers made from the organizational plan objects, you can perform career planning for employees in your company. An employee's position or related job can specify one or more careers available for him. Alternatively, by using the requirements profile for a job or position, you can search through careers to find matches based on an employee's qualifications match. In either case, the career planning scenarios are tightly integrated with the organizational plan data for jobs and positions, providing the most up-to-date information for planning purposes.

11.1.7 Training and Event Management Integration

Integration of OM with Training and Event Management (TEM) can occur through one of two mechanisms. First, when PD is integrated with TEM, you can generate training proposals in the process of comparing position requirements with personnel qualifications. In this process, the system suggests training courses that can fulfill missing requirements. From PD, you can also initiate processes to enroll the employees in the relevant courses, or request courses where none are presently scheduled.

The second option is that TEM functions can integrate with OM through the event and attendance management processes. In TEM, you create and maintain all of the training programs, courses, and events for the enterprise. Business events can also be created with organizational units identified as the organizer of the event (shown in Figure 11.12).

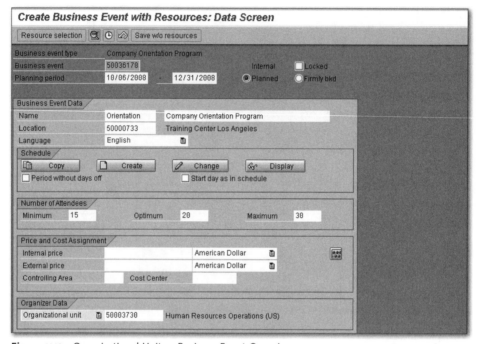

Figure 11.12 Organizational Unit as Business Event Organizer

In addition to the business event, OM is also integrated into attendance functions. When enrolling attendees in training courses, you have the option of enrolling entire organizational units into courses. Organizational units are read from the organizational plan in OM as possible attendee types, which you can see in Figure 11.13. When they are selected, you can view the people in the organizational unit using the employee list 👥 icon. This helps you know how many attendees to book for the business event.

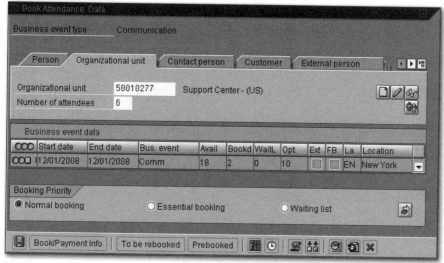

Figure 11.13 Booking Organizational Units to Business Events

Tip

Organizational unit attendees are simply placeholders in the business event; specific persons are not selected for enrollment. This is helpful when you are unsure which attendees will attend a class or program. So you can simply set aside a certain number of seats, and the attendees can decide at a later time who will actually attend.

The functions in PD and TEM are both meant to provide additional learning opportunities for your employees. As such, they rely on the organizational plan information to determine the job, position, and organizational unit objects and characteristics to help plan and administer learning programs effectively.

Let's take a look now at Recruitment integration with OM.

11.1.8 Recruitment Integration

You can use the Recruiting component to complete the entire recruiting process, all the way from identifying positions that need to be filled to hiring. OM plays a critical role in the early stages of the recruiting process by identifying vacancies. As we discussed in Chapter 3 (Section 3.5.3), positions can be identified as vacant, on hold, or occupied in OM. You can choose to identify positions as vacant proactively by creating an Infotype 1007 Vacancy record when a position is ready to be filled. Alternatively, you can set a system-wide setting that identifies all unoccupied positions as vacant. The vacancies shown in Recruitment represent your company's workforce requirements, and are the basis for starting the recruitment process.

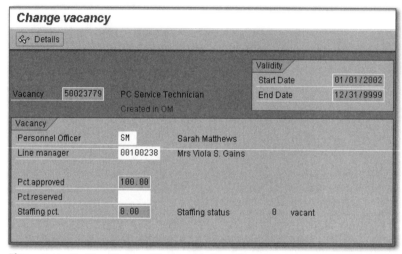

Figure 11.14 Position Vacancy Displayed in Recruitment

As you can see in Figure 11.14, the vacancy record as managed in Recruitment allows the addition of two data elements: personnel officer and line manager. These fields are used to simplify data selection in subsequent recruitment processing steps. The data can also be used to present the vacancy in the recruiter and manager's self-service inbox in either the Enterprise Portal or Business Workflow components. Vacancies are one mechanism that link data to Manager Self-Service, but there are additional functions, so let's look at those next.

11.1.9   Manager Self-Service Integration

Manager Self-Service (MSS) is an easy-to-use web application that empowers managers to conduct administrative and strategic functions via an enterprise portal. Functions in SAP ERP HCM that managers can conduct include recruiting the right people, performing budgeting and headcount planning, writing performance appraisals and rewarding employees, and initiating employee data change transactions. In most enterprises, managers have to perform a variety of functions all year round. MSS provides them with information, tools, and reports to do this efficiently and effectively.

For customers planning to implement MSS as part of their enterprise portal solution, knowing and maintaining the correct OM data model will ensure that MSS can identify relevant data so that managers are connected with their employees. For MSS to function properly, the portal must be able to identify the manager is and the employees for whom he is responsible. This information is determined in PA and OM through a four-step process as outlined in Figure 11.15.

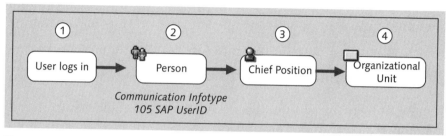

Figure 11.15 Manager Self-Service Login Process

The steps the portal uses to determine if a user is a manager are as follows:

1. The user logs in to the enterprise portal with a valid system userid.

2. The personnel number associated with the userid is identified. SAP system userids are stored in PA Infotype 105 Communication.

3. The person's Infotype 0001 Organizational Assignment is read to determine the holder's position(s). The system then checks OM to determine if the position is identified as a chief position.

4. The organizational unit for which the position is the chief is read, as are all subordinate organizational units. All positions and holders in those organizational units become available to the manager via self-service functions.

The MSS logic used to determine the manger of employees works in conjunction with the authorizations that are set up for the user. Any restrictions the user has because of standard or structural authorization profiles is also taken into account. You can read more about authorizations in Section 10.4.

Tip
Although you can assign object types external person (H) and user (US) to be holders of chief positions, these objects don't work for MSS. The system requires a valid personnel number (PERNR) in PA for MSS functions.

For MSS users, organizational plan integration is a critical component that keeps the information about who is a manager in the enterprise and for whom that manager is responsible.

So far, we've discussed integration of OM within SAP ERP HCM components, but no discussion of OM integration would be complete without mentioning SAP Business Workflow. This cross-functional component is uniquely tied to OM, using the organizational plan data to design and run workflow processes across the enterprise.

11.2 Workflow Integration with OM

Throughout SAP ERP components, you use SAP Business Workflow to define end-to-end business processes in the SAP system. In SAP ERP HCM components, workflow tasks typically consist of release or approval procedures or more complex business processes such as creating a new position and the associated coordination of the departments involved in that process.

11.2.1 Workflow Scenarios in SAP ERP HCM

SAP Business Workflow is particularly suitable for situations in which work processes have to be executed repeatedly and situations in which the business process requires the involvement of multiple agents in a specific sequence.

You can also use SAP Business Workflow to respond to errors and exceptions in other, existing business processes. You can start a workflow when predefined events occur; for example, an event can be triggered if particular errors are found during an automatic check.

> **Example**
>
> You may choose to notify payroll processors when employees error out of the payroll run. The workflow process can notify the processor via email of the error occurrence, the employee involved, and details about the error. This provides the payroll processor with information to research the error and make any corrections necessary for the payroll run to continue. Having this automated workflow notification eliminates the need for manual visual monitoring of the payroll run.

SAP provides many predefined workflow processes throughout the SAP ERP components. If a predefined workflow does not exist to meet your needs, there are also tools to create your own workflow scenarios or modify the delivered workflows. These tools include:

- **Workflow Builder** for displaying and making changes to workflows
- **WebFlow Functions** for executing workflows between different companies
- **Business Object Builder** to define and analyze business object types
- **Business Workflow Explorer** to get an overview of all existing tasks
- **Business Workplace** or the portal iView **Universal Worklist**, where users receive information about the workflows they need to carry out

SAP Business Workflow uses the existing transactions and functions of the SAP system and takes over control of routing the business processes to the appropriate individuals. The question of how SAP Business Workflow knows who to route workflow tasks to is answered by OM.

OM forms the basis for SAP Business Workflow. The organizational plan you create forms the framework for a routing structure that SAP Business Workflow uses to assign tasks to an employee. Using OM, you can use the organizational plan structure created there to have the relevant agents carry out the individual activities. Both OM and SAP Business Workflow are components of Business Management (BC-BMT).

A prerequisite to any use of SAP Business Workflow is the creation of the organizational plan. The organizational plan describes the organizational assignment of the employees. The aim of this in the SAP Business Workflow context is to determine the responsibility of employees for the execution of individual business activities in the form of activity profiles.

The organizational plan created for HR purposes can also be used in SAP Business Workflow, as long as the workflow functionality and the HR application are in the same client. If you've set up an organizational plan in a different client or a separate SAP HR system, you can use program RHMOVE30 to copy this data to the client of the SAP system in which the workflow is to be executed. (See Chapter 10, Section 10.3.5 for more information about moving OM data between SAP clients and systems.)

In the organizational plan, you typically have a structure that is composed of organizational units, jobs, and positions. If you're planning to use your organizational plan for SAP Business Workflow, you'll also incorporate the object types standard task, workflow template, and task group. These standard workflow objects are provided for setting up your workflow templates; these objects fulfill the most popular requirements for processing HR processes:

▶ Workflow templates you can use to execute purely technical process steps

▶ Standard tasks that depict editing, approving, and saving the data entered

▶ Standard tasks that control system actions such as automatically saving data, sending emails, or sending system messages for the exchange infrastructure

These elements combine with the agent assignment rules that determine the appropriate processor for each process step. Agent determination rules specify how the system is to determine the agent (processor) of a workflow step. These agents then receive a work item in their universal worklist. Alternatively, you can send an email to an agent.

As shown in Figure 11.16, the workflow task is assigned various organizational plan objects as agent. In this example, the new hire onboarding workflow process contains a task 🎩 Define equipment for work center. In this instance, the task agent is defined first by the job Assistant or Secretary, and second by multiple positions that are defined by that job category. At the third level, the position holders are also identified as potential persons who may subsequently process the task.

You can assign tasks to any of the object types in the organizational plan:

▶ **Organizational units:** In which all persons of the organization may be a possible agent

▶ **Jobs:** In which all holders of positions defined by the job are agents

▶ **Positions:** In which any holder of the position is an agent

▶ **Persons:** Direct agent assignment to specific persons in the company

▶ **Users:** Direct agent assignment to specific users in the SAP system

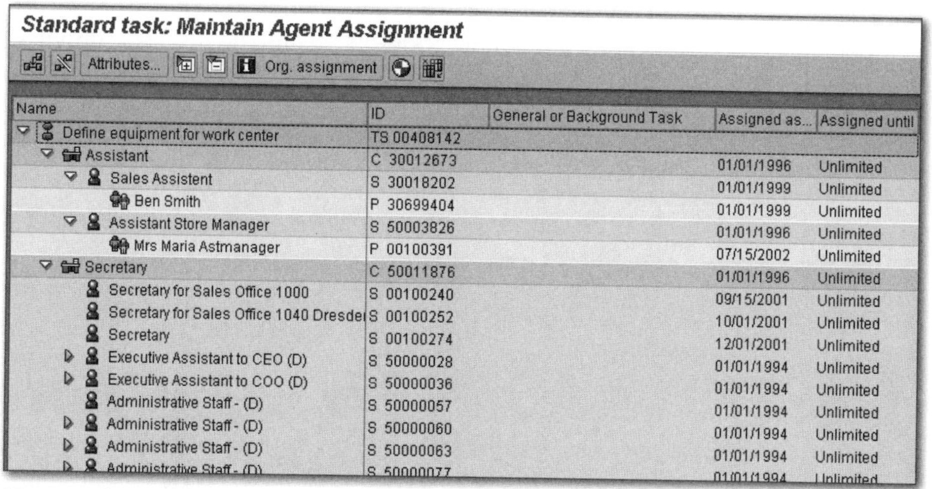

Name	ID	General or Background Task	Assigned as...	Assigned until
Define equipment for work center	TS 00408142			
Assistant	C 30012673		01/01/1996	Unlimited
Sales Assistent	S 30018202		01/01/1999	Unlimited
Ben Smith	P 30699404		01/01/1999	Unlimited
Assistant Store Manager	S 50003826		01/01/1996	Unlimited
Mrs Maria Astmanager	P 00100391		07/15/2002	Unlimited
Secretary	C 50011876		01/01/1996	Unlimited
Secretary for Sales Office 1000	S 00100240		09/15/2001	Unlimited
Secretary for Sales Office 1040 Dresde	S 00100252		10/01/2001	Unlimited
Secretary	S 00100274		12/01/2001	Unlimited
Executive Assistant to CEO (D)	S 50000028		01/01/1994	Unlimited
Executive Assistant to COO (D)	S 50000036		01/01/1994	Unlimited
Administrative Staff - (D)	S 50000057		01/01/1994	Unlimited
Administrative Staff - (D)	S 50000060		01/01/1994	Unlimited
Administrative Staff - (D)	S 50000063		01/01/1994	Unlimited
Administrative Staff - (D)	S 50000077		01/01/1994	Unlimited

Figure 11.16 Workflow Task Agent Assignment

Companies that use SAP Business Workflow will find that it is far more efficient and effective to use organizational units, jobs, and positions for agent assignment, rather than using persons or users. Relationships from tasks to the organization, job, and position objects don't need to be changed as people move in, out, and around the organization, because workflow dynamically searches the relationships of these objects to the holders (persons or user IDs) to determine who can then complete the tasks. If you assign tasks to specific people or user objects, the task relationship will likely need to be maintained, updated, and reassigned to someone else when the person moves to another role in your company.

The primary purpose of SAP Business Workflow is to get the right tasks to the right processors as soon as possible. OM provides the framework for a routing structure for task assignments that is fully integrated to your day-to-day HR operations. This helps ensure that the most up-to-date personnel information is reflected in the organizational plan and that business processes are completed in a timely manner.

11.3 Conclusion

We've reviewed a wide range of integration points to and from the OM organizational plan structure in this chapter. As we've demonstrated, OM is a core component of many functions throughout SAP ERP HCM. The objects, infotypes, and relationships used throughout OM are flexible and adaptable to nearly any business requirement. Whether integrating to SAP ERP HCM components or other SAP functions, OM is a central and powerful component, and when implemented properly, it can help you achieve great benefits from your SAP solution.

Appendices

A   OM Object Types

Object	Object Name
A	Work center
AC	Rule
AG	Role
AP	Applicant
B	Development plan
BA	Appraisal
BG	Criteria group
BK	Criterion
BL	Dev. plan group
BP	Business partner
BS	Appraisal model
BU	Budget structure
C	Job
CP	Central person
D	Course type
DC	Curriculum type
E	Course
EC	Curriculum
EG	Exposure group
EP	Inv. program position
ET	E-Learning
F	Location
FA	Application component
G	Resource
H	External person
I1	Personnel subarea

Object	Object Name
I2	Employee subgroup
I3	Employee group
IA	Company
IB	Credit control area
IC	Company code
ID	Business area
IE	Functional area
IF	Cons business area
IG	FM area
IH	Controlling area
II	Operating concern
IJ	Plant
IK	Location
IL	Division
IM	Sales organization
IN	Distribution channel
IO	Distribution chain
IP	SalesOrg-division
IQ	Sales area
IR	Sales office
IS	Sales group
IT	Shipping point
IU	Loading point
IV	Transp. planning point
IW	Plant storage area
IX	Purchasing org.

Object	Object Name	Object	Object Name
IY	Warehouse complex	ND	Application
IZ	Personnel area	NE	Candidacy
K	Cost center	O	Organizational unit
KA	Capacity (logistics)	OD	Request
KG	Cost center group	OJ	Learning objective
KI	Prospect	OR	Legal entity
KU	Customer	P	Person
L	Course group	PC	Profit center
LA	Logistics work center	PG	Business process group
LB	Career	PH	Profit center group
M	Material	PJ	WBS element (project)
M0	Process group	PR	Business process
M1	Process	PT	Contact person
M2	Local process step	Q	Qualification
M3	Process step	QK	Qualification group
M4	Process (scope)	QP	Requirements profile
M8	Local account group	R	Resource type
M9	Local MC/group	RA	Advertisement
MA	Account group	RE	Report (with variant)
MG	Central process group	RI	Recruitment Instrument
MM	Mgmt control/group	RQ	Requisition
MO	Control objective	RR	Requisition request
MP	Central process	RY	Responsibility
MR	Risk	S	Position
MT	Central process step	SO	SAP org. object
NA	Candidate	SR	Planned staff reqmt.
NB	Requisition	T	Task
NC	Posting	TG	Task group

Object	Object Name	Object	Object Name
TR	Transaction	WI	Work item
TS	Standard task	WM	Workflow object method
U	Company	WO	Workflow object
UG	User group	WS	Workflow template
US	User	WT	Workflow object type
VA	Appraisal template	XC	ALE filter object combin.
VB	Criteria group	XF	ALE split function
VC	Criterion	XG	Expert group
VE	Service	XO	ALE filter object
WA	Work area	XP	Expert
WE	Workflow event	XS	ALE logical system
WF	Workflow task		

B   Infotypes in OM

The following tables list the OM infotypes identified in this book.

Infotype Name	Number
Object	1000
Relationship	1001
Description	1002
Department/Staff	1003
Character	1004
Planned Compensation	1005
Restrictions	1006
Vacancy	1007
Account Assignment	1008
Health Examinations	1009
Authorities and Resources	1010
Work Schedule	1011
Employee Group/ Subgroup	1013
Obsolete	1014

Infotype Name	Number
Cost Planning	1015
Standard Profiles	1016
PD Profiles	1017
Cost Distribution	1018
Quota Planning	1019
Site-Dependent Info	1027
Address	1028
Mail Address	1032
Shift Group	1039
Job Evaluation Results	1050
Salary Survey Results	1051
SAP Organizational Object	1208
General Attributes	1222

United States–specific Infotypes

Assignment of EEO and AAP Categories	1610
Assignment of Workers' Comp Codes to Org Units	1612
Assignment of Workers' Comp Codes to Positions	1613

C Transaction Codes in OM

These are some of the more important transaction codes for organizational plan maintenance and reporting. This list does not contain all transaction codes available in OM.

Transaction	Name of Transaction
PPOCE	Create Organization and Staffing
PPOME	Change Organization and Staffing
PPOSE	Display Organization and Staffing
PP01	Maintain Plan Data (Expert Mode)
PP03	Maintain Plan Data (Actions)
PPOM_OLD	Maintain Organizational Plan
PPCO _OLD	Initial Screen: Organizational Plan
PPOC _OLD	Create Organizational Unit

Extended maintenance transactions

Transaction	Name of Transaction
PO01	Maintain Work Center
PO03	Maintain Job
PO10	Maintain Organizational Unit
PO13	Maintain Position
PO14	Maintain Task
PPCT	Task Catalog
PQ01	Actions for Work Center
PQ03	Actions for Job
PQ10	Actions for Organizational Unit
PQ13	Actions for Position
PQ14	Actions for Task
PSO0	Set Plan Version for OrgManagement
PSO1	Set Aspect for OrgManagement

Transaction	Name of Transaction
PGOM	Graphical Structure Maintenance
PPMS	Display Matrix Organization
PPME	Change Matrix Organization

Transaction codes for organizational plan configuration and settings

Transaction	Name of Transaction
OOOT	Maintain Object Types
OONR	Number Ranges
OONC	No. Assignment for All Plan Versions
OOPV	Plan Versions
OOAP	Set Active Plan Version
OOIT	Infotypes
OOSU	Subtypes
OOVK	Relationships
OOAS	Aspects
OOPPOMSET	T77SO: PPOM Settings
OOV2	Maintain Table T77SO
OOPP	Consistency Check for Integration
OOCR	Set up PD Transport Connection
OODT	Data Transfer
OOMV	Create Sequential File for PD
OOMW	Display Sequential File for PD
OOHQ	Integration: PLOG – PREL
OOFRAMEWORKCUST	Hierarchy Framework Customizing
OOOBJMANCUST	Object Manager Customizing
OOMT	Actions
OOPR	Authorization Profile Maintenance

D   Authorization Functions for OM

OM uses a long list of functions to determine what you can and can't do in OM. Following are the available function codes used in the OM authorization objects. These options can be used individually or together in specific authorizations and authorization profiles.

Func	Function Description
ABLN	Reject
AEND	Change
AENK	Change canteen field
AKTI	Change temporarily
BEAN	Activate
COP	Submit
COPR	Copy
COPY	Copy room
CUT	Copy object
CUTI	Delimit object
DEL	Delete
DELO	Delete object
DISP	Display
DUTY	Essential relationship
GENE	Approve
HITK	Career planning hit list

Func	Function Description
HITS	Career plan simulation
HITW	Hit list for E&T planning
INIT	Initialization
INSE	Create
INSG	Create from OS/2
INTE	Integration
LISD	List display
LIST	List display with change
MASS	Create
NEWL	New language
PLVG	Propose plan from OS/2
PLVO	Propose change
QUIC	Fast data entry
SIMU	Simulation
VORS	Succession plan screening

E Workflow Scenarios in SAP ERP HCM

Multiple workflow scenarios are delivered for SAP ERP HCM components. Following are some of the workflow scenarios SAP provides for SAP ERP HCM. A complete list can be found in the SAP documentation for your release.

Component	Workflow Scenario
Organizational Management	Create Vacancy for Position
	Generate Headcount Planning
Personnel Administration	HCM Processes and Forms (e.g., Hiring, Transfer)
	Preparations for Start of Work
	ESS Activities after Hiring
	Employment and Salary Verification
	ESS: US Address Change/Create
Recruitment	Receipt and Resubmission
	Planning and Holding Job Interviews
	Creating an Offer of Contract
	Preparation for Hiring
	Rejecting Applicants
Time Management	ESS Leave Request
	Approve Absence Request
	Shift Planning Approval
Compensation Management	Compensation Adjustment Approval Process
	Follow-Up Actions after Award Exercised
	Award Expiration
	Qualification Monitoring
Personnel Development	Approving and Following Up an Appraisal
	Changed Subprofile
	Profile Matchup for Transfer to Another Position

F   FAQs for Organizational Management

Q: Should a manager be in his own organizational unit or the organizational unit of his manager?

A: Managers should be in the same organizational unit as their employees. Their positions can be used to designate them as the "chief" of the organization. Evaluation paths and authorizations can be used to control how a manager accesses his employee information.

Q: How do I get a report of the responsible manager of an organization?

A: You can run report RHSTRU00 Structure Display/Maintenance using evaluation path BOSSONLY. This evaluation path displays the manager position and the holder for each organizational unit selected.

Q: How do you identify an "acting" manager or chief of an organizational unit while the position is vacant and being actively recruited?

A: There are two possible ways to handle acting manager assignments:

▶ Utilize the next-higher manager in the organizational unit hierarchy. The organizational plan will default the responsibility to the next-highest manager above if a chief position is vacant. Users may not want to do the work, but it might encourage them fill the vacancy faster.

▶ Assign the interim manager to the temporary position at <50%, leaving his regular position at >50%. On PA Iinfotype 0001 Organizational Assignment, the position with the greater percentage will be displayed on screen. You can use Other positions in the menu bar to display both assignments. By splitting the position assignment, the manager can perform duties for both organizations until recruitment is completed.

Q: We use Global Employment in PA. How does this affect the holder relationship of the employee to the position?

A: Using the Global Employment component in SAP ERP HCM activates the person ID concept. This ID is not used to integrate with OM. The personnel number (PERNR) remains the employee ID related to the position, so you shouldn't see any changes in how OM is managed.

Q: Is there an easy way to find out the infotype number in expert mode?

A: You can activate user parameter HR_DISP_INFTY_NUM with value "X" in your user settings. This will display the infotype number in the infotype header in expert maintenance transactions. This user parameter is used for both OM and PA infotype transactions.

Q: U.S. Infotypes 1610 U.S. EEO/AAP Information and 1612 and 1613 for Workers Compensation information maintenance require transport from system to system. Users keep getting the message "Client xxx has status of 'not modifiable'" in production. How can we avoid this or work around it?

A: This is a bit of a design flaw in the system. Even though it may appear that you are maintaining infotype master data, the OM screens that appear for EEO/AAP and workers' compensation data are actually table views. In a production system table, views are generally not maintainable. To be able to maintain the information in production, you have to correct the table or view attributes so the entries can be edited without users receiving error messages. Note 123383 in the SAP Service Marketplace (*http://service.sap.com*) gives instructions on how to correct the table view attributes.

For OM objects in general, the automatic transport connection should also be deactivated in your production system by changing the TRSP CORR to "X" in the system control table T77S0. This will ensure that users are not prompted for transport requests when they save any other OM infotype data.

Q: How long will it take me to implement Organizational Management?

A: As with any SAP component implementation, the answer is, "It depends." A rather interesting formula found on the Internet may prove useful:

v = complexity   w = knowledge   x = skill   y = luck   z = magic
# of days = (((records * v) / (w + x + y)) * z)

G   Glossary

The glossary contains terms that refer to SAP applications or have a special meaning at SAP.

ABAP   Advanced Business Application Programming – a programming language developed by SAP for application development.

Benefits   SAP ERP HCM component that manages employee health, welfare, and other benefit plans.

CRM   SAP product that provides functions for marketing, sales, and customer service.

Customer (user) exit   SAP customer exits for enhancements. Exits allow you to add your own functionality without modifying the original code.

ERP   Enterprise Resource Planning.

HCM   Human Capital Management.

IMG   SAP Implementation Guide, which provides tasks for customizing the system during implementation.

Infotype   Thematically linked data structure that allows you to enter and store object characteristics.

Job   Classifications of functions within a company as defined by the assignment of characteristics. Example: Administrative Assistant.

Job Index   The catalog of jobs in the enterprise.

NetWeaver   SAP technical platform for applications.

MSS   Manager Self Service.

Object   An item that can be selected and maintained individually.

OM   Organization Management.

OOP   Object-Oriented Programming.

Organization Management   SAP ERP HCM component that manages the organizational plan and hierarchy structure.

Organizational plan   Representation of the task-related, functional structure of the enterprise.

Organizational unit   A functional unit in a company or enterprise. Can represent departments, functions, divisions, projects, and so on.

PA   Personnel Administration.

PD   Personnel Development.

Person   An individual, as defined as an employee or other person category in Personnel Administration.

Personnel Administration SAP ERP HCM component that manages employee and other personnel transactions and information.

PLM SAP product that provides functions to manage, track, and control product-related information over the product lifecycle.

Position A post that can be occupied by a person. Defined by a job. Example: HR Assistant.

PY Payroll.

SCM SAP product that provides functions to enable adaptive supply chain networks.

SRM SAP product that provides functions to optimize procurement operations.

Staff assignment All the persons and positions belonging to an organizational unit.

Standard report Executable programs written in the SAP ABAP language that read data in database tables and sometimes also make updates. You can display, print, or save the resulting output list.

TEM Training and Event Management.

Time management SAP ERP HCM component that manages employee time recording and evaluation.

H Author Biography

 Sylvia Chaudoir has been a Consultant on SAP ERP HCM components since 1994 and has expertise in several SAP HCM functional areas, including SAP HR Personnel Administration, Organizational Management, Benefits, Time Management, and US Payroll. She started her work as a consultant for SAP and finally became a platinum consultant and client manager.

Sylvia was part of the first group of HCM consultants in the US and participated on customer co-development projects for US Payroll and Time Management, as well as over 30 US and global implementations of SAP ERP HCM solutions, so she has been doing SAP HR consulting work for about as long as the R/3 HCM product has been in existence. Sylvia also supported US and global HCM operations management for SAP. She was the also the project/product manager and lead content author of Accelerated HR, which is currently branded SAP Best Practices for HCM.

Following her career with SAP, she was a managing consultant for Emeritis USA and then managed enterprise applications for Genentech, Inc. She's been a trainer of SAP HR courses and also presented at multiple SAP conferences on Organizational Management and other topics. She is currently a Senior Lead Consultant at Deloitte Consulting LLP in their Human Capital group. Sylvia lives in the San Francisco bay area with her husband and two children.

Index

Best Practices for Payroll, Time Management, Personnel Administration, and much more

Expert advice for integrating Personnel Planning and SAP Enterprise Portal

Based on R/3 Enterprise and mySAP ERP HCM 2004

629 pp., 2006, 69,95 Euro / US$
ISBN 1-59229-050-7

Mastering HR Management with SAP

www.sap-press.com

C. Krämer, S. Ringling, Song Yang

Mastering HR Management with SAP

Get a step-by-step guide to the entire personnel management process, from recruiting, to personnel controlling, and beyond. This book comes complete with practical examples regarding user roles, and covers all of the new enhancements, improved features and tools that have been introduced with R/3 Enterprise. Uncover the ins and outs of e-recruiting, organizational management, personnel administration, payroll, benefits, quality assurance, rolebased portals, and many others too numerous to list. The book is based on Release 4.7 (R/3 Enterprise), and mySAP ERP 2004 (HCM)

Increase company productivity
by learning to use HCM
Performance Management
efficiently

Prepare for, design, implement,
and configure your HCM
implementation

302 pp., 2007, 69,95 Euro / US$ 69.95
ISBN 978-1-59229-124-3

SAP ERP HCM
Performance Management

www.sap-press.com

Jeremy Masters, Christos Kotsakis

SAP ERP HCM Performance Management

From Design to Implementation

This comprehensive book is an indispensable reference for HR professionals, analysts, and consultants
learning how to implement SAP ERP HCM Performance Management. The book teaches you everything you need to know about the Objective Setting
and Appraisal (OSA) module within SAP so that you
can identify and retain key talent within your organization. You'll take a step-by-step journey through
the design and implementation of your own performance management application that will help you
improve your companies' performance and talent
management processes. The book covers all the
latest releases, including the R/3 Enterprise Release
(4.7), SAP ERP 2004 (ECC 5.0) and SAP ERP 2005
(ECC 6.0).

**Solves difficult
US Payroll-related problems**

**Create custom wage types and
learn about the schemas and rules
specific to US Payroll**

**Discover advanced topics, such as
overpayments, accruals, payroll
interfaces, garnishments, and more**

332 pp., 2007, 69,95 Euro / US$ 69.95
ISBN 978-1-59229-132-8

Practical SAP US Payroll

www.sap-press.com

Satish Badgi

Practical SAP US Payroll

„Practical US Payroll" has everything you need to
implement a successful payroll system. Readers will
learn how to create custom wage types, process
deductions for benefits and garnishments, handle
accruals, report and process taxes, and process
retroactive payrolls. From the hands-on, step-by-step
examples to the detailed wage type tables in the
appendix, this book is your complete guide to the
US Payroll system.

Covers standard SAP reports, queries, SAP
NetWeaver BI, and the
creation of customer reports

Provides practical examples for report
creation in the different
SAP ERP HCM components

Examines reports in area menu,HIS,
MDT, and SAP NetWeaver Portal formats

Up-to-date for SAP ERP 6.0

431 pp., 2008, 69,95 Euro / US$ 69.95
ISBN 978-1-59229-172-4

HR Reporting with SAP

www.sap-press.com

Hans-Jürgen Figaj, Richard Haßmann, Anja Junold

HR Reporting with SAP

This comprehensive book describes how you can use the
powerful reporting tools of the SAP system efficiently and in
a goal-oriented manner. You will first get to know the
details of the reporting tools, Standard SAP Report, Query,
SAP NetWeaver BI, and Customer Report. The book then
describes various real-life examples in order to demonstrate
how you can use the tools in the different HCM modules in
the best-possible way. You will get to know selected
standard reports as well as the SAP NetWeaver BI Standard
Content for each module. In addition, you will learn how
you can make the reports available to users. The book is
based on SAP ERP 6.0 and can be used with Release R/3
Enterprise or higher.

Interested in reading more?

Please visit our Web site for all
new book releases from SAP PRESS.

www.sap-press.com